MODERN AMERICAN SNIPERS

MODERN AMERICAN SNIPERS

From *The Legend* to *The Reaper*—
on the Battlefield with Special Operations Snipers

CHRIS MARTIN
Foreword by Eric Davis

ST. MARTIN'S GRIFFIN
NEW YORK

Designed by Kathryn Parise

THE LIBRARY OF CONGRESS HAS CATALOGED THE HARDCOVER EDITION AS FOLLOWS:

Martin, Chris, 1974–
    Modern American snipers : from the legend to the reaper—on the battlefield with special operations snipers / Chris Martin ; foreword by Eric Davis. — First edition.
        p. cm.
    Includes bibliographical references.
    ISBN 978-1-250-06717-3 (hardcover)
    ISBN 978-1-4668-7623-1 (e-book)
    1. Snipers—United States.   2. Sniping (Military science)—History.   3. Special operations (Military science)—United States—History—21st century.   4. United States—History, Military—21st century.   I. Title.   II. Title: From the legend to the reaper, on the battlefield with special operations snipers.   III. Title: On the battlefield with special operations snipers.
    UD333.M313 2014
    356'.162—dc23

                                                                          2014040098

ISBN 978-1-250-07645-8 (trade paperback)

Our books may be purchased in bulk for promotional, educational, or business use. Please contact your local bookseller or the Macmillan Corporate and Premium Sales Department at (800) 221-7945, extension 5442, or by e-mail at MacmillanSpecialMarkets@macmillan.com.

First St. Martin's Griffin Edition: December 2015

10   9   8   7   6   5   4   3   2   1

Contents

Foreword

There's no doubt in my mind that American special operations has produced the finest and most technologically savvy snipers the world's battlefields have ever seen. This book is a back window into some of the most accomplished marksmen deployed against America's enemies.

I had the honor of serving as a Navy SEAL instructor at the Naval Special Warfare Group One sniper cell, and later at the Special Warfare Center's basic sniper course. The instructor cadre that I worked with at both units sacrificed long hours, and put their hearts and souls into the training in order to ensure that our guys were ready to deploy at the tip of the spear, and rain down hate on the enemy. These were some of the finest men I've had the pleasure to work with in my career.

Outside of the schoolhouse we came to work with other units' sniper instructors in different branches of the U.S. and coalition militaries. Always on the lookout to share ideas and improve our courses even more, we shared one thing in common, a desire to produce the best student possible. What this also did was let us get to know coalition programs, the USMC's Scout Sniper course (we even sent some SEALs there), and the Army's Special Operations Target Interdiction Course (SOTIC) , and to know them with great respect and mutual admiration of the work we were all doing.

Reflecting back it was a rare moment in history and time. While most of the instructor cadre had real-world sniper experience, most of it was limited to doing airborne support or reconnaissance and aerial targeting. We had no idea that the men we were training, in our newly modernized sniper program, would go on to become some of the deadliest snipers the American military has ever produced. Guys like Chris Kyle (*American Sniper*), and Marcus Luttrell (*Lone Survivor*) would come through our schoolhouse, and go on to do different but great things in their own way. These men have been highlighted in the media but they would likely defer attention away from themselves and toward many of the other unknown snipers in the community that have equally incredible accomplishments against the enemies of America.

While I'm admittedly biased to the product we put out in the SEAL sniper program, the accomplishments of the U.S. Special Operations Command (US SOCOM) sniper community cannot, and should not, go unknown. These are their stories. Whether it was Chris Kyle giving sniper support to the Marines in the hot and dirty streets of Iraq, or Nick "The Reaper" Irving providing sniper overwatch for the SEALs, one thing is clear to me: It's one team, one fight.

Eric Davis,
Former Navy SEAL Sniper Instructor

MODERN AMERICAN SNIPERS

1

Next-Gen Force Multiplication

Some three hundred miles off the coast of Somalia in the dead of night, everything was black. Even the silhouettes of the hulking floating structures that surrounded their little vessel could not be made out against the sky behind them—at least not well enough to discern that those shadows were growing larger.

The three remaining pirates had been played—convinced it was in their best interest to accept a tow from the USS *Bainbridge*, the destroyer on point of the shepherding armada.

The enterprising teenagers were exhausted, weary, and growing increasingly agitated. Only a few days before, they had accomplished something no others had in nearly two centuries: the successful seizure of a United States Merchant Marine vessel.

The hijacking had not gone exactly to plan and now they found themselves in an awkward-looking lifeboat, cramped and breathing stale air. Their single source of leverage was the man who not long before was in charge of the cargo ship they had boarded—Captain Richard Phillips of the MV *Maersk Alabama*.

However, that bargaining chip was significant enough to prove considerably more than they had actually bargained for, bringing the maritime might of the United States Navy down on top of them. And that might was expressed not only by the mammoth naval destroyers, frigates, carriers, and aircraft those boats ferry.

Unbeknownst to the pirates, an advance team of DEVGRU operators had materialized on the scene, taking up station on the *Bainbridge*. The commandos had jumped in following a short flight from their operational base in Manda Bay, Kenya, and they were soon joined by a larger force that flew in from the States on a C-17 and also parachuted into the shark-infested waters of the Gulf of Aden.

Earlier there had been four pirates threatening the life of the captain on the lifeboat. But one, the wounded and desperate Abdiwali Abdiqadir Muse, had surrendered and voluntarily placed himself in the hands of the SEALs.

Despite its cramped quarters, the bobbing orange lifeboat had already been the backdrop for plenty of drama. Phillips attempted an ill-advised escape at one point but was fished back out of the water and yanked back into the craft.

Troublingly, Phillips's captors had grown more and more unpredictable as the days wore on. At times they would crack shots from their Kalashnikov rifles at the Navy ships, and at others they would communicate via satellite phone with potential reinforcements of their own—a makeshift Somali pirate armada consisting of five additional hijacked ships loaded with additional hostages.

And almost comically, the pirates also provided occasional real-time updates to the international press corps as the world became entranced by the ratcheting drama.

The FBI negotiations cycled between promising and nonexistent. Lockheed P-3 Orion and Boeing ScanEagle ISR (intelligence, reconnaissance, and surveillance) platforms circled overhead while the DEVGRU assaulters readied on the USS *Boxer*, just waiting for the green light to launch.

For days the unit's snipers—members of its shrouded Black Team—had rotated through gun positions fanned out the back deck of the *Bainbridge*.

While waterborne operations are the historic calling card of Navy SEALs and maritime hostage rescues DEVGRU's raison d'être, the reality is that by April 12, 2009, these SEALs had spent nearly a decade dismantling terrorist networks in the jagged mountains of Afghanistan. Even the most senior of DEVGRU's men were far more familiar with operating at an elevation of ten thousand feet above the sea rather than in it; their particularly demanding tasking requires they be prepared for any mission, in any environment, at any time. And the more impossible it's deemed, the more likely it will come their way.

The SEALs who had come to save the captive American hailed from Red Squadron, one of DEVGRU's four assault squadrons. It had shed blood in the region before. In 1993, four of its snipers had taken part in Operation Gothic Serpent—more popularly known as Black Hawk Down—in Mogadishu, Somalia, in 1993 and earned four Silver Stars for their considerable trouble.

One of Red Squadron's own was also the first make the ultimate sacrifice following 9/11. Petty Officer First Class Neil Roberts died fighting alone atop the peak of Takur Ghar in Afghanistan during Operation Anaconda.

And over the decade following that loss, the squadron had doled out vengeance in spectacular numbers and with unapologetic efficiency.

Now the SEALs were back in the water, preparing to add three more to their monumental toll. Execute authority had been granted by *the executive authority*: President Obama provided the team with the permission it needed to intervene should they judge the captain's life to be in grave and immediate danger.

While the night was pure blackness from the pirates' perspective, through the DEVGRU snipers' advanced night-vision optics they could clearly see the beams of the infrared lasers that stretched out from their accurized SR-25s across the *Bainbridge* and danced across faces of the fleeting targets.

And then an AK-47 was driven into Phillips's back. The frantic shuffling inside the lifeboat's cabin exposed all three heads simultaneously for just a fraction of a second.

DEVGRU's snipers—collectively known as Black Team—offer commanders a 100 percent headshot guarantee within a certain range. Its snipers are regularly tested to demonstrate that they can actually deliver on that promise. Reeled in to a range nearly ten times shorter than that magic distance, the pirates had become the closest possible literal realization of the idiom "shooting fish in a barrel."

Three mechanical clicks of suppressed Mk 11 Mod 0 semi-automatics registered almost as a single hushed sound as the weapons issued forth three 7.62mm rounds. At that distance the bullets traveled precisely down the path shown by the lasers. Barely slowing from their initial velocity of over twenty-three hundred feet per second, they found their marks in near-instantaneous fashion.

Almost as quickly, two DEVGRU snipers traversed the two ropes to secure Phillips.

A complex situation had been resolved in shockingly simple, almost elegant fashion.

Three bullets equaled three dead pirates. And those three bullets also meant one American life had been preserved while the entire globe watched on at full attention.

The dramatic rescue provided a rare and fleeting glimpse of the wealth of capabilities that had been acquired by the nation's spec ops snipers during the Global War on Terror.

What went unseen to the world at large were the vast multitudes of operations executed by these marksmen and others like them. Their work is largely performed behind a veil of secrecy, hidden by special access codes and other gray mechanisms of classification.

A former Black Team sniper said, "As impressive as that was, I can guarantee you it wasn't that big of a deal to those who did it. They're used to being in a much more difficult environment than they were that night. I know that's difficult for people to conceive. Difficult as those shots were or that scenario seems to be to the average Joe, for those guys, it was just another night at work."

The dead pirates were only three of thousands—if not tens of thousands—that have perished at the discretion of America's modern special operations snipers.

And Richard Phillips was just one of an even greater number saved by those same actions—whether directly, more broadly, or abstractly.

◆

Depending on how much slack the definition is allowed, the first sniper arguably came into existence before the first human did; newly discovered evidence suggests that ancient hominids were throwing spears nearly 280,000 years ago. You have to figure it wasn't too long after that an enterprising prehuman devised one a little straighter that flew a bit truer. Later, archers dominated battlefields for hundreds of years, striking from distances of hundreds of yards.

Even snipers in the more modern sense of the word brought dread to their enemies long enough ago to seem downright prehistoric. Snipers have acted as force multipliers in every major conflict dating back to the Revolutionary War. Their exact role, along with their tactics and composition, have altered with time, matching technology with the particulars of environment and engagement.

However, even with the celebrated rescue of Captain Phillips—a rescue followed by millions as it happened, re-created for millions more by way of a blockbuster motion picture that received a slew of Academy Award nominations, and compounded by the latter-day celebrity status of Navy SEALs—the popular image of the sniper had already been permanently seared into the collective consciousness.

The word "sniper" evokes images of the silent hunter stalking his prey through the jungle. He is utterly unshakable in his concentration, and relentless, deliberate, and precise in his actions. Fearless and unstoppable, he is Gunnery Sergeant Carlos Hathcock II.

Hathcock's exploits during the Vietnam War not only established him as a legendary figure bordering on the mythical, but also elevated the very concept of the sniper in the process. That impact has been spread equally to the public at large, his successors who continue to follow in his footsteps to this very day, and the military leaders who employ them.

Carlos Hathcock grew up with his grandmother, but in many ways, he was raised by the Arkansas woods. There he developed an innate sense and natural affinity for fieldcraft.

He also proved to be an unusually gifted marksman. Hathcock was actually a decorated competitive shooter prior to his experience as a sniper. In fact, he won the prestigious Wimbledon Cup in 1965 as a young Marine, which directly led him to the profession he would soon embark upon—and revolutionize.

His Wimbledon Cup success led to his recruitment by Captain Edward James Land, who sought to rapidly muster an elevated sniper presence for the USMC during the Vietnam War.

Even among the rest of Land's "Murder Inc." at the 1st Marine Division, Hathcock proved to be an exceptionally adept sniper, far outstripping even what his competition-proven accuracy predicted. Not merely a Mozart of the Model 70, Hathcock's mental makeup made him the ideal specimen for what may be deemed by many to be a rather disagreeable discipline.

Utilizing prodigious skills and an ingenious mind, Hathcock silently haunted the rainforest near Hill 55. He racked up a remarkable number of confirmed kills—ninety-three—which are widely thought to be less than a third of the genuine tally.

And for every kill, there seemed to be an associated tale of note. Routinely on the hunt for days at a time with just his spotter at his side, Hathcock assembled a division's worth of war stories all on his own.

Legend has it that he once volunteered for a "suicide mission" before he himself was made aware of the particulars. Having been given his orders, Hathcock crept into position. He had imperceptibly eased his body across a mile of terrain out over the course of four long days to pull the trigger on this North Vietnamese general. Surrounded by enemy patrols some seven hundred yards from the heart of the encampment, Hathcock went unnoticed in the brush. Camouflaged by an improvised proto-ghillie suit of sticks and vegetation, he was nearly stepped on by an NVA (North Vietnamese Army) troop before he finally caught sight of his target.

Hathcock put the general down with a direct shot to the heart and then made a measured retreat in the same manner in which he had come even as the compound exploded with the confused frenetic activity of a disturbed anthill.

And then there's the one about the time the Marine sniper eliminated the sadistic Viet Cong guerrilla leader, Apache. A sniper, interrogator, and torturer of inhuman note, Apache skinned alive a captured Marine within screaming distance of Hill 55. Those shrieks served as Hathcock's new mission orders and he tracked Apache down to end her reign of terror with precise finality.

And for more than three decades his name was etched in the record books, laying claim to the longest recorded sniper kill. Showing every bit as much ingenuity as accuracy, Hathcock is credited with a twenty-five-hundred-yard kill, accomplished by using a Browning .50 Caliber Machine Gun fit with a customized scope mount.

The legend grew on both sides of the lines during the course of his two tours as a sniper. In what must be considered the ultimate sign of respect, his petrified adversaries tagged him with the nickname "Long Tr'ang"—"White Feather"—after the adornment on his boonie hat.

That notoriety was followed by scores of countersnipers who flooded the region, including one known only as Cobra. A worthy opponent, the predator-prey balance continually shifted as the two snipers sought the upper hand in a dual destined to be decided by a single round. Hathcock caught a glint of light reflecting off the lens of his nemesis's optics, prompting the Marine to fire a headshot directly down through his enemy's scope moments before a lethal round could be sent in his direction.

Gunnery Sergeant Hathcock had been blessed with the innate tools to become the prototypical sniper. He could "dope" (read and adjust accordingly to) the wind with uncanny accuracy. He also boasted rare focus: when necessary Hathcock was able to go into single-minded bubble. It wasn't only his rifle and bullet that seemed to become an extension of himself, but the environment itself.

He also had rare charisma about him and a cult of personality gradually took shape. White Feather became the subject of endless books while inspiring numerous films and television programs. He remains a near-religious figure in the sniper community.

"I think I was one of many, many snipers who grew up reading the books about him," said Jack Murphy, who himself later became a sniper who served in the 75th Ranger Regiment and 5th Army Special Forces Group.

"I read that as a teenager—and I thought that was cool as hell. I really liked the idea that this guy was doing operations with just one other guy . . . and he was even going out by himself sometimes. They really were a force multiplier. They were harassing and killing the enemy. There was one point where Carlos Hathcock and his spotter pinned down an NDA company in the Elephant Valley for, like, six days and kept calling in artillery strikes on them. When I read that I was like, 'Damn, that's cool.' "

Following the war, Hathcock put that profile—along with his refined skills and years of accumulated knowledge—to good use.

"Look historically at snipers as a tradecraft and you'll see it would get stood up—like during World War II—and then after the war there would be this decline in training and focus," explained Brandon Webb, former U.S. Navy SEAL Sniper Course Manager. "And then Vietnam comes around and all of a sudden we had to revive the tradecraft again. Only since Vietnam has there really been continuity among the training programs."

Hathcock took an active role in ensuring that subsequent generations of snipers would be shaped in his image. He was a driving force behind the establishment of a permanent sniper presence for the Corps, rather than waiting and only raising specialized sniper units in times of need. GySgt Hathcock leveraged his knowledge and influence to develop the USMC's Scout Sniper Basic Course in Quantico, Virginia.

For decades, the Scout Sniper Basic Course secured the Corps's leadership in the field. The course became recognized as the gold standard and served as *the* template that other leading courses throughout the world would subsequently follow.

Hathcock's individual accomplishments and the legacy he left behind transformed him into a symbol. Although he died in 1999, his impact still reverberates loudly in the sniper community.

❖

Although the lessons learned by Hathcock and his ilk are still passed along to aspiring snipers and the popular image of the craft he forged remains ubiquitous, the modern-day special operations sniper has evolved into a new species—one that comes in a variety of lethal breeds.

The SOF (special operations forces) sniper has emerged the dominant hunter in a war without distinct boundaries. This new generation of sniper retains that edge that has always been granted a stealthy marksman capable of delivering precision fire at great distances. But bleeding-edge technology multiples that capability; it's not only rifles that serve as an extension of today's elite snipers, but fleets of tightly integrated aerial and satellite platforms as well.

Wielding the combined power of highly specialized SOF training, ballistics mastery, unblinking surveillance, close air support, and a team of dozens of subject-matter experts lending aid from afar, in the eyes of his adversaries the post-9/11 SOF sniper is nothing short of a technologically-enhanced warfighting demigod.

These are the men who turn the tide of battles both large and small. They do so with shots delivered across valleys, shots fired across rooms, and shots never fired at all.

They implement foreign policy at the ground level with their wits, skills, and technology. The world is subtly shaped from the shadows by men in MultiCam who exert more real-world influence than your average senator.

These are the virtuosos of precision warfare and reconnaissance. Tasked with the impossible, they are the ones who penetrate behind enemy lines, across borders, execute their orders, and escape unseen.

"If you ask any general who has commanded special operations forces on live operations, they will give great credit to the snipers—there is no more efficient mechanism," said Craig Sawyer, a former DEVGRU sniper.

"It's a capability that is very, very valuable and effective. They carry out several functions for any special operations mission and it's always a vital one. They play a huge role."

They also come in a variety of forms. Some of today's spec ops snipers are clearly derived from the Hathcock line, simply remade for the modern world. Others are so far removed from that representation that their traditional sniper lineage is nearly unrecognizable.

Utilizing stacked skill sets to drive forward a truly revolutionary era of special operations, the new legends are every bit as epic as the old.

2

Set the Conditions

The wider impression made by America's special operations forces in Vietnam was nearly as indelible as that of the sniper, although the mammoth and high-profile role spec ops have played throughout the Global War on Terror has done much to alter this.

The idea of bandana-and-bandolier-adorned Green Berets and Navy SEALs sneaking through the jungle deep behind enemy lines remains a popular one. But it's been joined in the collective consciousness by the veiled operator decked out with insectoid panoramic night-vision goggles (NVGs) and suppressed weaponry moving through urban strongholds in the dead of night.

The rise of terrorism in the modern sense during the 1970s forced the United States to reconceptualize its approach to SOF. Actually, "forced" is perhaps a bit strong, but it did crack the door open wide enough to allow an indomitable Special Forces officer by the name of Charlie Beckwith to eventually smash through the established order. Despite facing numerous stumbling blocks along the way, Beckwith ultimately triumphed in his campaign to provide the nation with a specialized and exceedingly well-trained counterterrorism (CT) component to combat this new threat.

Closely patterned after the British Special Air Service—a fabled unit in which Beckwith served as an exchange officer—1st Special Forces Operational Detachment-Delta was stood up in the late 1970s.

Delta Force soon faced its trial by fire in the attempted rescue of more than fifty Americans held hostage at the U.S. embassy in Tehran, Iran.

The unfortunate reality of counterterrorism units of this sort—tasked with the most politically sensitive, highest priority, or, frankly, impossible missions (and quite often all three at once)—is that their triumphs typically take place out of sight while their failures are flooded by the spotlight of national catastrophe.

And the unfortunate reality for Delta Force was that Operation Eagle Claw proved to be a leading example of this fate. The audacious rescue plan was overly ambitious in its construction and it devolved into an embarrassment of global proportions. The already aborted operation turned to tragedy when a Marine Corps RH-53 helicopter collided with an Air Force EC-130 transport plane during the attempt to exfiltrate Iran.

The incident not only struck a blow to the United States' reputation, it also tarnished Delta—who only became publicly known as a result—despite its operators being powerless victims.

Danny Coulson, who would later found the Hostage Rescue Team (HRT), the FBI's civilian equivalent to Delta Force, compared the reaction to blaming a quarterback for losing the Super Bowl if the team's bus had crashed on the way to the game.

Nevertheless, the development served to make leaders gun shy when presented with the option of calling into action an elite force whose missions—which often straddled the line between traditional military and law enforcement activities—could have vast political consequences.

The debacle also forced the nation to further redefine the command structure of its special operations forces. In Eagle Claw's wake, the Joint Special Operations Command (JSOC) was founded to coordinate high-priority, national-level missions—a decision that would have massive implications decades down the line.

It also provided yet another crack of the door, this time spotted by another enterprising Vietnam-era officer by the name of Richard Marcinko, who sought to create Delta's Naval equivalent.

◈

In other quarters of the military, Delta Force—internally referred to simply as "the Unit"—was viewed with equal portions of awe and suspicion. Its operators had undeniable skills—practical marksmanship and rigorous training not found elsewhere—and organizationally it was scientifically adept and forward thinking.

However, it was also considered insular, secretive, and arrogant.

But if Delta's soldiers were considered iconoclastic cowboys, Marcinko's new unit was nothing short of a gang of pirates.

Marcinko eschewed conventional notions when determining the sorts of men and missions that should define SEAL Team Six. His idea of outside-the-box flirted with the lines of legality. He required SEALs that were loyal to him, dedicated to achieving the desired end result, and willing to break rules to make both happen.

"Demo Dick's" pragmatic approach to this gray world—which demanded operators who could operate independently, decisively, and unnoticed in the darkest pits of the world at a moment's notice—was not easily rationalized by those who did not see its mandate in the same fashion.

While Marcinko could present an argument in defense of almost every questionable procurement, activity, and team-building exercise (code for nightly drinking sessions), to others the unit was simply out of control.

Marcinko deftly wielded his considerably charisma and developed intense loyalty from his enlisted SEALs. Meanwhile, he undercut and ran off any straitlaced officers who didn't get with the program (eventual JSOC commander William McRaven was one such example). He wanted outlaws to combat outlaws and not everyone was comfortable with that idea. But "Six" also possessed capabilities no other unit maintained.

SEAL Team Six had grown out of an existing SEAL intercept/CT initiative dubbed Mobility 6 (or MOB-6). However, it too followed the UK model and was assembled in a largely similar fashion to Delta Force. Rather than platoons, the unit was organized into squadrons and further subdivided into troops, with teams beneath that.

Included in this arrangement was a robust, dedicated sniper capability, necessary for the types of surgical direct action (DA), hostage rescue (HR), and special reconnaissance (SR) missions for which the two units were designed to excel.

Previously, snipers and special operations forces had largely been separate, parallel force multipliers in the American military rather than a single compounded asset.

◈

"You know why the Unit is so good?" one of its recently retired snipers asked in a clearly rhetorical fashion. "It's all about unbroken continuity from one guy to the next for the past thirty years. Guys have access to every single hit that's ever been done and they learn from that and build on that."

That continuity traces its lineage back to Larry Freedman, one of the earliest and most influential figures of all Delta's snipers.

A character among characters, Freedman was both animated and idiosyncratic. Just five eight but with an impressive physique (its maintenance said to be driven as much by narcissism as the physical demands of the job), he proudly went by the code name "Super Jew."

While his custom-made cape brandishing the Hebrew letter "S" may have just been for show, Freedman's concentration and marksmanship were regarded as effectively superhuman by his peers.

A decorated Special Forces veteran, Freedman proved fiercely protective of the snipers under his watch and worked hard to impart his knowledge to them—as they would for the next generation and so on down the line.

Super Jew intentionally tested the boundaries of personalities and situations just to find their limits. As a result, he was reportedly "fired" by Beckwith six times but returned after each dismissal to continue molding the fledgling CT force.

Freedman technically left Delta Force in 1982, but he continued to school its prospective snipers while serving as the Non-Commissioned Officer in Charge (NCOIC) of the Special Operations Target Interdiction Course (SOTIC)—the primary basic sniper course to which the Unit sent its men. He later returned to serve Delta more directly, acting as an instructor for the Unit into the early '90s.

Then in his fifties and with a long white ponytail, Super Jew looked more like a Harley-Davidson-riding grandfather—which he in fact was—than a restless, motivated commando. However, that he was as well. Despite a deep-seated mistrust of the CIA that reflected his various dealings with the Agency while a Delta operator, Freedman signed on as a Paramilitary Officer of the CIA's Special Activities Division.

In that capacity, he continued to shape future generations of spec ops snipers, although his reach widened significantly.

In the summer of 1990, just prior to the first Iraq War, a group of six CIA, DIA, and NSA intelligence operatives were keeping tabs on troop movements. However, they found themselves stranded and surrounded near the Iraq/Kuwait border when Iraq's invasion came quicker than expected.

With nowhere else to flee, they secreted to Baghdad, hoping to find a means of escape in the heart of the enemy.

After U.S. requests for help were refused by the British, French, and Russians, Polish intelligence—driven by a desire to win over their new Western allies—came to the rescue. Operation Simoom—something of a Polish "Argo"—was successfully executed and the Americans were spirited away to freedom.

Following the triumph, the United States expressed its gratitude by assuming a hands-on role in the subsequent formation of a special Polish military unit called Jednostka Wojskowa GROM.

"Naval," a recently retired fourteen-year veteran of GROM, reflected on Operation Simoom: "Nobody wanted to do it. We were the only ones and we succeeded. Officially, GROM was created afterwards and then the magic began. This was also the moment that the Americans offered their support in providing us with weapons, money, and training."

Working in collaboration with the CIA, Polish General Sławomir Petelicki envisioned a unit that would blend the best characteristics of Delta Force, the British SAS, and Germany's crack CT team, GSG 9. And indeed, Delta played a major role shaping the new unit from its earliest training.

"In 1991, thirteen GROM soldiers were sent to Delta Force for training shortly after the unit was officially formed," Naval said. "They actually went through the first selection to GROM somewhere in the mountains in America and that was conducted by Delta Force."

During one of the training marches, a Delta officer teetered on the edge of a cliff and would have fallen if not for the execution of another impromptu Polish rescue operation. An especially powerful GROM operator, "Artur," reached out and caught the American.

Following GROM's initial schooling from Delta, a special training group was formed by the CIA to send American trainers to Poland. A familiar face was among these original trainers.

"Larry Freedman, one of the best Delta Force snipers ever, was actually the first sniper instructor in GROM," Naval said.

Working as an operative of CIA's Ground Branch, Freedman showed the Poles the ropes. And then a few months later, the white-haired Freedman was right back in hostile territory, seeking the ground truth in a fast-devolving Somalia during the opening weeks of Operation Restore Hope.

On December 23, 1992, his vehicle hit a Russian-built land mine near Bardera City, in the Juba Valley. He was the first American casualty of the conflict in Somalia. His Delta Force progenies would add to that list in the following months as Operation Restore Hope was superseded by Operation Gothic Serpent.

The CIA honored Freedman with an Intelligence Star dedicated to his memory while GROM showed its gratitude by naming a street at their base after him.

The Joint Special Operations Command (JSOC) . . . is charged to study special operations requirements and techniques, ensure interoperability and equipment standardization, plan and conduct special operations exercises and training, and develop joint special operations tactics.

The Combat Applications Group (CAG) . . . tests special operations methods, equipment, tactics, and combined arms interoperability with a focus of the development of doctrine. . . .

The Naval Special Warfare Development Group (DEVGRU) provides centralized management for the test, evaluation, and development of current and emerging technology applicable to Naval Special Warfare forces.

By the early '90s, the nation's deeply classified direct action units and the larger command that controlled them were no longer quite the secret the Department of Defense would have preferred. Colonel Beckwith and Captain Marcinko both authored books detailing the origins of the units they founded, and Hollywood quite naturally jumped on the concept of priority-one CT units that existed on a constant war footing and were assigned a global area of operations.

Movies starring Chuck Norris and Charlie Sheen did not exactly lend credibility to the Pentagon's stubborn denial of the units' existence either.

Partially in an attempt to put the genie back in the bottle, the units were rebranded CAG and DEVGRU, respectively. And, like JSOC as a whole, they were purported to be nothing more than glorified test-and-development-centric organizations.

While it's certainly true they carefully studied and advanced the military in the application of surgical violence, this was work that was tested in the field, not in some lab as their charters attempted to imply.

At least that was the idea. Although the units had captured the imagination of the public, those with the power to actually send these unique solutions into motion remained haunted by the failure of Operation Eagle Claw and thus less likely to get caught up in the hype.

They had not been sidelined completely. During their formative years, Delta Force and SEAL Team Six—collectively referred to as JSOC special mission units (SMUs)—represented the last option a number of conventionally minded military leaders and timid politicians wanted to call upon during a time of need. But in the most pressing cases, they also represented the only option.

Both units had scored significant victories and demonstrated their value multiple times over. Delta executed the first successful hostage rescue of an American civilian on foreign soil when it stormed the Carcel Modelo prison in Panama City in 1989 and freed Kurt Muse. And SEAL Team Six played a key role in capturing Panamanian strongman Manuel Noriega just days later.

But those were very much the exceptions. While "all show and no go" is certainly not a fair description, the reality is that the dog and pony shows—CAPEX (capability exercise)—far outweighed the green lights granted. The units regularly underwent extensive mission workups in response to some larger crisis or another before moving on to start training in preparation for the next mission that would never come.

However, the worsening situation in Somalia demanded an overwhelming response. In August of 1993, President Bill Clinton approved Operation Gothic Serpent in order to hunt down Somali warlord Mohamed Farrah Aidid.

The operation was built around Task Force Ranger. And while the soldiers of the 75th Ranger Regiment's 3rd Battalion (3/75) were the most numerous in its overall composition, the centerpiece of this 160-troop-strong manhunting task force was unquestionably Delta Force's C Squadron.

They were further enabled by the Night Stalkers—the elite helicopter pilots who manned the specialized aircraft of the 160th Special Operations Aviation Regiment (160th SOAR)—along with their usual complement of attached Air Commandos from the 24th Special Tactics Squadron (24STS), JSOC's Air Force special mission unit.

The manifest also happened to show the inclusion of a small four-man DEVGRU sniper element, although it was considered nothing more than a token representation for the Navy unit.

Ultimately, Operation Gothic Serpent merely replaced Operation Eagle Claw as the fiasco that reminded leaders exactly what can go wrong when it commits its most elite troops to the sorts of extreme-risk, extreme-reward operations for which they were designed.

But even as an already risk-averse SOF environment hardened while the specter of terrorism continued to rise, the manhunt in Somalia also served as a precursor of what was to come . . . eventually. Though primitive by today's standards, the technology and tactics innovated in Mogadishu served to add to that unbroken continuity that "makes the Unit so good."

Over time—and following a tectonic shift regarding the nation's stomach for combating terrorism—the somewhat clumsy, uncoordinated attempts to take down Aidid would be transformed into the most efficient and lethal capability ever envisioned.

It would also offer a preview of the capability and courage that exists within the ranks of JSOC's snipers—capability and courage that would come to play such a defining role in subsequent conflicts.

◈

The SEAL snipers from Red Squadron—Richard Kaiser, John Gay, Howard Wasdin, and Homer Nearpass—weren't exactly embraced by their Delta counterparts. They weren't exactly shunned either, but the tension in the air was irrefutable, as was the general feeling among the Delta operators that the presence of the SEALs added no particular value to the operation.

This was a bitter rivalry born with SEAL Team Six's very inception. While initially sold as a maritime complement to Delta Force—one that could, for example, rescue hostages aboard hijacked cruise ships—that would serve to round out the nation's total CT solution, it was never truly envisioned as such.

Founding commanding officer Richard Marcinko joked (or perhaps more accurately, opined) that a mud puddle or a canteen in the general vicinity was enough to justify SEAL Team Six's right to an operation.

Operators from both units presumed their superiority in their shared core competency of precision direct action, and thus considered their respective unit the more deserving when any potential high-profile operations surfaced (or landed). Delta Force and DEVGRU represented two apex predators claiming domain over a hunting ground barely large enough to feed one.

"Unfortunately, the units have been politically pitted against each other; they compete for the same missions," said former DEVGRU sniper Craig Sawyer, who experienced this frustration firsthand. "It's unfortunate because both units are filled with heroes—highly capable men with red, white, and blue in their eyes. Brave as they come. Capable as they come. Mean as they come. Dedicated as they come. But they hated each other because they were pitted against each other."

The lack of delineation largely worked in opposition to Marcinko's grander scheme. While Delta Force may have been continually stymied by operations rehearsed for but never executed, ST6 was discouraged to an even greater degree.

The relatively rare missions that did come around were generally snared by the Army unit while SEAL Team Six found itself pushed aside again and again.

According to those on the losing end, this wasn't down to any assessment that Delta was the more capable unit (both had their champions and detractors), but rather a question of parentage.

JSOC—which has operational control of both units—was dominated by Army generals throughout the first two decades of its existence. In fact, its first ten commanders came from the Army, including multiple officers who had served inside Delta Force.

"I see them like two boys on a Little League baseball team who could pitch," Sawyer explained. "But one of their daddies is the coach. So who do you think is going to get to pitch come game day?

"It's a horrible situation. It didn't matter which unit was appropriate for the job, it just mattered whose daddy ran JSOC at the time. The politics cause the units to resent each other but it's not their fault. That's the situation that they're in. If you took the guys and just let them hang out together, they'd probably get along like brothers."

On one occasion, DEVGRU even suffered the indignity of having its OTB (over the beach) gear commandeered by Delta Force to conduct a clear maritime op. At times the situation seemed so dire that some experienced SEAL Team Six operators—including Sawyer—actually considered leaving the Navy to take a shot at joining the Unit.

Sawyer said, "When I was at DEVGRU, we kept training, developing solutions and equipment, and staging for certain operations and then losing them. . . . They would get handed to Delta. I realized, okay, the politics are stacked in their favor. Their dad is the coach."

Still exasperated by the experience, the former SEAL Team Six sniper continued, "I went to the Navy because SEAL Team were the baddest motherfuckers on the face of the planet; that's what I had read and that's what I was told. So I went to SEAL Team. Once I got in there I started learning about SEAL Team Six and that's like the all-star team. If you really want to operate and to roll the dice and volunteer for something even riskier, more hard-core, but get a lot of sophisticated support and opportunity, then you go to that league there. I was like, 'That's me. That's where I'm going.'

"Once I saw that one unit was going to get most of the work and the other unit was going to get kicked to the side for political reasons, well, shoot, I'm going to go to the unit that is getting work, period. I don't care what you call it. I wasn't after a career in the military. I wasn't after a collar device. I wasn't after all the chest candy they loaded me down with after each campaign. I didn't care about those things. I cared about kicking some ass. And not anybody's ass—the ass of those who directly meant to do harm to those I care about. That's where my head was at and that's what I wanted to do."

Both ultimately chose not to ("My teammates were so bitter at me [for talking about it] . . . They would have hated my guts"), but the mere consideration serves to illustrate just how unloved the ST6's operators felt by JSOC.

◈

One of those former Delta commanders who had moved to the top seat at JSOC, General William Garrison, was the man in charge during Operation Gothic Serpent. He threw the SEALs a bone—a small one—but a bone nonetheless with the inclusion of the four DEVGRU snipers in Task Force Ranger.

The SEAL Team Six snipers leveraged the fact that they weren't as tightly integrated into the mission's primary HVT (high-value target) effort, freeing them up to conduct the full spectrum of their expansive mission set. The snipers of DEVGRU and Delta Force specialize in executing extraordinarily demanding reconnaissance operations, the sort more typically associated with intelligence operatives, although often with an even greater degree of danger attached. As a result, both units refer to their snipers with the term "recce"—British for "recon" and indicative of their British heritage.

Rather than stay in the relative safety of the hangar where the bulk of the task force was based, the DEVGRU snipers coordinated with the CIA and teamed with SIGINT (signals intelligence) specialists from the Army's enigmatic Intelligence Support Activity, or ISA.

The ISA remains among the "blackest" organizations in the DoD's arsenal. Even insiders who casually toss around references to other JSOC units rarely make mention of "the Activity." In Somalia, they came complete with their own dedicated aircraft, directional microphones, and other specialized equipment, which enabled its specialists to intercept communications traffic among the warlord's men. While relatively basic by today's standards, this allowed them to begin mapping out Aidid's network, providing them the actionable intelligence Delta needed to strike.

Operating from their shared safe house deep in the heart of Mogadishu, DEVGRU recce operators Nearpass and Wasdin pulled clandestine vehicle reconnaissance despite the volatile nature of a city primed to explode.

Masked behind keffiyeh headdresses and the flowery shirts favored by the locals, they helped to further pinpoint ISA's potential targets armed with a 35mm camera. The four-man Black Team element also utilized their rare low-visibility surveillance skillets to map out escape and evasion routes and identify potential landing zones for 160th SOAR helos.

Wasdin captured photographic evidence of weapons disguised as babies and bricks being transported by noncombatants.

Commenting on their low-vis tasking and the nuances it can entail, the Georgian said, "I can tell you for a fact, we were the only ones issued a [keffiyeh]. Sometimes we wore it and sometimes we didn't; it depended on which part of booger-eating country we were in.

"We found out real quick that just because you were wearing a headdress didn't mean you were wearing the right one. You'd find out the red-and-white-checkered one is good in some parts of town but in other parts it means something—like with the Crips and the Bloods over here. They each had their own headdress and body language."

The snipers also leveraged the more lethal aspects of their advanced training. After climbing a six-story tower to make a positive identification of Osman Hassan Ali Atto, Delta Force launched a raid on the target building.

While Atto—a powerful figure in the khat (a local narcotic) trade and Aidid's second in command—escaped minutes prior to the assault, Wasdin came up big in the clutch. Spotting a Somali armed with a rocket-propelled grenade (RPG) and with a circling Black Hawk in his sights, the sniper connected from 846 yards away with his .300 Win Mag.

The shot went straight through the militiaman's face and erased the threat, earning the SEALs a bit of respect from onlooking Unit snipers in the process.

Wasdin admitted the shot wasn't quite as precise as it appeared, although he kept the Delta snipers in the dark about that fact at the time. He said, "You have to have a little bit of luck, because at those ranges, even the rotation of the Earth is going to be playing with it one way or the other. Just a tiny bit of wind at a thousand yards can move a bullet eight to ten inches laterally. I have no qualms telling people I was actually aiming for the sternum. I just got lucky to not miss left or right, but vertically. It would have been just as easy to shoot him in the groin as it was in the head."

Days later, Atto was successfully ensared. The Somali warlord's Fiat 124 sedan was brought to a halt when a 160th SOAR helicopter swooped into position and a Delta sniper destroyed its engine block from the air. Atto attempted to flee the scene but was run down by Delta assaulters who swarmed down from the helo as Atto's gun-toting bodyguard was incapacitated by sniper fire.

The small SEAL sniper contingent also added to their significant contribution to the overall mission by pulling "Eyes of Mogadishu" duty—utilizing conventional military QRF (Quick Reaction Force) UH-60 Black Hawks of the 101st Airborne Division as aerial sniper platforms—as well as escorting CIA assets throughout the threatening city.

◈

Less than two weeks after the apprehension of Atto, Task Force Ranger attempted a daylight raid to round up more of Aidid's top lieutenants. The resulting events have been extensively covered across books, television, and film.

The full package of 160th SOAR Black Hawks and Little Birds hit the target location. Delta operators flowed through the objective and rounded up the prisoners precisely as planned. 3/75 Rangers fast-roped in to cordon off the area, while an awaiting twelve-vehicle convoy was in position to extract the assaulters and their quarry back to the hangar.

The initial outburst of hostile fire was greater than anticipated, and a Ranger—PFC Todd Blackburn—was gravely wounded when he missed the rope and fell seventy feet to the earth.

This already chaotic situation ripped free of any semblance of control or coordination when Super 6-1—the MH-60L Black Hawk piloted by Chief Warrant Officer Three (CW3), Clifton "Elvis" Wolcott—was hit by RPG fire and crashed several blocks away.

Delta snipers Dan Busch and Jim Smith had survived the Super 6-1 crash and actively attempted to defend the site. Busch eventually succumbed to injuries he suffered in the attempt.

Three vehicles from the convoy—including one with SEAL sniper

Richard Kaiser—immediately transported Blackburn back to base so that he could be rendered aid. The miniconvoy was torn apart by withering enemy fire in the process with another Ranger—SGT Dominick Pilla—killed as they attempted to negotiate their way back to the hangar.

The remainder of the extraction vehicles later became known as "the lost convoy." They would ultimately fail in their bid to make the short drive to the Super 6-1's crash site just a few blocks away but were repeatedly foiled by a bewildering series of events, marked by delayed instructions, wrong turns, and massive bloodshed.

SEAL snipers John Gay, Howard Wasdin, and Homer Nearpass were among this unfortunate lot. Early in the engagement, Wasdin and a Unit operator silently advanced through an alley on foot and eliminated a pair of Somali gunners who were firing down on the assault element from a nearby fifth-floor window.

Then Wasdin was hit in the knee by a ricocheted round. While others rushed to the downed Wasdin, Nearpass stepped in and dropped multiple targets. He calmly aimed down the Trijicon ACOG of his suppressed CAR-15 to pick off one rushing attacker after another.

An attached 24STS Air Force Combat Control Team (CCT) later described Nearpass as the embodiment of what SEALs were meant to be. Utterly unconcerned for his safety in those moments, he even flashed a broad grin as the action intensified.

Back in their vehicle and trapped in the center of a blistering spherical attack, Nearpass and Wasdin went through their ten thirty-round magazines and then several more taken off an injured Ranger. Out of ammunition and with the entire city seemingly descending upon them in a nonstop barrage of AK-47s and RPG fire, Wasdin drew his SIG P226 9mm sidearm.

Face-to-face with an adversary at near-point-blank range, the SEAL's first shot somehow missed. The Somali's did not; the Georgian was struck in the right shinbone, nearly ripping the limb from his body. Wasdin instinctively pulled the pistol's trigger twice more, putting his attacker down with a tight group to his head.

Nearpass dragged the incapacitated half of his shooting pair to the passenger seat, draped his mangled leg over the hood, and took the wheel himself, all the while keeping the badly wounded Wasdin as calm as possible. As the crippled Hummer limped along, the injured SEAL was struck with yet another round, this time to the left ankle.

The Humvee finally expired. Completely surrounded and with militiamen from multiple factions closing in fast, the QRF at last arrived to rescue the lost convoy.

"There is a Bible verse that says, 'Greater love has no one than this: to lay down one's life for one's friends,'" Wasdin said. "To be a SEAL sniper, you're on the cutting edge, you're on the tip of the spear. You're more likely to die than anybody else. You have to have it in your heart that you love your country and your fellow Americans so much that you are willing to be that person to lay down your life. In Somalia there was no doubt in my mind that I was going to die."

He reflected on making the sniper shot to prevent a Black Hawk from being hit weeks earlier yet being haunted by not being able to do again. "I shot those guys in Mogadishu that were trying to shoot down the Black Hawk. . . . I was happy that that happened, but you know what? It still eats my butt to this day that I wasn't able to get the one guy who shot down the bird that my buddy Dan Busch was on. What would I give to be able to make that shot? I'd love to be able to go back. And make that shot and kill the guy in the doorway who shot me in the Humvee that almost shot my leg off.

"I think any elite warrior isn't going to be patting themselves on the back going, 'Look what I did here.' Because that's not perfection. Of course, we always strive for perfection but that's unattainable, unachievable."

◈

As the convoy—along with a number of Delta operators and Rangers who left on foot following the initial takedown—attempted to make their way to the Super 6-1 crash site, another MH-60L Black Hawk was impacted by an RPG and helplessly circled down to a shattering collision with the dirt several blocks away.

Initially, the Super 6-4 survivors were defended from a distance, as Delta snipers Brad Halling, Gary Gordon, and Randy Shughart thinned the initial rush to the site with accurate sniper fire from aboard Super 6-1.

However, that was only a temporary measure and there were no reinforcements available. The entire ground force had already been committed to the first crash site and was now either lost or pinned down.

A mob collected and strode toward Super 6-4 pilot CW3 Michael Durant and his crew. Sniper team leader Gordon requested that he and Shughart be put down to defend Super 6-4. His request was denied.

He made another request. Again, denied.

The third request was accepted.

Super 6-1 pilots James Francis Yacone and Mike Goffena maneuvered their bird into position and the sniper pair fast-roped in some one hundred meters away. From there they rapidly made their way through a maze of shanties to arrive at the downed Black Hawk.

Similar to the way Nearpass was described, Durant later recalled the sense of composed efficiency with which his two-man cavalry operated. They matter-of-factly moved the crew into defendable positions and then set about whittling away at an onrushing bloodthirsty flock.

Eventually, Maine-native Gordon reported that he was hit, more with a sense of irritation than fear or pain. After he fell, Shughart retrieved Gordon's CAR-15 and handed it to Durant to use in his own defense.

Nebraskan Shughart returned to tend to the pack with his M14, firing deliberate, precise shots. He inevitably ran out of ammunition and was overrun.

The two Delta recce operators killed an estimated twenty-five assailants before making the ultimate sacrifice. With no one left to protect him, Durant was beaten savagely, but taken hostage rather than murdered. He was later released and lived to tell the tales of the heroism he saw that day.

Despite being in different Sabre Squadrons, retired Delta Force assaulter Larry Vickers—who took part in A Squadron's successful rescue of Kurt Muse a few years earlier—knew both Gordon and Shughart from their shared time in the Unit together.

Vickers said, "Gary was more of a hard charger while Randy was a real quiet, reserved guy. They were both well-liked dudes. The thought process was always—no one will ever know this for sure because they are both dead—but Gary was kind of the one who would jump first and ask questions later and that's almost possibly what got them in the situation they were in with Durant. That's neither here nor there, that's speculation.

"But the reality is, that's just an example of the kind of courage and sacrifice you'll find inside the Unit. It could have been any two guys to go down there, but those guys actually did it. They saw what was going on and they saw that things were going sour and made the request three times."

After Gordon and Shughart were on the ground and battling to save Durant, Super 6-1 too was hit with an RPG. Brad Halling—the Delta sniper who remained aboard the Black Hawk to man its minigun after a crew chief was injured—had his leg torn off in the resultant explosion, which also rendered Captain Francis Yacone unconscious. CW3 Mike Goffena somehow managed to set the Black Hawk down in a controlled crash in the safety of a nearby port facility.

◈

Ultimately, eighteen American servicemen were killed and another seventy-three wounded in the day-long clash. Additionally, a Malaysian soldier was killed and a handful of Malaysian and Pakistani troops were wounded in the QRF rescue.

Estimates place the enemy losses anywhere from five hundred to three thousand.

The American public—the vast majority of whom were unaware of any military action taking place—were aghast to turn on CNN and see images of the mutilated, naked corpses of Delta snipers Gordon and Shughart dragged through the streets of Mogadishu.

The hunt for Aidid was promptly canceled and the men returned home soon afterward.

While a Delta Force assaulter who took part in the battle considered it an overwhelming victory ("one of the most one-sided battles in American history"), it only served to cement the United States' unwillingness to pro-actively use its most elite troops.

General Peter Shoomaker, a onetime Delta Force squadron commander who succeeded Gen. Garrison as JSOC commander just months after the Battle of Mogadishu, lamented, "It was like having a brand-new Ferrari in the garage, and nobody wants to race it because you might dent the fender."

Meanwhile, the fallout also emboldened emerging terrorist networks, who termed the nation a "paper tiger" that would shirk whenever its nose was bloodied.

According to *The 9/11 Commission Report,* President Clinton openly dreamed of sending JSOC after bin Laden ahead of the September 11 at-tacks. Speaking to Gen. Hugh Shelton, then-Chairman of the Joint Chiefs of Staff, Clinton said, "You know, it would scare the shit out of al-Qaeda if suddenly a bunch of black ninjas rappelled out of helicopters into the middle of their camp."

He was right, although the United States was institutionally unwilling to take such bold action with its world-leading collection of "ninjas," still haunted by the failures of the past. Even as America fell under an increas-ing threat, not once during the '80s or '90s was Delta Force or DEVGRU sent to hunt down terrorists.

It would take a massive occurrence to change that mindset.

That something massive came on September 11, 2001.

◈

Delta Force snipers Gary Gordon and Randy Shughart were posthumously awarded the Medal of Honor, the first recipients since the Vietnam War. They also both had naval vessels, the USNS *Gordon* and USNS *Shughart,* named in their honor.

Captain James Francis Yacone was awarded the Silver Star for braving intense enemy fire to Super 6-1 so that Gordon and Shughart could fast-rope to the rescue of Super 6-4.

Unit sniper Brad Halling was fit with a prosthetic left leg. He mastered his new leg sufficiently to return to active duty, resuming his role as operator in one of the most physically demanding military units to ever exist. Halling left the Army with eighteen years of SOF experience under his belt to become a prosthetist. He now serves as president of Innovative Prosthetic Solutions.

All four DEVGRU snipers were awarded the Silver Star for their actions in the Battle of Mogadishu.

Sniper team leader Richard Kaiser returned to the fray after their three-vehicle convoy made an early return to base to race the wounded back for immediate care. That team—the so-called relief convoy—was joined by SEAL officer Eric Thor Olson, who was in Somalia merely to observe a JSOC task force in action in anticipation of taking command of DEVGRU in the following months. Olson borrowed body armor and a CAR-15 and braved the erupting city to come to the aid of the dozens who were trapped and under heavy fire. For that, Olson was also awarded a Silver Star.

Kaiser had entered the Navy at the tender age of seventeen and served in the SEAL Teams from 1980 to 1990, the last five with DEVGRU. He took some time away while in the Enlisted Education Advancement Program (EEAO) and earned a bachelor's degree before rejoining SEAL Team Six as a sniper in '91.

The Milwaukee, Wisconsin, native served as the training chief for DEVGRU from '93 to '95 before assuming the role of DEVGRU sniper cell leader in 1997. And in that capacity he deployed to Bosnia to hunt down PIFWCs (Persons Indicted for War Crimes).

Kaiser retired in August of 2000 following twenty-two years of active duty. However, he continued as a civilian government employee with DEVGRU, serving as ST6's deputy operations officer from 2001 to 2012. He's now the executive director of the Navy SEAL Museum.

John Gay was spared serious injury when a bullet fired from an AK-47 deflected off his trademark oversized Randall Bowie knife. The blade shattered but Gay was only left with superficial wounds. He hoped to cash in with a knife endorsement but was denied—much to his teammates' amusement. Gay continued with SEAL Team Six long past Operation Gothic Serpent, serving well into his forties.

Howard Wasdin recuperated from his serious leg injuries and returned to DEVGRU, but he medically retired a short while later. Besides becoming a bestselling author of titles such as *SEAL Team Six* and *The Last Rescue,* Wasdin also found a second life as a chiropractor.

"People always ask how you go from being a SEAL sniper to being a chiropractor," he noted with a laugh. "I tell them it's the exact same job; I just put people out of their misery in a different way now."

3

Ground Truth

The wisdom gleaned by Homer Nearpass in Somalia was directly called upon as the Joint Special Operations Command was at last sicced upon its enemies following the devastation of 9/11 and the nation's requisite monumental shift in mentality.

This did not occur as quickly as one might assume. Jawbreaker—an initial advance team of Central Intelligence Agency officers sent to Afghanistan in the weeks following the attacks—requested a JSOC component; however, that request was denied. Much to Delta Force's dismay, military leaders deemed the assignment lacking in clarity and overly risky.

The CIA, joined later by Army Special Forces, took the reins to spearhead a classic (if technologically sophisticated) unconventional warfare campaign that toppled the Taliban. Meanwhile, Delta operators waited for weeks to at last receive orders to set off after Osama bin Laden and his chief associates (and DEVGRU even longer than that).

JSOC, then commanded by Gen. Dell Dailey, finally established an HVT-hunting presence known as Task Force Sword, at the recently seized and converted Bagram Airfield in late October 2001.

Initially fronted by Delta's B Squadron, Dailey's strategy was to prestage the bulk of Task Force Sword's direct action forces at the base so that they could be immediately launched for kill-or-capture missions in the event of an HVT spotting.

However, there was a much smaller component of the task force, known as AFO (Advance Force Operations), that actively attempted to root out these targeted elements.

AFO actualized the leadership philosophies of its commander, Lt. Col. Pete Blaber. "Imagine the unimaginable," "when in doubt, develop the situation," and "always listen to the guy on the ground," were among AFO's central tenets in 2001 as it scoured hundreds of thousands of square miles with a force of less than fifty men divvied up into six teams.

The amorphous, proactive initiative was a bespoke effort meant to exploit the unique strategic reconnaissance skill sets contained within the rank of JSOC's sniper teams. AFO was only loosely defined and each team was adaptable and independent—self-organized and then self-operated to best suit its particular set of circumstances.

Nearpass was Blaber's right-hand man as these recce teams sprawled across Afghanistan. Now close to forty, the venerable DEVGRU sniper still regularly flashed the same fearless grin he displayed to his enemies in Mogadishu. His unflappable attitude and dedication proved to serve Blaber well in offering up his no-nonsense advice and counsel . . . well, maybe with just a touch of nonsense at the appropriate times.

"Homer is tireless and dedicated in his attention to detail," recalled Wasdin. "He's never going to stop. After the day was done, Homer would still be working on his field sketches or redoing his DOPE notes. He would get up at three o'clock in the morning and go for an eight-mile run . . . I never did that. You've got to respect that."

Effusive in his praise, Nearpass's former shooting partner continued, "You never had to worry about him being thorough and sniping is an exact science. Some guys get to be snipers by busting their hump and putting in the work. There are others that just have a lot of talent. I was probably more talent than busting my hump to be honest. And then there's that combination, guys who have the talent and who put in the work to be an elite sniper. Homer had equal measures of both."

And Nearpass's USMC Scout Sniper Course schoolmates got a small preview of his ability to keep on smiling when the world is falling apart around him.

Following an especially difficult day in which almost the entire class failed their stalk, the class collectively hung their heads in the film room, readying for a United States Marine Corps–caliber browbeating from the instructor. The projector kicked on and threw light up onto the screen at the front of the class. On it appeared Nearpass's silhouette, which suddenly broke into full *Flashdance* mode.

"We all busted out laughing," Wasdin recalled. "It really lightened the mood and then everybody got themselves squared away. It was one of those things you just can't plan. You have to be in tune to when to do it and when not to and that was Homer's gift. He could keep it light. If there was a tense situation, Homer always had a good way of dissipating it."

◈

In December 2001, an high-value target worthy of the larger task force was thought to be pinpointed. And not just any HVT, HVT-1—Osama bin Laden himself.

"UBL" in military parlance, bin Laden was believed to have taken refuge in Tora Bora, the cave complex stronghold in the White Mountains that had served the Mujahideen so well in their long existential struggle against the Soviets.

Delta's B Squadron had just been rotated out of country to make room for A Squadron, which readily accepted the challenge of bagging bin Laden.

While JSOC was in country and on the hunt, it was still hampered by risk-averse decision making. While the public, the politicians, and military generals demanded results, the men they expected to actually deliver them were not consistently afforded the full authority or support required to make that a reality.

Though an overwhelming tactical victory, the Battle for Tora Bora ultimately failed in its chief goal of neutralizing bin Laden, foiled by mechanisms well above the pay grade of the men on the ground.

Multiple operational plans made by the Unit were rejected, including a brazen scheme to scale the fourteen-thousand-foot peaks that border Pakistan in order to shock a trapped al-Qaeda from behind.

Too much faith was placed on the efforts of ambiguous allies—some local (Afghani tribal militias more concerned with their own power struggle than the elimination of al-Qaeda or the Taliban) and others international (Pakistan was gifted the princely sum of $1 billion in new economic aid in exchange for sealing off the border, which was later judged to have been executed in a halfhearted fashion—at best).

Finally, according to Senator John Kerry's 2009 report, "Tora Bora Revisited: How We Failed to Get Bin Laden and Why It Matters Today," the critical—and repeated—request that the campaign be rounded out with the addition of a 75th Ranger Regiment battalion was denied by order of JSOC commander Dailey and CENTCOM commander Gen. Tommy Franks.

Despite these crippling limitations, A Squadron managed to kill scores of al-Qaeda fighters and send the terrorist network into disarray. It did so following the same underlying game plan that Blaber's AFO put into practice: leveraging the abilities of Delta's recce snipers.

Augmented by CIA paramilitary officers and contractors, a small team of British Special Boat Service (SBS) commandos, and Army SF soldiers, the Delta Force snipers assumed the lead role in executing devastating terminal guidance operations (TGO), i.e., directing air strikes via laser and GPS guidance.

Multiple snipers made crucial contributions to the campaign. This was largely made possible by their advanced mountaineering training, as they conquered the terrain to identify observation posts and then utilize them to locate entrenched enemy positions and rain down death in the form of hundreds of thousands of pounds of ordnance over three consecutive days.

They took a more hands-on approach as well. Recce operators led multiple surveillance missions up the mountain to close in on their adversary's ranks, while also delivering precision fire of their own; one Delta sniper made a (unconfirmed and previously unreported) kill with a .50-caliber sniper rifle at an astonishing range of twenty-five hundred yards—among the longest in the history of warfare.

◈

Among the recce operators who demonstrated proficiency and bravery beyond any realistic expectation was sniper team leader Sean "Scrawnee" Walker.

Walker's legend inside the world of special operations had been secured more than a decade earlier.

In December of 1989, he may have already seemed like an old hat by most standards with seven years of service with the 75th Ranger Regiment under his belt, but he was still a relatively inexperienced operator, less than a year removed from OTC—Delta Force's initial half-year-plus Operator Training Course that takes accomplished soldiers and transforms them into world-class commandos.

That night the young assaulter was assigned a position on a roof alongside the Unit's snipers. Their task was to provide overwatch security while an element breached the Carcel Modelo prison in Panama City to rescue imprisoned American citizen Kurt Muse.

Inserted by a 160th SOAR MH-6 Little Bird and armed with an M249 Squad Automatic Weapon (the fire-breathing machine gun's first real test in combat), Walker proceeded to unleash nine hundred rounds and two grenades to decimate a heavy reinforcement force as Muse was pulled from his cell. In less than six minutes, Walker racked up fifty-five confirmed kills, earning himself the apt nickname "the Punisher" in the process.

Four years later, Walker would join the snipers again—this time as a member of the recce troop himself, having traded in the M249 for an M14 (and later, an SR-25). There he would remain for the next eleven years, adding significantly to that invaluable unbroken continuity of experience.

During that time he would deploy to Somalia, Bosnia, and elsewhere—adding Operation Just Cause, Operation Desert Storm, Operation Fervent

Archer, and Operation Relentless Pursuit to his résumé while earning multiple Bronze Stars with "V" devices for valor in little-known operations—before finally arriving in Afghanistan as one of the recce troop's most seasoned operators.

Alternately dubbed "Scrawnee" despite boasting the shredded physique of a professional bodybuilder, Walker distinguished himself yet again during the Battle of Tora Bora.

As part of Jackal Team, Walker and two other snipers negotiated a seemingly impassable vertical rock cliff to claim a superior vantage point of the mountainous battlefield—among the closest Task Force Sword would attain throughout the clash. Once in position, he called in precision air strikes old-school-style, using just a compass and his experience to obliterate DShK heavy machine gun and al-Qaeda (AQ) personnel positions over the following two days. When an AQ patrol narrowed down on their prime location, Scrawnee and the other snipers scrambled over the side of the cliff to its rock walls to avoid discovery.

Ultimately, his actions at Tora Bora would earn him another Bronze Star.

The intensity of the overwhelming firepower was seemingly too much for bin Laden, whose frantic communication with his followers was intercepted by the DoD's SIGINT wizards at the Intelligence Support Activity. Wounded and desperate, an apologetic bin Laden was heard granting his followers permission to surrender while he expected his death was fast approaching.

As it turned out, he would escape that fate for almost a decade. After the battle, bin Laden's condition and whereabouts were unknown for years. His death at Tora Bora was deemed a distinct possibility until he put an end to the mystery with the resumption of AQ's propaganda campaign, praising America's enemies and taunting his pursuers.

Tora Bora turned out to be the last, best chance the United States had at vengeance for the entirety of the '00s.

Following the frustrations of Tora Bora, Delta's A Squadron's deployment came to a premature halt. General Dailey replaced Delta's Task Force Green with DEVGRU's Task Force Blue. This made Red Squadron the primary direct action component of Task Force 11 (formerly Task Force Sword) and bypassed the Unit's C Squadron in the process.

This decision only served to inflame the already bitter friction that existed between the competing special mission units. Delta's soldiers judged the sailors to be the martial equivalents of "fish out of water" in the mountainous Afghanistan, inadequately outfitted or prepared to operate in the harsh and unforgiving terrain. Meanwhile, DEVGRU considered its men more than ready for the fight, both operationally and motivationally, having been held by the collar dating back well before 9/11.

However, as the unified team of Delta Officer Pete Blaber and DEVGRU sniper Homer Nearpass illustrated, the units' rivalry didn't extend to its recce elements—at least not with the same burning ferocity, anyway.

"The snipers cross-train and work together much more than the assaulters do," former Red Squadron sniper Craig Sawyer confirmed. "As a result, you don't find that same level of animosity."

JSOC's snipers also opened their Afghanistan manhunt having recently worked in unison toward similar goals in Bosnia, increasing the familiarity between the units.

In early 2002, following the crushing, one-sided encounter at Tora Bora, a sizable collection of anti-American forces was suspected to have amassed in the Shah-i-Kot Valley.

As Task Force 11's primary assault force remained leashed in Bagram awaiting word on the location of one of the big three—bin Laden; his AQ number two, Ayman al-Zawahiri; or Taliban leader Mullah Mohammed Omar—Blaber's approach continued to contrast (and in some ways clash) with that of his boss, Dailey.

AFO recalled snipers from B Squadron's recce troop to headline a series of arduous reconnaissance operations designed to "prepare the battlefield" in anticipation of a significantly larger military operation that was being formulated: Operation Anaconda.

Multiple trial runs meant to test both the brutally difficult terrain and the defenses of the enemy were made by two AFO field teams: India and Juliet.

India was initially just a two-man affair, but one stocked deep with talent and experience nonetheless. It comprised a pair of master hunters from the south—Master Sergeants Kevin "Speedy" Short of Kentucky and Robert Horrigan from Texas. The two were an ideal pairing—silent and unyielding infiltrators with boundless endurance. Those traits were mission critical as they trudged and scaled their way deep into enemy-laden territory marked by vertical cliffs and snowdrifts at an elevation of greater than ten thousand feet. Later, as they continued penetrating defenses, India added a SIGINT specialist from the ISA to round out their effort.

Meanwhile, Juliet was led by another southerner—the accomplished and devoutly religious Master Sergeant Kristofar Kosem of West Virginia. Kris's team included two additional Delta recce snipers along with an Air Force Combat Control Technician (CCT) from JSOC's 24STS and yet another soldier from the ISA.

Desperately in need of additional men boasting those same rare polished talents in order to completely blanket the expansive valley, Nearpass suggested that Blaber turn to Bagram and invite his fellow snipers from Red Squadron's Black Team to join the effort.

Blaber's request to SEAL Team Six commander Joe Kernan was partially met—one of the squadron's two Reconnaissance and Surveillance elements was redirected to assist AFO in the Shah-i-Kot. Blaber's new five-man DEVGRU recce team addition was given the code name Mako 31. Meanwhile, the remainder of Red Squadron hunkered down an hour away, awaiting the call to action should an HVT be sighted during Operation Anaconda (or elsewhere).

The trial runs complete, India went in on foot to claim their final observation points, Short armed with an M4 and Horrigan with an SR-25. The team endured a steep overnight march from the west and ascended to an elevation of 10,500 feet over a four-mile trek. Their assignment was to assume an overwatch position over the valley's southwest.

Juliet, meanwhile, chose to ride in from the north of the valley. Piloting virtually silent hybrid electric-powered ATVs (which were classified and practically magical vehicles at the time) through the dark with the aid of similarly cutting-edge NVGs and GPS technology, the team narrowly avoided being compromised on multiple occasions. It infiltrated the small enemy-occupied village of Menewar, skirted past a minefield, and dodged an enemy machine-gun position before finally establishing a position overlooking the valley's east. Once set up in overwatch, Juliet immediately identified an AQ infestation in the surrounding areas.

Mako 31's SEAL snipers (along with Air Force CCT Technical Sergeant Andrew Martin) reported in to the AFO safe house in Gardez just ahead of the commencement of Operation Anaconda and therefore lacked the benefit of the advance penetration ops. Their mission was to lay claim to a position overlooking the valley's southern edge via a grueling path earlier blazed by India.

Mako 31 completed a laborious multiday, seven-mile climb through thigh-deep snow while subjected to extreme cold and high winds in order to approach its assigned observation point unseen. However, as they neared their intended destination, they discovered the position had already been claimed by an AQ-heavy machine gun team armed with a Soviet-built DShK. Deemed a tactically critical position by AFO, the AQ fighters were ideally situated to tear apart the impending air assault that the coalition conventional forces planned to conduct the following day.

◈

Despite the AFO teams warning that a significantly larger-than-anticipated force existed in the valley and its surrounding mountainsides—perhaps a thousand strong and owning vital strategic territory in some cases—Operation Anaconda had become a strategic freight train.

The battle plan was complex to the point of convolution and lacked effective unity of command—and therefore coordination and control. It involved multiple task forces across multiple nations in a misguided attempt to weave together a wide range of conventional and SOF forces—both air and ground—into a single, cohesive (yet rigid) operation.

Unfortunately, the cumbersome op's momentum alone seemed to cause leaders to ignore updated intelligence and willfully choose to make poor decisions.

The existence of a single DShK in precisely the wrong spot from the coalition's perspective had the power to upend Anaconda with spectacularly disastrous results despite its two thousand well-equipped men and technological might.

Mako 31's unwelcome discovery certainly fit that bill. With Operation Anaconda's leaders unwilling to adjust their assault plan, the SEAL Team Six snipers were forced to devise an audible of their own. An hour before the official launch of the offensive, the recce team sprang a surprise raid on the al-Qaeda camp. They eliminated two terrorists in the opening instants of the attack and incapacitated another. A circling AC-130H then unleashed its overwhelming firepower to mop up the remainder of the pack.

As Operation Anaconda steamrolled into action, India, Juliet, and Mako 31 called down devastation on the entrenched AQ and Taliban militants they had located, tallying up scads of casualties. Meanwhile, a number of the larger coalition force were not so effective while enduring less enviable circumstances—from being immediately pinned down by enemy gunfire to a convoy that was on the wrong end of a punishing and tragic blue-on-blue strike from an AC-130.

A conventional nine-man tactical command element had infiltrated the valley aboard a pair of Black Hawks but now found themselves sustaining considerable enemy fire. The lethal Black Team snipers linked up with the soldiers and immediately cut down an advancing enemy force. Thinning the herd through the course of the day to enable the soldiers' exfiltration that night, the DEVGRU element dissipated in the manner they had earlier materialized, ascending back up to their OP to resume calling down air strikes on their enemy.

Ultimately, Anaconda was a massive and unsynchronized operation that had all the makings of yet another debacle. In the end, it was deemed a victory—albeit a costly one.

Without the wildly disproportionate contributions of the nation's elite snipers, even that costly victory would have been all but impossible. As had been the case at the Battle of Tora Bora, JSOC's recce operators were the carpenters that skillfully cobbled together tactical triumphs from strategic blunders.

Delta and DEVGRU's snipers had demonstrated a capacity to redirect battles beyond assessment. They served as the pivotal, centerpiece component at Operation Anaconda despite comprising less than a single percent of its overall strength in terms of sheer numbers.

The efforts of India's team leader, Delta sniper Kris Kosem, and Mako 31's 24STS CCT attachment, Andrew Martin, were recognized with the awarding of Silver Stars. It's reasonable to assume those were far from the only medals awarded to AFO troops for their participation in Operation Anaconda; troves of commendations earned by JSOC operators deep enough to stock a museum remain classified.

However, the story of Operation Anaconda did not end with Juliet, India, and Mako 31—not by a long shot.

◈

Back at Bagram Airfield, Task Force 11 got antsy when the action of Operation Anaconda proved hotter than it had anticipated—particularly for its wayward AFO subcomponent. Motivated to work its forces more deeply into the mix, General Dailey's in-country deputy, Air Force Brig. Gen. Gregory Trebon, along with ST6 commander Joe Kernan, sent forth "reinforcements" from Task Force Blue to swoop in and assume control of the air strike operations from AFO.

The new arrivals at the Gardez safe house were directed by Lieutenant Commander Vic Hyder, who two months earlier had evoked unwanted comparisons to SEAL Team Six's riotous past. On New Year's Eve of '01, a group of SEALs, led by Hyder, blasted through Afghan militia checkpoints in a reckless "joyride." The vehicle was fired upon and its driver struck, forcing the DEVGRU operators to pull over and surrender their equipment to the tribesmen in humiliation.

Now Hyder came with a group of SEALs looking to seize rather than surrender. Although Lt. Col. Blaber had been informed to the contrary, upon arrival, Hyder was not only in command of the teams he brought with him, but also the AFO recon teams already in position. And at TF 11's behest—and in direct opposition to Blaber's recommendations—he immediately set about replacing them with the three new ST6 teams (despite their lack of familiarity with the terrain and the situation).

Complicating matters further, both Hyder and Blaber believed they were in command, and, unbeknownst to Blaber, the two did not use shared communication channels as subsequent events rapidly unfolded.

Of the three SEAL teams preparing for immediate insertion, two, Mako 21 and Mako 22, consisted of assaulters. Both were emplaced without resistance, although, lacking the specialized training and equipment required for an operation of this sort, they produced rather mixed results.

A third team, Mako 30, consisted of the other half of Red Squadron's recce element that Blaber had earlier requested but been denied. This Black Team sniper element was tasked with the most challenging and potentially pivotal of the operation: the 10,469-foot peak of Takur Ghar, which teased a dominant overwatch position towering over the entire valley below.

The seven-man team was led by a SEAL named Britt Slabinski. "Slab," a wiry-framed and reflective sniper in his midthirties, was the converse of the stereotypical image of a Navy SEAL.

He was joined by heavy metal aficionado Stephen "Turbo" Toboz, and Kyle Defoor, an avid motorcyclist and relative newcomer to recce. There was also a member of the secretive ISA, along with Air Force Technical Sergeant John Chapman of the 24th Special Tactics Squadron. The team was rounded out by three additional SEALs, including thirty-two-year-old Neil "Fifi" Roberts, sporting curly red hair and an M249 SAW.

Blaber knew and respected Slabinski. The two had operated alongside one another extensively prior to 9/11 in Bosnia and elsewhere.

After the two had conferred, Mako 30 planned to infiltrate some thirteen hundred yards short of their ambitious objective, providing them adequate time to complete the demanding four-hour climb with the advantage of night on their side.

This was later scrapped, however. Multiple delays had encouraged a decidedly dicier approach, and instead of marching to the peak, they chose to shift their intended LZ (landing zone) directly to the top of the mountain. This was viewed as extremely dangerous for any number of reasons—not the least of which it would signify their placement to any nearby fighters. Making matters even more dire, there was compelling evidence that suggested the "nearby" fighters would be even closer than that, with an entrenched al-Qaeda force thought to have already claimed ownership of the prized turf.

In their earlier discussion, Blaber urgently argued against an impetuous attempt of this nature. However, despite retaining notional authority, he had since been removed from the loop and was unaware of this late development. Slabinski requested that the operation be pushed back to the following evening; however, he was overruled and instructed by Task Force Blue's TOC in Bagram to immediately go forward with the daring—arguably reckless—mission plan.

The eight-man JSOC team was ferried into position above the peak of Takur Ghar aboard a 160th SOAR MH-47E Chinook. Ignoring still more warning signs on approach, the Night Stalker set the bulky tandem-rotor craft down on top of the mountain. Within moments, the night sky strobed with a barrage of intense RPG and small arms fire.

The crew immediately reacted and wrenched the unwieldy helicopter back into the air in hopes of limping it to a safer landing zone. However, Petty Officer 1st Class Roberts was already preparing to disembark, one foot off the ramp. The DEVGRU operator was knocked off balance and he slipped out of Toboz's grasp and into the blackness ten feet below.

Moments later he found himself all alone on the mountain peak, lying in the snow and surrounded by a pack of fanatical jihadists closing on his position. At that instant, the remainder of his team was helplessly drifting away from him in a crippled Chinook, which had suffered massive damage to its electronic and hydraulics systems in the onslaught.

The DEVGRU sniper element frantically requested for immediate reinsertion in hopes of saving Roberts but Anaconda's ineffectual command and control (at multiple levels) magnified an already dire situation.

A second Chinook arrived at the scene of their controlled crash, but they were ordered back to Gardez. This was due to an unwillingness to abandon the downed helicopter's crew when nearby friendly forces were mistakenly believed to be an advancing pack of enemy combatants.

Roberts's condition and predicament were a mystery. A soupy-thick fog of war had enveloped the chaotic situation as AC-130Hs and various ISR (intelligence, surveillance, and reconnaissance) platforms had changed stations and were scrambling in hopes of locating the abandoned SEAL.

After hauling the spare 160th crew back to Gardez, the remaining five from Six and their CCT were finally allowed to charge back to Roberts's aid. However, it was already too late. The precise details of his demise have been debated. There is some speculation he died almost instantly while other reports claim he fought off a mob of onrushing attackers for as long as thirty minutes, undone only after his M249 had jammed and he had run through his secondary weapon's ammunition and stock of grenades.

Additionally, the manner in which he was killed is unclear. The rumor mill is filled with (allegedly) Predator-feed-informed anecdotes that range from an execution-style bullet to the head to tortuous brutalization at the hands of savage enemies.

Unaware that Roberts had already been killed, Mako 30 touched back down on Takur Ghar in hopes of a hasty rescue. They immediately split into three pairs and were engaged straight away in intense, close-range combat. Several al-Qaeda gunmen were dispatched in the opening frenzied moments, but the hopelessly outnumbered recce force quickly took casualties. Three of the DEVGRU commandos were wounded—including Toboz, who took a round from an RPK "Super Kalashnikov" to the left calf, ripping a baseball-sized chunk out of his lower leg.

Tragically, the 24STS Combat Controller, Technical Sergeant John A.

Chapman, joined Roberts as KIA (killed in action) on the peak of Takur Ghar, downed in the firefight (though there remains some dispute concerning the particulars of Chapman's death as well).

Forced to make a desperate escape, the JSOC snipers leapt over the crest of the peak and plowed down a seventy-degree embankment at speed before clambering to cover hundreds of feet below.

SEAL Team Three sniper Brandon Webb was aboard a QRF (Quick Reaction Force) helicopter at Bagram Airfield and heard the confused radio calls as the operation spiraled deeper and deeper out of control. Ready to race to the mountain to support the cornered DEVGRU element, his Task Force K-Bar team was ordered off the helo in order to make room for an Army Rangers QRF just prior to liftoff—further evidence of Operation Anaconda's shattering miscommunication and lack of coordination.

Webb later observed the footage captured by an MQ-1 Predator drone of the battle atop Takur Ghar.

"Part of the feed is just burned into my mind," Webb said. "These guys sliding down this mountain with their kit. . . . I'm not sure what the pitch would have been, but it was incredibly steep."

The Ranger Regiment-led QRF, which was split between a pair of Chinooks, attempted to assist the SEALs. However, one of the helicopters was mistakenly directed into the firing lines of the awaiting AQ combatants atop the peak while the other flew to Gardez before finally inserting some eight hundred meters away (now with SEAL officer Vic Hyder, who joined in the rescue effort).

The QRF ultimately took "Roberts Ridge"—as the deadly peak would come to be known—but not before the lives of five additional American warriors were taken.

While the Rangers aboard the second QRF scurried to the ridge, Hyder went in search of Mako 30.

The sniper element had been engaged for hours on end as they attempted to fight their way back to safety. Slabinski controlled the chaos throughout, alternately urging his men on and shredding through packs of assailants via the liberal application of surgical fire courtesy of "Barney"—his 7.62mm semi-automatic rifle.

Webb later discussed the day's events with Toboz. "When they got down to the bottom of the mountain, [Toboz] just wanted to lay down and die. But that Slab guy just smacked him in the face. *'Dude, get your shit together.'* They basically patched him up but Turbo had lost a lot of blood. He said that literally Slab would drag him for a while and then run into the woods for, like, twenty or thirty minutes and Turbo would just hear a bunch of gunfire. And then he would come back and move Turbo again. He did this a bunch of times. He just told me, 'That guy is a fuckin' hero.' Literally, he would run off, just picking off guys, run back, until the helicopter extracted them.

"Turbo said it was surreal. The guy was a fucking maniac."

Hyder finally tracked down his SEALs. In addition to Slabinski's astonishing proficiency and heroism, the recce team had been sheltered by the combined firepower of a circling AC-130H Spectre gunship, F-15E Strike Eagles, and a CIA MQ-1 Predator drone that happened to make aviation history that day by executing the first-ever instance of UAV ground-to-air support.

Though wounded—Toboz in mortal danger—the SEALs completed a six-hour, fifteen-hundred-meter march to escape. Unable to make contact with the Task Force Blue TOC by radio, Hyder resorted to placing a call via satellite phone to DEVGRU's compound in Dam Neck, Virginia, so that they could pass along word and arrange for their extraction.

Like Operation Anaconda as a whole, the Battle of Takur Ghar proved to be a mixed victory. It was undeniably an awesome display of courage under fire by the Black Team sniper element along with the 1/75 Rangers who bravely came to their aid. However, it was just as clearly an utter C2 (command and control) debacle. Multiple opportunities to avoid or correct mistakes were missed—mistakes that were instead compounded with tragic results.

In the weeks following Operation Anaconda, the CIA tracked down a collection of foreign fighters who had escaped the onslaught in the Shah-i-Kot Valley. Initially spotted by a U.S. Navy P-3 Orion and then passed off to a CIA-controlled Predator drone, the convoy was positively identified as being among the forces that had scattered in the wake of Anaconda.

They were subsequently redirected by a joint CIA/Afghan ground team as they attempted to race for the Pakistan border. Successfully shepherded back into play, the convoy was subsequently intercepted by a heliborne SEAL Team Six strike force that included Mako 30 sniper element leader Slabinski.

The DEVGRU SEALs disembarked from the 160th SOAR choppers and proceeded to annihilate their terrorists with measured fury, leaving no survivors among the fleeing Chechen terrorists while absorbing no additional casualties.

The loss of Roberts—the first SEAL killed in the Global War on Terror—was a turning point for DEVGRU. This was particularly the case for Red Squadron, who would earn a reputation inside the special operations community for taking no prisoners.

◈

Toboz first joined the Navy in '91 after drifting through a couple of colleges and being inspired to seek a new start after reading Richard Marcinko's memoirs, *Rogue Warrior*. After becoming an operator of SEAL Team Six himself and later being maimed on the battlefield, he continued to demonstrate his dedication and desire.

Toboz was awarded a Silver Star and Purple Heart for refusing to give in despite his life-threatening injuries. He continued to serve as an inspiration long after that fateful day.

Following multiple surgeries to his lower leg, Turbo ordered the doctors to amputate and fit him with a prosthetic leg. Like Delta operator Brad Halling before him, Toboz returned to active duty, redeploying to Afghanistan nine months later.

However, unsatisfied with operating at 95 percent, Toboz changed paths and instead passed his wisdom downrange: he became an instructor for the U.S. Navy SEAL Sniper Course.

Neil Roberts was awarded the Silver Star posthumously, while John Chapman received the Air Force Cross posthumously.

Vic Hyder received a Silver Star for the critical role he played in Mako 30's rescue and recovery.

Kyle Defoor was awarded the Bronze Star for valor. He left DEVGRU in '03 and took on training positions with Blackwater and Tigerswan before later establishing Defoor Proformance Shooting.

Slabinski was awarded the Navy Cross for his actions, the second highest military award available to a member of the United States Navy, ranked only behind the Medal of Honor.

4

Three Seven Five

Barely a year after the Battle of Takur Ghar and the conclusion of Operation Anaconda, Britt Slabinski and his squadron were again the linchpin of a high-profile operation.

Far removed from the granite peaks of Afghanistan, 160th Special Operations Aviation Regiment Black Hawk and Chinook helicopters ferried a rescue force through the blackness of the early-morning hours above Nasiriyah, a city of a more than a half million people in southeastern Iraq.

While a Marine platoon provided a diversionary attack and an AC-130 circled overhead, the DEVGRU operators hit the ground and stormed Saddam Hospital, which had served as an improvised command post for the Iraqi military in these opening days of the Iraq War.

Backed by 2/75 Rangers of B Company and 24STS Air Force Pararescue Jumpers, the ST6 SEALs located and retrieved Pfc. Jessica Lynch without incident.

Lynch had been captured just days after the Global War on Terror expanded its boundaries. Her 506th Maintenance Company convoy wandered off course early in the invasion and drove directly into an ambush. Eleven American members of the company were killed and six others captured.

The rescue captured the nation's attention—and later suspicion—as detractors viewed the April 1 operation as a bit too neat and tidy. Combined with exaggerated reports of heroism on Lynch's part that served as a rallying cry for the escalating war effort, rumors flew that the operation was little more than a staged April Fool's joke.

In reality, the cynicism was largely unwarranted. While perhaps overplayed to the media, the operation itself had been genuine and its success very real, the first American POW rescue since Vietnam.

◈

Delta Force too had been busy in the early days of the Iraq War. Well, before its earliest days actually, as B Squadron kicked off its invasion a day ahead of the larger coalition force.

Like ST6's Red Squadron, Delta's B Squadron had also shifted its area of operations (AO) following the standout performance of its recce operators in Operation Anaconda a year before.

However, it was still plagued by the operational friction that had prevented the vast capabilities of the special mission units from being fully leveraged in Afghanistan. Gen. Dell Dailey was still in command of JSOC and continued to prefer that Delta Force and DEVGRU prestage and wait for the call in the event that a high-value target was located. Meanwhile, the unit's squadron commanders sought to put their men in the mix more actively, rooting out those HVTs rather than taking on the more passive stance.

CENTCOM commander Gen. Tommy Franks had proven something of an obstacle for the SMUs in Afghanistan as well. Franks, Dailey, and Secretary of Defense Donald Rumsfeld were later assigned much of the blame for allowing bin Laden to escape Tora Bora, primarily for not allowing the CIA/Delta-led force the operational autonomy and support it had requested.

One year and a new war later, Franks had been transformed into an ally and enabler, having witnessed the improbably large role a small handful of JSOC snipers played in ensuring Anaconda's ultimate success.

Rather than be confined to the Arar base in Saudi Arabia, B Squadron marauded across the border and launched multiple hit-and-run raids with a small armored component that allowed it to take on the appearance of a considerably larger force. The tactic struck fear into an already overwhelmed Iraqi military and forced it to tie up its forces, further enabling the broader invading forces elsewhere.

B Squadron commander Lt. Col. Pete Blaber immediately capitalized on this early success by requesting that Delta's C Squadron join the effort, as the coalition raced for Baghdad and toppled Saddam Hussein's regime in swift, convincing fashion.

While a promising start, Delta's situation in Iraq, along with its larger influence over the war, would soon be radically changed for the better.

◈

Dailey's tenure as JSOC commander would come to an end shortly after the opening of the Iraq War and a new "Pope" would be appointed in the following months.

Dailey, an aviator with, and later commander of, the fabled 160th SOAR, was a much admired leader in many quarters. He was considered inspiring and thoughtful by his subordinates and later went on to be named Ambassador at Large as the State Department's Coordinator for Counterterrorism and was inducted into both the U.S. Army Aviation Hall of Fame and the Ranger Hall of Fame.

However, despite his assignment as a Ranger officer, JSOC's direct action components viewed Dailey as painfully risk-averse and too inflexible to obtain the most from them and their specialized skill sets.

In mid-2003, he was replaced by another legendary Ranger—onetime commander of 75th Ranger Regiment, Gen. Stanley McChrystal.

McChrystal, a tireless and pragmatic leader, brought a fresh outlook to the position and immediately implemented changes in how the secretive command would operate moving forward. He sought to better integrate and coordinate JSOC—and not solely internally between its elite, diverse components, but also externally with the wider network of units and agencies that it regularly interacted with (or at least should have regularly interacted with).

And while he strove to tear down artificial, ego-fueled barriers and transform JSOC's "tribe of tribes" into a "team of teams," he also recognized the potential in empowering the individual units.

Among his first acts as JSOC commander was to travel to Delta's expansive compound at Fort Bragg and inform Delta Force's commander, then-Colonel Bennet Sacolick, that the Unit now "owned" Iraq. Delta Force would be the primary counterterrorist and direct action force in country until the battle was won. Additionally, a Delta officer would head the wider JSOC-led task force in Iraq (which rotated its names—TF 20, TF 121, TF 6-26, TF 145, TF 77, etc.—and exact composition as the effort evolved) and direct not only the Unit's efforts, but those of the Rangers, 160th SOAR, the ISA, and so on.

Delta Force wanted Iraq. Now it had it.

McChrystal's reasoning was not entirely out of step with the "total quality control" management philosophy that was utilized by Japanese firms to rapidly transform the nation into an economic power following World War II—in effect, counterterrorism the Toyota way.

This sense of ownership shifted the perspective of Delta's men. No longer were they a small, interchangeable part of a massive coalition effort. In their minds—and in large part, in reality—they were responsible for the overall outcome of the war.

The Unit's men readily embraced the challenge put before them. Operators would voluntarily stay in country past their scheduled deployments to help ease the transitions between squadrons, building uninterrupted institutional knowledge and fostering the innovation that would pay massive dividends in time.

Some of the earliest hints of what was to come were seen as a newly empowered and intel-enabled Delta Force showed greater and greater proficiency in hunting down the "Deck of 55"—the most wanted members of Hussein's toppled government who had since gone into hiding.

By the end of '03, the Unit had removed all four aces from the target deck.

The first man down was Lieutenant General Abid Hamid Mahmud al-Tikriti—the Ace of Diamonds. With 1st Battalion, 22nd Infantry Regiment, 4th Infantry Division (Mechanized) scouts cordoning off an expansive compound in Cadaseeyah, a suburb of Tikrit, Delta operators breached and banged, taking Mahmud alive.

Up next were Hussein's notorious sons, Uday and Qusay—the Ace of Hearts and the Ace of Clubs. They were tracked to a safe house in Mosul, ultimately turned in by the keeper for being ungrateful and unpleasant houseguests.

Once the barricaded brothers were dispatched by Unit bullets (after a round of TOW [Tube-launched, Optically-tracked, Wire-guided] antitank missiles had more or less leveled the building), all attention focused on the Ace of Diamonds himself.

Following multiple takedowns of suspected accomplices, Delta Force captured a man who proved to be the key. He led them to a farmhouse in Ad-Dawr, a small village near Tikrit. There, in Operation Red Dawn, a Delta operator finally dragged a dazed and disheveled deposed dictator from his spider hole before handing him off to soldiers from the 4th Infantry Division (Mechanized) and fading from the scene.

◈

When McChrystal put Delta in charge of JSOC's activities in Iraq, he simultaneously did much the same in Afghanistan, handing ownership of that AO to SEAL Team Six and the 75th Ranger Regiment (although the considerably larger Ranger force would continue to maintain a significant presence in Iraq throughout the war there as well).

In October of 2001, nearly two hundred Rangers from the 3rd Battalion jumped into combat from four Lockheed MC-130 Combat Talons near Kandahar, Afghanistan, to seize Objective Rhino. They continued to play a pivotal early role in Afghanistan—both by their absences at Tora Bora and with their arrival at Takur Ghar.

The opening days of the Iraq War took similar shape. In March of '03, 3/75 jumped to seize an airfield near the Syrian border and three days later conducted another air assault to lay claim to an Iraqi fighter base dubbed Objective Serpent.

A misguided run on a dry hole—the Al Qadisiyah Research Center, aka Objective Beaver—resulted in serious injuries for two Rangers with B/3/75. The 160th SOAR helos that carried the assault team to the objective were waylaid by armor-piercing rounds en route to a suspected chemical and biological weapons facility in the (largely) futile search for weapons of mass destruction.

The 3rd Battalion next set its sights on Objective Lynx: the Haditha Dam—a massive complex on the Euphrates River over five miles long that fed a third of the nation's electrical grid.

The objective was later portrayed by CENTCOM—the regional command tasked with overseeing the wars in both Iraq and Afghanistan—as a critical strategic target in order to prevent Hussein from self-sabotaging resources similar to his actions when faced with defeat in the First Gulf War. And while there was certainly some truth to that, the mission was cobbled together late as JSOC commander Dailey et al. sought out a significant operation to task to the Ranger Regiment and no other obvious targets were available.

"There was supposed to be nothing out there," said Pete Careaga, one of four Ranger snipers assigned to the op. "It was supposed to be an abandoned dam."

However, the Haditha Dam op certainly turned out to be significant. The Iraqi Army was well prepared in their defense, readied with men and machines of destruction awaiting the 3/75 Rangers, backed by Delta Force's C Squadron and other supporting elements. The battle for the dam erupted on April 1—the same day Britt Slabinski and the DEVGRU SEALs, backed by 2/75 Rangers, rescued Jessica Lynch on the opposite side of the nation.

Even after successfully seizing the dam, the Rangers could not breathe easily. They were forced to fight back heavily armed reinforcements for several days, repeatedly calling down devastating air strikes from the Air National Guard F-16s and A-10s supporting the operation.

The 3rd Battalion's top marksmen provided an outsized contribution throughout the multiday clash. A pair of two-man teams, each armed with a Barrett .50 caliber weapon, delivered a constant rain of precise fire throughout. Careaga and his teammate, "BT," were attached to Bravo's 1st Platoon and on the near side of the military compound while Robby Johnson and another sniper were attached to 2nd Platoon and located on the dam itself.

"We were pretty much just direct action on that one," Careaga explained. "We were right there with the guys, just engaging, and a lot of times calling for fire. There were just so many air assets there and we only had a couple TACPs [tactical air control parties]. Half the time they were out of range for us so I just called mortar strikes.

"It was pretty much direct action sniping—engaging targets from sub-100 meters to 2000 meters and calling for fire. Pretty straight forward. But it was a target-rich environment."

Early in the assault, Staff Sergeant Johnson engaged a harassing Iraqi RPG team from a range of nearly a thousand meters with his .50-caliber sniper rifle. The heavy round ripped clean through its intended victim with enough velocity to penetrate a propane tank located directly behind him. The resultant explosion also killed the two other Iraqi fighters of the RPG squad.

In addition to the sniper platoon's pivotal involvement, CSM Greg Birch also demonstrated the shock and awe one sniper and his weapon are capable of delivering.

Already long cemented as a mythical figure in the realm of special operations, Birch had only recently returned to the Regiment to serve as the 3/75 Command Sergeant Major following a fifteen-year tenure with Delta Force.

At the Unit, "Ironhead" served as an A Squadron sniper team leader for several years before ascending to the position of Sabre Squadron

Sergeant Major. In that role he distinguished himself during the Battle of Tora Bora for which he was awarded a Bronze Star for valor.

Even during his lengthy run with the Unit, Birch never forgot his Ranger roots and regularly kept tabs on the Regiment before finally returning in 2002. The Rangers hadn't forgotten Birch either. Now Rangers from both the pre- and post-9/11 eras pass along stories of this forward-thinking yet uniquely disciplined leader.

At the Haditha Dam, Birch showcased his well-practiced lethality with an SR-25 7.62mm semi-automatic, taking more than twenty enemy soldiers off the battlefield. He also came to the rescue of three wounded Iraqis during the clash while generally keeping the younger Rangers focused during the extended, multiday clash. He was later awarded a Silver Star for his actions.

Birch would be promoted to 75th Ranger Regimental Command Sergeant Major and later became the first Command Sergeant Major of the Army's fledgling Asymmetric Warfare Group (AWG).

CSM Greg Birch retired in 2007 following more than thirty years of service.

◉

As is too often the case with the Ranger Regiment as a whole, Ranger snipers are frequently overlooked and underestimated, having failed to capture the public's imagination in the way that Navy SEALs or Army Special Forces have.

While widely unrecognized, the 75th Ranger Regiment boasts perhaps the purest expression of sniper in the inventory of the United States Special Operations Command (USSOCOM, JSOC's ostensible parent organization). They represent a rare breed in the United States military: dedicated snipers who focus on that demanding job full-time.

By contrast, SEAL Team and SF snipers can be considered "part-time." They have undergone extensive training to earn their sniper qualification— and they often go on to pursue more advanced, follow-up courses—but they also continue to serve in their previous positions once they reintegrate with their platoon or ODA (Operational Detachment-Alpha or "A-Team").

The amount of actual sniper work they receive can vary, from extreme workloads—as would prove to be the case for a number of SEAL snipers in Iraq—to being just one of several Green Berets on an experienced, flexible ODA that carry that particular qualification, along with countless others.

Jack Murphy, who served as a 75th Ranger Regiment sniper and later an Army Special Forces Weapons Sergeant, explained, "In SF things are a little bit different. An ODA is expected to do everything. You take a guy—you can even take me as an example. I was a senior Weapons Sergeant. I had been to sniper school. I had been to SERE. I had been to language training. I had been to the HALO school. I had been to off-road driving schools. . . . That's normal in SF."

Any given Special Forces sniper may also be scuba qualified and a French linguist. He may have also received medical training on top of all that. Murphy said, "You do have ODA guys sent to the Special Forces Sniper Course as slots become available; guys get sent and that happens all the time. But sniper is one of many, many hats those guys have to wear.

"It makes things problematic. All the things I'm listing—you know how much time it takes to become proficient at all these different skill sets? What ends up happening, because you are a Green Beret, this sniper role just becomes one of many things you have to be and have to do. It's not something you necessarily get to specialize in and go out to the range and do every week."

Besides the SF and SEAL part-timers, the conventional Army's trained snipers often perform more mundane duties when actually deployed, and even the snipers of JSOC's special mission units exist more in a hybrid, advanced reconnaissance role.

Murphy said, "I would point out that the Rangers and the Marine Scout Snipers are close to being the only two elements that are dedicated full-time snipers in the military. Even the Delta guys, yeah, they're snipers, but they're also recce dudes and everything else."

Isaiah Burkhart, another former 3/75 Ranger sniper, added, "It might not be the old-school, 'Hey, we're going to set up in a hide site type thing' that people think of when you say the word 'sniper.' We do more of a direct action thing, but we definitely placed accurate, effective fires on guys."

◈

Each Ranger battalion operates semi-independently from one another and the details may differ, but they each followed a similar path in revamping their sniper elements. Formerly, a small allotment of snipers were assigned by each rifle company to a dedicated "weapons platoon" that could be detached to support the company's individual rifle platoons as necessary.

"The problem with that was, Rangers have always been shorthanded," Careaga explained. "When we go through the selection process, we'd rather be shorthanded than a bunch of guys who don't meet the standard. So every time the line [rifle] platoons were short, they'd take guys from the snipers section."

Eventually, the snipers were consolidated under their respective Battalion Headquarters and Headquarters Company into dedicated sniper platoons, one per battalion.

Even among the Ranger Regiment, the 3rd Battalion snipers are something of an outlier due to a convergence of factors. For 3/75, the transformation took place in the summer of '98—just after 1/75 made the adjustment and prior to 2/75 following suit—and the battalion's setting at Fort Benning played a contributing factor in forging a uniquely effective capability.

The platoon was initially stood up by Tom Fuller in July '98 and then quickly handed over to its second platoon sergeant, Lindsay Bunch.

"GM," a former 3/75 sniper, said, "Every battalion does their own thing, you know what I mean? I know in 1st Batt, they call it SNOT—Sniper Observation Team. We never called it any of that stuff. It's sniper section or sniper platoon. That's it.

"But 3rd Batt—here's the deal—3rd has the worst quality of life because there's nothing out there; it's a military town, unlike Seattle or Savannah. But they have a lot of ranges, and they have the Army Marksmanship

Unit there—the Army shooting team—ammo, ranges, all that stuff. Seriously, out of the three battalions, it's the best one to train at because they have all those resources. The environment dictates that 3rd Batt has a good sniper platoon. Granted though, those guys have no lives."

The tremendous upside associated with being based in proximity to the U.S. Army's Marksmanship Unit was cited by more than one Ranger sniper. The AMU was originally devised by President Dwight D. Eisenhower in the '50s with the intent of defeating the Soviet Union . . . not on the battlefield, but in international shooting competitions.

The unit still exists in largely the same capacity, with a focus on competitive shooting, although it also serves in a recruiting, training, and R&D capacity.

AMU boasts its own Custom Firearms Shop and develops weapons and ammunition of unequaled precision. And its success in the role for which it was originally founded is undeniable, having garnered dozens of Olympic medals.

Its shooters are widely regarded as ballistic wizards. Shared ranges and ready access to that knowledge only pushed the 3/75 Ranger snipers to elevate their games accordingly as the sniper platoon took shape.

"The AMU is a huge resource," GM said. "You have the best shooters in the world. And you're not talking about, 'Hey, this guy is a good really shot.' No, you flip through a magazine and you see he's number one in the world. And you're training with those guys. These guys went to other places throughout the U.S. and trained other tier units as well. They knew how to train special ops guys. At 3rd Batt you have that in your backyard at all times, to go shoot, pistol, rifle, whatever."

Burkhart added, "[AMU] are the best shooters out there. And the coach of the service rifle team, the high-power team, Emil Praslick . . . that guy— he can read wind better than anyone I've ever seen. It's crazy when you're sitting there and he would come out there and do a wind call. You'd shoot and he'd say, 'Why don't you try this?' and then, yep, you're dead on. You see a huge difference between someone who has the experience and a guy who just has a natural ability for it."

Over time, the 3/75 sniper platoon came to shoot at an AMU level while maintaining its operational, real-world focus.

"Pre-GWOT, all they did was go to schools and shoot—that's it," GM said. "With the Army Marksmanship Unit there, they had the best shooters in the Army—in the world—there, at their fingertips. So the guys would go down and shoot all the time. Iron sights, M16s, out to one thousand yards plus, just really honing their skills."

The 3rd Battalion sniper platoon established a powerful foundation, honed their skills religiously on the ranges at Fort Benning—which far outstripped what existed in Savanah, Seattle, or just about anywhere else— and constantly cycled through other sniper schools. During this time of peace, the results of all that hard work manifested in a dominant stretch across a number of sniper competitions.

GM said, "These guys got a lot of trigger time. A *lot* of trigger time. It was the perfect storm for guys to really hone their skills. These guys set up the foundation, set up the platoon, set up the standards of shooting, and built the relationships throughout the gun industry to make it a success. Guys liked it so much, they'd stay on for years on end which was unheard of. Three, four, five years, they'd stay a squad leader. Some of them would reject rank, too. They didn't want to get promoted; they wanted to stay there."

Pete Careaga was one of the Ranger snipers who helped build that foundation and stayed on far longer than was initially proposed. He was in on the ground floor, having served in a rifle company's weapon platoon's sniper section before the 3/75 sniper platoon was consolidated.

"The creation of Sniper Platoon did a few things to our benefit," Careaga explained. "Beforehand, snipers kept rotating too fast in the sections. So nobody really knew how many rounds this rifle had—any of that stuff. But once the platoon came around training went up immeasurably.

"Before most snipers just went to the sniper school at Fort Benning and that was it. But once it became a platoon, we started sending guys through every sniper school we could think of. The Marine Scout Sniper Course, Canada, the SAS course, the Navy SEAL Sniper Course, all sorts of advanced courses . . . Pretty much any school you could think of, military or civilian, we would send guys there.

"It was just an incredible training environment. We were shooting pretty much every day and night. We had, like, one week for maintenance and the other times we were just shooting. When I was there, my M24 was re-barreled twice, that's how much we shot just training. The amount of weapons we had too . . . I had two M24s, SR-25, and Barrett, an M4, a pistol just assigned to me. It was just insane. It was actually the best place to be a sniper. I had talked to some Special Forces guys and they do go to the schools and they are kind of designated snipers but they don't do it enough.

"I was there exactly seven years even though initially it was supposed to be an eighteen-month billet. We soon realized we can't do eighteen months. There's too much training required. Once the guys get the training, they are very valuable."

All of that training quickly developed a reputation for the 3/75 sniper platoon.

"We did get a lot of notoriety on our skills," Careaga confirmed. "We would send the guys to all the schools, but we also sent them to all the competitions. And we won. The 10th Special Forces Group [Airborne] International Sniper Competition in Colorado, we won that like every time we went. The Marines Scout Sniper comp, the Canadian International Sniper Concentration . . . We were just winning competitions because we trained so much. That also contributed to us sending so many snipers to the AMU. We started sending guys for the summer trips. Before that there were pretty much zero ex-Rangers in the teams. The AMU used to hire just junior shooters who had already been doing that style of shooting. And once we started going there, they realized these guys actually have some skill and they started hiring from Ranger Battalion."

Among the other Ranger snipers who built the pre-9/11 foundation were Jared Van Aalst ("VA") and Robby Johnson ("RJ")—the Ranger who would later make the video-game-like propane tank triple kill at the Haditha Dam.

The close relationship between the AMU and the Rangers resulted in significant cross-pollination. Burkhart explained, "When I got there, Jared Van Aalst and Robby Johnson were the guys who were in charge of the section. They were both guys who had been in the platoon before and then got picked up by Army Marksmanship Unit to be summer shooters and then they ended up staying on there for a couple years. They went and shot competitions and then came back and took over the sniper platoon."

Van Aalst graduated high school in 1993—the same year eighteen members of Task Force Ranger died in the Battle of Mogadishu. After taking a year to travel the world, he returned home to attend college and got a small taste of soldiering in ROTC. That was all that was required to decide the life of a Ranger was the one he would pursue.

Following a few years in the battalion, Van Aalst joined the newly revamped sniper platoon in '98 in its formative months. He ascended to the role of squad leader in '01 before leaving for the AMU—just prior to the attacks of September eleventh.

What he had pegged as a plum assignment was transformed into a ball and chain that kept him out of the fight. Anxious to earn his stripes in combat, Van Aalst sought a return to the Regiment and was finally brought back as the 3/75 sniper platoon sergeant in 2003.

Described as "idiosyncratic," Van Aalst had developed a taste for fine wine and good cigars. He also brought a corporate attitude to the sniper platoon, devouring leadership handbooks and emulating the techniques of successful businesspeople . . . to mixed reception.

However, while it was sometimes difficult to decipher, behind the cold façade, Van Aalst managed to see his soldiers as people and not merely sub-MOA machines.

VA and RJ developed a pipeline for their snipers. New recruits would typically go straight to the U.S. Army Sniper School and, if time permitted, follow that up with additional, advanced training, whether taught internally or via outside courses.

With his first deployment as a sniper looming, Isaiah Burkhart had yet to go through the basic Army Sniper course. He explained, "A couple other of the new guys in the section got slots and I was really pissed off about it. *'This is bullshit!'* I felt I was doing better than these other guys."

Van Aalst pulled Burkhart aside: *"Hey, since we're getting ready to go on this deployment, I didn't want to send you off to school and then directly to Iraq and not give you any time to spend with your wife."*

"That was cool," Burkhart said. "Maybe that was an excuse and I was a turd, but it seemed legitimate. He actually cared about the personnel in his section."

The reality was, the training inside the sniper platoon was so strong that 3rd Battalion snipers were being given the tools to excel before they had even attended the Army's baseline training course.

GM, a former sniper with the battalion, explained, "They'd start out with the basics. They had a template. You'd take a new guy, you'd put him on iron sights with an M16A2—old school M16—and if he can shoot iron sights with the M16A2 out to a thousand, he can do anything. They had a little pipeline. You start with this, you bump up to this, you go onto this. After that you were constantly doing ranges or constantly going to schools."

Burkhart continued, "I went on my first deployment [as a sniper] and I hadn't even gone to sniper school. But we had been training at the range four or five days a week, and these guys who were teaching me were just amazing shots. And our whole section went to the Marine High Angle Course."

Even as the wars in Afghanistan and Iraq raged, the 3/75 Ranger sniper platoon continued to run roughshod through competitions. During Burkhart's time with the section, they had teams that won the International Sniper Competition, the Canadian International Competition, and the Special Operations Sniper Competition, defeating snipers from Delta Force, SEAL Team Six, and Special Forces in the process.

"Our guys were really on point so I was learning from amazing marksmen," Burkhart said. "I didn't feel like I was really far behind."

Van Aalst finally made his first combat deployment in 2004 to Afghanistan. But just as Iraq was heating up, Afghanistan had begun to cool, with the initial postinvasion flurry of activity followed by a slower-paced game of cat and mouse.

"Most of the time we were in support of actual direct action elements," said Murphy, who went to Afghanistan on his first deployment as a 3/75 sniper a few months later in late '04. "It wasn't like Carlos Hathcock stuff, going out with a spotter for five days and hiding out, looking to shoot some communist general or something like that. We were going out there with actual rifle platoons and we would support them however they could best employ precision fire."

During Murphy's three-month deployment, they ran a couple dozen missions. That pace would pale in comparison to what was to come in subsequent deployments. However, the more measured speed did allow the snipers to operate with the sort of creativity that would prove impossible due to the punishing operational tempo the Rangers would inflict on their adversaries in the more target-rich Iraq AO in the months and years ahead.

The 3/75 snipers pushed their operational boundaries in search of targets with a dearth of obvious objectives to keep them busy.

Additionally, the line platoons still did not know how to best leverage the battalion's potent sniper capability. However, Careaga saw that as an opportunity rather than a handicap and one that resulted in two combat jumps in the opening months of the Afghanistan War for the sniper.

"They just didn't know how to use snipers properly, so we just told them how we could best be used. And that was just awesome," Careaga said. "They didn't know but we did. It wasn't a bad thing. I think it actually worked better for us. It allowed us to pretty much pick our own missions."

On multiple occasions, Van Aalst led a team of six snipers through the night, a loose pack of shadows shifting from observation post to observation post. In the final hours of darkness they built hide sites so they could scan the valley below for targets in the following hours.

"We did that quite a bit," Careaga said. "Afghanistan, with all that open terrain, was more permissive to that kind of mission."

Their initiative and ingenuity resulted in a handful of kills in what otherwise was an uneventful deployment.

Murphy and his sniper partner also conducted a handful of recon patrols that bordered on clandestine. At various times decked out in civilian attire, traditional Afghani robes, or Afghani military uniforms, they traveled in NSTVs—nonstandard tactical vehicles—to scout out potential overwatch positions for upcoming raids.

Most memorable of these atypical ops were the aerial platform support missions.

"Of course those stand out in my mind," Murphy said. "On one occasion we went out at night—me and the other sniper on one side of a Little Bird and a rifleman on the other side just in case we needed to get off the helicopter and take someone prisoner.

"I never knew that a Little Bird could fly that fast. You're just hanging outside the aircraft. Like *'holy shit.'*

"We got to the target area just as the assault elements were rolling up in their Humvees. We pulled security over the objective, watching specifically for anyone running up on the objective or maneuvering on our guys while they captured the HVT on that objective.

"But nothing really happened."

3/75 along with elements from its sniper platoon would next deploy to Iraq. The days of nothing really happening were about to come to an end.

5

Triple Threat

As the Global War on Terror altered in shape, so too did the role of the nation's most elite snipers.

In Afghanistan, al-Qaeda and the Taliban had been overwhelmed by the initial onslaught. Forced to accept the military and technological superiority of the presumed "paper tiger," terrorist leadership and foot soldiers alike scattered into hiding. Some sought the shelter of borders while others dispersed among the local population.

As a result, Herculean efforts to scale perilous mountainsides no longer granted AFO teams a vantage point in the clouds from which they could call death down from the sky on collected masses of enemy fighters with any sort of regularity.

Instead, the Joint Special Operations Command became more and more focused on executing surgical snatch-and-grabs and decapitation strikes aimed at high-value targets. As such, JSOC's special mission units were presented with the opportunity to demonstrate their highly vaunted capabilities in dark arts such as close-quarters combat.

Despite contrasting political and geographical considerations in Iraq, the same was not only also true there, but especially so. Delta Force had begun storming compounds with increasing frequency as it made its first steps toward developing a powerful capability to systematically tear apart loosely connected networks of enemy combatants, strategic piece by strategic piece.

The rounding up of Hussein and his cronies who represented Iraq's 55 Most Wanted was only a minor preamble to the statement JSOC was about to make. The hard-hitting, up-close nature of this next phase of GWOT had shifted the spotlight over to the assaulters.

Even when special operations forces are viewed through a relatively microscopic lens, the assaulters that lend the line squadrons at Delta and DEVGRU their heart and soul are regarded as exemplars of soldiering in its highest form . . . and for good reason.

Potential operators are first identified through methods that are custom designed and proven over time. They sift through the nation's most battle-hardened and accomplished warriors and then choose only those with the traits required to excel at an even higher level.

Those who pass selection are then subjected to months of exhaustive training that forces their bodies and minds to push the upper bounds of human limits. If one actually succeeds in making it through to see the light at the other end of this demanding pipeline, they are issued customized and technologically advanced gear available nowhere else that allows them to effectively leverage their extensive training. They are then given the operational support necessary to conduct the most high-priority and tactically challenging operations in existence at a breakneck pace.

The vast majority of well-proven SOF veterans who attempt to enter their ranks never make it to this point. Those who do now occupy the uppermost stratum in the warfighter hierarchy.

And yet, there exists an even more advanced tier to which they may eventually ascend.

◉

Even though the mission had evolved, the importance of JSOC's recce assets did not diminish in the least. Rather, these snipers' stacked skill sets were called upon in new ways, and they again responded by demonstrating a total mastery of modern warfare.

Collectively, Delta and DEVGRU's snipers stand as the most seasoned, capable, and versatile human assets in the nation's arsenal.

The term "sniper" is actually something of a misnomer when discussing the special mission units. The word naturally directs one's mental images downrange in a Hathcockian trajectory centered around ghillie-suited soldiers stalking their prey with bolt action rifles.

And while it's certainly the case that the recce snipers must be capable of delivering precision fire at great distance and with superior accuracy, that is just one of the three primary—and in some ways, contradictory—roles with which they are tasked.

In addition to the expectation that they outshoot even single-purpose snipers hailing from other units, JSOC's recce operators must also be capable of executing violent, close-range raids with the same surgical exactness as their Tier 1 assaulter brothers. On top of that, they must be able to blend in to hostile, nonpermissive environments to conduct high-risk reconnaissance and surveillance that may be considered too dangerous for even the most brazen intelligence operatives.

Each of these three broad disciplines is extreme in its demands, requiring intensive training across a wide range of tactics and techniques that test one's physical, mental, and psychological strength.

They also require different approaches, from the distant (physically and emotionally) sniper, to the hyperaggressive assaulter, to the unassuming clandestine operative.

It is a position that requires maturity and experience in addition to inordinate amounts of training.

"They're assaulters first; rarely does anyone go straight to sniper troop out of OTC," explained Larry Vickers, who spent fifteen years in Delta Force as an assaulter and combat marksmanship instructor.

With few exceptions, JSOC's recce ranks are filled with operators who registered years of exceptional service as an assaulter before transitioning to the sniper role.

Vickers himself trained as an SF sniper prior to his arrival in the Unit, attending the Special Operations Target Interdiction Course (SOTIC). He's far from an unusual case in that regard. But established—even celebrated—snipers start the process all over again when they graduate to the next level due to unique demands required of SMU snipers.

Combined with their previous time spent in high-speed units such as the Army's Special Forces, the 75th Ranger Regiment, or the Navy SEALs, it's not unusual for an operator to have already accumulated a decade of special operations experience before he first begins to learn the ropes as a Tier 1 sniper.

"Once you become a sniper at DEVGRU . . . the performance requirement is so high," said former DEVGRU sniper Craig "Sawman" Sawyer. "You end up in a spot and you try for all your worth to become the best in the world at it. You get a lot more time on the rifle and a lot more support. You have no excuses for failure."

◈

While the individual operators would strongly disagree, Delta Force and DEVGRU are largely similar units, at least from a broader perspective. There is, perhaps, an 80–90 percent agreement in their respective organizational structures and mission sets. And certainly, they are more similar to one another than Delta is to Army Special Forces or DEVGRU is to the other SEAL Teams in this regard.

However, it's an oversimplification, and often inaccurate, to simply group the two units, their snipers, or the methods by which they are chosen into a single explanation.

The transition for a SEAL who moves from one of the regular Teams to ST6 is less abrupt in some ways than it is for a solider progressing to Delta Force from any other command. The separation between the two levels is not viewed quite so great by many inside the Teams, and the reputation a prospective DEVGRU operator previously earned as a vanilla SEAL will play a significant role determining whether he'll be given a shot at "the big leagues."

Meanwhile, the chances of a would-be Unit operator—whether he is a Green Beret, Ranger, Marine, or even Information Technology Specialist—is weighted more heavily on their performance during the selection process.

And just as this basic recruitment methodology differs, Delta and DEVGRU also tend to approach tabbing an assaulter for sniper duty differently as well.

Here too the Army unit is more structured and formalized. Following the conclusion of each round of its taxing selection process and follow-up Operator Training Course (OTC), rookie operators are divvied up among the line squadrons via a draft that would not be unfamiliar to fans of professional sports. Similarly, experienced assaulters can be drafted to the recce troop in the same manner.

A selected sniper remains with his previous Sabre Squadron, and again kicks off another round of in-depth training to obtain the skills required to operate in a recce capacity.

With SEAL Team Six, progression tends to be driven more by the career aspirations of its operators. DEVGRU also utilizes a draft following Green Team (its version of OTC), but after that, at a certain point, assaulters may be given the chance to volunteer for a sniper position. While a three-year minimum is the loose guideline, there are examples of SEALs being given the opportunity much sooner based on need and prior experience.

To get technical, the Naval Special Warfare Development Group's four Tactical Development and Evaluation Squadrons—Red, Blue, Gold, and Silver—are split up into three troops of approximately twenty operators apiece. Each troop contains a small sniper element ("RECCE") to complement its assault teams.

In addition to augmenting the troops of their individual color squadrons, DEVGRU's snipers are viewed as a modular, separable asset (hence the collective "Black Team" nickname for the unit's snipers across the squadrons). And as such, the sniper teams not only seamlessly integrate with assault teams during direct action missions, they are also capable of conducting low-visibility operations on their own. (Delta's basic assaulter/sniper troop structure is thought to be roughly the same.)

Should a DEVGRU squadron require a rapid injection of talent into its sniper ranks, exceptions to the seniority rule have been known to be made at the Squadron Master Chief's discretion. Howard Wasdin was one of those rare examples. "Waz-man" was still just an FNG (new guy) when he was given the green light to become an ST6 sniper.

Another example is fellow Red Squadron alumnus Sawyer. In fact, the Texan only served as an assaulter for a matter of weeks before he was allowed to join Black Team.

He explained, "Normally that's a senior position—you need to be in an assault team for a period of years before they consider letting you go back there, because you do operate more autonomously with more equipment and responsibility relative to an assaulter.

"But I was already a decorated combat veteran when I went to DEVGRU. At the time I went there, that was rare. And I had been a sniper instructor—not just a sniper. And I had prior service—I had been in the Marine Corps. So I came in with a higher set of experience and qualifications than my peers did at that time. So when there were several senior snipers that retired in rapid succession, they had a need to push somebody back there to fill those empty slots."

Sawyer admitted he was torn. He was looking forward to filling the assaulter role and the camaraderie that comes along with it, "but when you're given an early promotion, so to speak, you don't refuse it."

Once in, the advanced training begins and is handled largely in-house. Sawyer explained, "We trained ourselves. There was nobody really training us because who on the face of the planet knew what we needed to do more than we did? We were afforded every luxury and support item that was required. And as professionals, there was no excuse to fail. We knew that was on us, so we trained ourselves accordingly. We traveled all over the place, in different locations, and under every condition, just to be prepared for anything."

⊕

In the earliest days of Delta Force, back when it was still racing to assemble an operational force, it could not afford to take the time to scout and groom sniper prospects over a matter of years. To hasten the process, the Unit's psychologist identified several key traits thought to predict success in that role.

According to the Unit's founder and first commanding officer, Colonel Charlie Beckwith, they sought operators boasting such traits as "poise, patience, concentration, stability, calmness, and meticulousness about details."

B Squadron plank owner Eric Haney noted in his memoirs, *Inside Delta Force,* the original Unit snipers selected with these characteristics in mind came across as intelligent men, almost academic in their mannerisms.

Following decades of evolution shaped by each successive victory and failure, Delta Force now targets a slightly different breed of warrior for the recce role. While those originally cited traits retain their value in the position, they alone are not enough.

As explained by a retired Delta sniper who served multiple combat deployments post-9/11, "Do-gooder can't fight. You have to be a good person—have a good heart and good intentions—but you also have to be ready to fuck these motherfuckers up and get bad, only to see the job through."

◈

Since 9/11, the Unit's recce team rooms have been occupied by men who go by "Don," "Bob," and "John." While those names may lack a certain marquee-ready quality, the warriors themselves are far from average. To those behind the curtain of black operations, they are legends.

That "John"—John McPhee—serves as a prime example of the sort of overwhelming talent, training, courage, and accomplishment that has been boasted by the recce ranks over the past decade.

Lethal from any range and a wide variety of weaponry, McPhee epitomized all aspects of the impossibly demanding position during his long tenure with the A Squadron recce troop.

Raised on the South Side of Chicago, the former Army Ranger and Green Beret was already well established as a Delta sniper when the towers fell in September 2001.

McPhee was a key player in the initial post-9/11 hunt for the likes of Osama bin Laden, Ayman al-Zawahiri, and Mullah Mohammed Omar.

While he took part in the first Battle of Tora Bora in December of 2001, McPhee's legend was cemented (at least in a mainstream sense) in 2002 when he conducted a "singleton" operation that was later detailed in *Kill Bin Laden,* which was authored by A Squadron officer Dalton Fury.

Listed there by his call name "Shrek," the book's opening vignette describes how McPhee—thickly bearded and decked out in perahan tunban and pakol-style hat—effortlessly melted into the Afghan population in order to secure actionable intelligence—actual eyes on one Awal Malim Gul.

Gul, a suspected al-Qaeda sympathizer, was believed to have sheltered a desperate and wounded bin Laden after he escaped Tora Bora. It was thought the al-Qaeda emir fled north to Gul's home in the Pachir Agam valley near Jalalabad.

McPhee casts an imposing figure—his size, attitude, and skills make for the perfect storm of intimidation. An alpha even among a legion of type A's, the sniper carries himself with a confidence that can border on menacing. Almost by definition, that should make him the antithesis of the "gray man"—those with an unexceptional presence that allows them to be exceptional undercover operatives.

However, McPhee was not only able to turn that quality on, but do so in hostile territory. He went unnoticed in an alien country on the other side of the planet, with customs, dress, and language far removed from those most Americans are comfortable with—one of the hardest targets imaginable.

"That comes down to demeanor," explained McPhee. "And demeanor is a learned skill."

It also comes down to being blessed with rare intelligence—McPhee registered one of the higher IQ scores ever to be recorded by an operator during the selection process. While the Unit prizes mental acumen—and boasts men with Ph.D.'s and master's degrees in its operator ranks—there's a ceiling at which point a stratospheric intelligence quotient is actually considered a detractor. It's been said men who are too smart won't run toward machine-gun fire, but, as Shrek discovered years later over beers with the Unit psychologist, the shrink showed his intelligence by giving the Chicago native the green light despite an unacceptably high score on his entrance exam.

Shrek traveled among the locals unnoticed and closed in on Gul's residence, hidden alongside a ridgeline in the immediate vicinity of nearly forty other homes. Leveraging the 360-degree, total situational awareness that is drilled into recce operators, he invisibly gathered video evidence and the exact coordinates of Gul's location.

Once McPhee had enabled the assault team's advance—showcasing impressive creativity and composure despite the immense pressure—the target was detained in a lightning assault on the compound.

The captive was later transferred to Guantanamo Bay, where he remained until 2011. Gul, who the Taliban requested in a proposed trade for captured American soldier Bowe Bergdahl, collapsed and died while exercising on an elliptical machine only months ahead of the raid that killed bin Laden.

The HVT capture of Awal Malim Gul was the Unit's first after 9/11. It would be followed by hundreds more—if not thousands more—over the next decade.

While the tracking of Gul is Shrek's only singleton op known to the public, it is far from the only one to have been executed.

He added to his legend as Delta Force continued to hone its manhunting capabilities during subsequent deployments to Iraq.

While the sprawling, tightly assembled mazes of buildings that hid the enemy in Iraq was in stark contrast to the rural, fortified compounds that did the same in Afghanistan, recce operators like Shrek relied on the exact same skill sets to conduct close target reconnaissance and pinpoint the location of prey in both countries. The lessons learned were directly applicable despite the divergent conditions.

"It's the same philosophy either way," the Unit sniper explained. "There's more technology involved in Iraq—there isn't just one building every one thousand meters. . . . In Iraq if you're off by ten meters, you're in the wrong location, but the approach is the same."

McPhee also expanded his collection of war trophies that heavily hint at the pivotal role he played in that warzone as well. To go with Mullah Omar's green and red Korans, McPhee added one of Saddam Hussein's most iconic hats, a sweater that belonged to the deposed dictator (now complete with a Shrek-sized, stretched-out neck hole), and a new moniker: "the Sheriff of Baghdad."

A master practitioner of low-visibility operations and practically all relevant forms of armed combat, McPhee may very well be every bit as deadly when unarmed, as evidenced by the 2005 Budweiser World Cup Super Heavyweight Jiu-Jitsu Championship. Further emphasizing that notion is the fact that Shrek served as a one-on-one room instructor with the Unit, actively training other operators in hand-to-hand combat. That position is not assigned—it is earned. A prospective teacher must first defeat five fighters in a row before being awarded the role. And there's no concern an instructor will act like a tenured professor once he's in as that same standard is required to retain the position.

McPhee retired in 2011 following more than twenty years of service. More than a decade of that was spent in combat during a period marked by the most intense special operations campaign in military history.

The vast majority of McPhee's work over those years remains completely unknown outside the smallest of circles, but even the slivers that have come to light are worthy of modern-day folk hero status.

◈

Once selected for duty with a recce team, a newly minted JSOC sniper doesn't so much change careers as he accepts additional tasking and responsibilities.

The reconnaissance aspect of the position in particular requires an extra layer of maturity and savviness, and that drives the multiyear process.

However, a fortuitous by-product of this grooming system is that the sniper teams are loaded up with operators who rank as some of the preeminent assaulters and close-quarter combat experts in the world, fresh from years of training and experience operating at the highest level.

Shrek explained, "The recce troops recruit the guys who are good at everything. When I was an assaulter, I didn't want to be a sniper. I thought they were the fat, old guys. But once I was drafted, I learned in a hurry that these were actually the best guys in the Unit at CQB [close quarters battle]. No one in the world can touch them in combat marksmanship.

"All that matters is training and experience. Your average assaulter has two years of experience at that level. Most guys in a recce troop have five or six years in the Unit, and a team leader there usually has more than a decade."

This reality has earned Delta's snipers an alternate designation—"advanced assaulter"—that presents an entirely different mental image.

Vickers added, "They want guys over there on the sniper side of the house who are still assaulters at heart."

Not only are those CQB skills retained, they are continually refined. While perhaps originally just a secondary consideration (at best), the snipers' expertise in this regard pays significant dividends during direct action missions, and in multiple ways.

When tasked with overwatch duty—covering the raid from a nearby position as the assault team hits an objective—the snipers' intrinsic knowledge of this exacting and highly dangerous science allows for tighter integration. This is true even when doors are breached and bullets are slung in confined spaces while the sniper is on the glass of magnified optics from afar.

"You need to be an assaulter first so that you understand what they do—what they are going through and what they are thinking," ex-DEVGRU sniper Sawyer explained. "When you are covering them, you can do it much more effectively. The better you understand them, the more effective sniper for them you can be."

While somewhat removed from the fray, direct action overwatch is a critical task and one taken very seriously by the snipers who are charged with watching over their teammates' safety. Sawyer said, "I'll tell you what . . . having been there, I always wanted to carry the biggest, most powerful weapons I could as a sniper to make sure I covered for my brothers against any potential threat.

"It was a heavy responsibility and one that I appreciated and was glad to be able to provide to cover my brothers as they solved problems in the worst possible circumstances—halfway around the world in the middle of the night in enemy territory where you stirred up a hornet's nest and they're all coming to get you. The snipers' job is to keep people off of the assaulters and eliminate any threats upon initiation of the hit and afterward. It's definitely a heavy responsibility, but one that I welcomed."

Additionally, a sniper's assaulter background may need to manifest itself at a moment's notice as the overwatch assignment transitions into something else in a fast-moving raid. According to the former SEAL Team Six sniper, "At any moment, you may need to perform that room clearance to unite directly with the main assault team to work in with them. And it happens often. It always remains a part of your job."

And these sharpened talents are frequently called upon in an even more direct manner. The snipers are not confined to overwatch duty during take-down operations. In fact, to maximize its effectiveness at shredding through enemy networks, the Unit exploits the prodigious door-kicking and room-clearing skills of its snipers "every night, every assault," according to McPhee.

"Every operator in the Unit is an assaulter—that's job one," he continued. "The next thing is your specialty. If your specialty is needed on a given night, you'll do it. Otherwise, you're in the stack and hitting the building right alongside the rest of the assault element."

◈

It's not only outsiders who have a misperception of what snipers are and what they do, especially in Tier 1 units like Delta Force and SEAL Team Six.

In many ways, the basic assaulter role is the glamour position of these DA/CT-centric units. Not every established assaulter aspires to move to a recce role and some assaulters tend to view the snipers as too far removed from "the mix"—a more passive and solitary gig.

And in general—despite the undeniably vast experience and training contained within the recce ranks—the assaulters don't particularly look to the snipers with any sense of awe.

When asked if other operators admire the Unit's snipers, McPhee, the same former Tier 1 commando who considered the recce troop the "fat, old guys" before he became one himself laughed and said, "Fuck no. They're only worried about themselves and doing their job—which is how it should be. They're just looking to improve. When I was there, I was only worried about me, just trying not to get fired. You can't worry about anyone else's bullshit.

"The assaulters get pissed when they have to wait on the snipers for five minutes to hit a target. Well, we just hiked in here from twenty kilometers away at record pace—you can wait five minutes."

There is something of a cultural divide separating the two sides of the house within SEAL Team Six as well. The assaulters tend to face more logistical obstacles, with larger groups and regular meetings to deal with. Meanwhile, the snipers have less equipment to haul around and operators to coordinate. Rather than sit around the table, DEVGRU snipers can brief in a team truck en route.

"Back in my day, the assaulters called us the Rod and Gun Club," Sawyer said. "They were under the impression that all we did was lie in the dirt and shoot at our leisure, which couldn't have been further from the truth. But we had nicer equipment and we had more responsibility and more leeway in training.

"The culture is more that you're detached and it's more of a 'big boy rules' kind of thing. We had a lot more leniency to do things our own way, and that's resented by the assaulters, you know. They want to be the tip of the spear—and they are the tip of the spear—but if there's somebody that's allowed better equipment and more autonomy and more control over their training—their existence—that's of course resented by those who are not. It's just human nature."

◉

But perhaps most valued of all are a JSOC sniper's ability to conduct exceptionally high-risk reconnaissance and surveillance operations. It is certainly the most sensitive and unique, and the one that, when over-lapped with their multifaceted offensive skills, separates them from any other solution the United States can bring to bear.

This matrix of talents weaves across distinctions that typically separate black military ops and pure espionage work. It may involve operating from safe houses or conducting close target vehicle reconnaissance while in disguise, such as the work Black Team performed in Mogadishu, or traversing mountain peaks the way B Squadron's recce teams did in advance of Operation Anaconda, or even blending in among locals and then stealthily creeping through villages like McPhee to pinpoint the location of an HVT. And as Delta Force and DEVGRU gained the operational experience and confidence that came with the faster and faster tempo at which they began to work, these specialists became even more audacious and adept. Eventually, it was the norm that more than one of their three primary functions—the sniper, the advanced assaulter, and the recce operator—would be tapped into simultaneously, as B Squadron would demonstrate down the line in Iraq.

To effectively blur the lines between warrior, assassin, and spy, these assets often operate in very small elements. They regularly separate from their squadrons to deploy to the most dangerous corners of the world in teams of six or less. They are then given perversely difficult tasks and granted considerable autonomy with the expectation they will complete them.

DEVGRU will readily scale its recce teams down to as few as two. "We try not to go any less than two men for redundancy purposes," Sawyer explained. "There's a benefit of teamwork, you know? Two guys can move and shoot and cover each other out of a bad situation but one guy has got nobody to cover him. Especially if he medically goes down or something like that."

As evidenced by McPhee's operational history, under the right conditions and with the right man at its disposal, Delta Force has been known to push even lower. While the one-man army is more Hollywood legend than real-world ground truth, the Unit does in fact task some of its most skilled recce operators with singleton missions.

Shrek explained, "Rangers are most effective at the company size. With

SEALs, they're best as a sixteen-man platoon. Special Forces, it's the twelve-man ODA. In the Unit, it's one; you're the lone wolf and the jack of all trades. And that one has to be able to do everything the SF team can do. In the recce troop you have to be good at everything, because when you're out there alone, there's no one else to help.

"To teach someone to be able to do this, I'd make them go out and steal something every day—go to the gas station and steal bread," he added. "People always ask the same questions: 'What if you're out on a singleton op someone tried to grab you and you have to shoot them?' Well, you fucked up if you're in the situation in the first place. You should never get to that point. There'd have to be eight doors locked behind me before that would happen. You need to have 360-degree total situational awareness.

"There is no recce mind-set. Training is everything. And it's the system someone is trained in that matters, 100 percent."

While an outstanding illustration of the enormous capabilities contained within the recce troop, McPhee was not the only "Kingpin" in its ranks, as the looming First Battle of Fallujah would so clearly illustrate.

6

Tex

Afghanistan and Iraq were not the only parallel wars being waged by special operations forces. While that particular divide was obvious, the separation in the other was more subtle, more nuanced, and more philosophical.

Collectively, JSOC and its subordinate units are sometimes termed the National Missions Force—a pacified way of saying they exist largely outside the typical military bureaucracy. JSOC is freed up by an abbreviated chain of command, tying it directly to the highest levels of the government.

In a way, that has been true since its inception, as the impetus for creating the Joint Special Operations Command was the emergent requirement for surgically precise units that could conduct politically sensitive operations in response to terrorist actions, such as rescuing hostages on foreign soil. Any mission of that sort would quite naturally necessitate the president's direct input.

However, following 9/11, the concept of terrorism and the options for combating it radically expanded. And with that, so too did JSOC's reach.

In the wake of the 2001 attacks, then-Secretary of Defense Donald Rumsfeld initially showed his ignorance of JSOC's capabilities when he wistfully yearned for the sort of force needed to counter al-Qaeda. What he described—to a collection of JSOC officers no less—was precisely what he already had in the Delta Force and DEVGRU.

Once Rumsfeld became better educated as to the assets at his disposal—and later saw what they were capable of once the results began to roll in—he empowered and unleashed them.

The Global War on Terror would be waged by a global fighting force, largely unshackled by increasingly obsolete notions of geographic areas of operation and enabled by nearly unlimited budget and support.

Rumsfeld signed into effect a series of secret directives (the Al Qaeda Network Execute Order being of particular prominence) that freed JSOC so that it could more proactively combat global terrorist networks such as al-Qaeda.

In addition to the more narrowly defined war zones of Iraq and Afghanistan, JSOC was allowed to deploy its trigger pullers to such exotic locales as Pakistan (and did so as early as '02), Somalia, Syria, Lebanon, Yemen, Madagascar, and Iran, following nation-specific constraints.

While Multi-National Force – Iraq (MNF-I) and International Security Assistance Force (ISAF) may have technically managed the wars in Iraq and Afghanistan, respectively, JSOC did not answer to either of them. The Command operated inside those nations semiautonomously and with impunity as part of its larger, global campaign, and did so with varying degrees of coordination with those entities.

◈

The descriptor "Tier 1" signifies the role of Delta Force and DEVGRU as the principle direct action components of this National Missions Force.

Units that either belong directly to JSOC or are freely borrowed from SOCOM and regularly utilized to directly support the efforts of the Tier 1 units are considered Tier 2.

The Intelligence Support Activity—the shadowy specialized signals intelligence (SIGINT) and human intelligence (HUMINT) collection unit—was absorbed by JSOC shortly after 9/11. Rumsfeld sought ways to maneuver free from reliance on the CIA during what had become a heated turf battle between the DoD and the Agency, and bringing the ISA under JSOC's authority helped toward those ends. One of the most tightly secretive units in the American military, the exploits of "The Activity" have largely been left to the imagination, although a number of its wide assortments of aliases—including the Mission Support Activity (MSA), TORN VICTOR, CEMETERY WIND, and GRAY FOX—have found their way into the public.

The ISA serves as an example of a Tier 2 unit, as one of its core functions is securing actionable intelligence for Delta and DEVGRU.

Similarly, the Air Force's 24th Special Tactics Squadron is also considered a Tier 2 entity. The unit's PJs and CCTs regularly attach to Delta Force and DEVGRU elements in training and in the field. This is so much the case, in fact, that these top-tier USAF Air Commandos actually take part in the initial training pipeline alongside their Tier 1 counterparts so they'll later be able to operate together seamlessly.

The 160th Special Operations Aviation Regiment, home to the crack Army pilots known as the Night Stalkers, are also considered Tier 2. The pilots are admired throughout the military for their tremendous courage and aptitude in placing their tricked-out helos into the tightest spots under even the most compromising of conditions.

Not technically a JSOC unit, the 160th SOAR is one of the aforementioned "borrowed" assets, as is the 75th Ranger Regiment, another Tier 2 organization that regularly details its soldiers to JSOC.

These tier labels have become progressively blurred over time. For example, The Activity's priority level, budget, and ability to operate independently are more indicative of a Tier 1 outfit—and thus it has been referred to as such in some quarters. Meanwhile, others term it as a "Tier 2 unit performing Tier 1 functions."

Similarly, while the Rangers were not asked to undertake the full spectrum of mission sets tasked to the Tier 1 units in Iraq or Afghanistan, the Regiment began to operate more along the lines of an equal partner as the pace quickened. It routinely planned and executed its own direct action missions to cut down HVTs in Iraq and rotated command and operations with ST6 in Afghanistan.

Buried even deeper behind a curtain of classification is a wide assortment of supporting commands either owned or controlled by JSOC, some of which help secure or decipher intelligence by specialized and technical means, while others serve as streamlined procurement offices that rapidly usher emerging technologies from the drawing board into the field.

Yet another term that is frequently used to describe JSOC and its missions is "black," as in "black special operations." This refers to their covert nature and classified, sometimes unacknowledged existence (even if the wink-wink, nudge-nudge denials can at times strain credulity).

The flipside to this are the so-called white SOF—the unclassified special operations forces such as the regular "vanilla" SEAL Teams and the Army's Special Forces. Considered Tier 3, they traditionally answer to, and are directed by, regional combatant commanders. Although the rising influence of SOCOM has altered this dynamic somewhat, it often means that the unique capabilities of these particular forces are called upon in support of wider conventional campaigns.

While JSOC's HVT hunter-killer task forces took on an ever-shifting set of generic, largely numeric designations as the war in Afghanistan continued and the war in Iraq kicked off, the wider (and whiter) special operations forces were organized under the umbrellas "Combined Joint Special Operations Task Force–Arabian Peninsula" (CJSOTF-AP) and "Combined Joint Special Operations Task Force–Afghanistan" (CJSOTF-A).

These CJSOTFs were established by SOCCENT—Special Operations Command Central—a subunified command of CENTCOM.

The Iraq-focused CJSOTF-AP included SEAL Teams from both coasts, along with the 1st, 5th, and 10th U.S. Army Special Forces Groups. Meanwhile in Afghanistan, CJSOTF-A was heavily weighted toward SF with the 3rd and 19th among the Groups supplying its headquarters element.

◈

While there is some overlap in what is brought to the table, Navy SEALs and Army Special Forces have each carved out their own particular niche during the course of their proud histories. The units' roles within the task forces generally reflected these differences.

The Army's Green Berets are renowned for the skills in the areas of unconventional warfare and foreign internal defense. This allows them to operate alongside the local populace, train them, and effectively weaponize their sympathies.

Alongside small teams from the CIA's Special Activities Division, Special Forces ODA's played a critical role in the opening stages of the Afghanistan War. Among the enduring images of that initial rush are Task Force Dagger Green Berets on horseback, astonishing their Northern Alliance allies while devastating their Taliban enemies with air strikes. In Iraq, their expertise often meant bringing local special police and military units up to speed and then leading them in the field.

Meanwhile, SEALs are most effective when conducting kinetic operations, unleashing their quick-strike capabilities in direct action missions.

If used properly, these complementary core strengths can allow both units to make invaluable contributions across a wide variety of scenarios.

However, they haven't always been leveraged to the maximum of their capabilities. As the Afghanistan War campaign ramped up, the vanilla SEAL Teams were assigned to Task Force K-Bar, a hodgepodge of allied SOF that also included Australian SASR, Canadian JTF-2, and German KSK commandos.

While deep in talent and motivation, the task force was often sidelined or given lower priority targets to chase as JSOC's task force assumed the role of the AO's dominant hunter.

And later, as a new war kicked off in Iraq, the National Missions Force largely operated where and when it chose while monopolizing limited ISR (intelligence, surveillance, and reconnaissance) resources, particularly the emerging robotic air force—the MQ-1 Predators and other drone platforms.

The SEAL Teams expected to play a crucial role in Iraq. Naval Special Warfare made a splash at its opening, executing high-profile operations timed to the start of the invasion. However, as the war started to evolve, their impact was rendered nearly nonexistent.

◈

As the Iraq War broke out, Lieutenant Larry Yatch was on his second deployment, serving as the AOIC (Assistant Officer in Charge) of a Team Three platoon. Yatch had already earned himself an outsized reputation as a new-guy "third O" while taking part in the visit, board, search, and seizure (VBSS) operations that earned Team Three its pre-9/11 status as the place to be—the *only* Team doing actual SEAL work in those days. There he had developed a new method for breaching ships that was utilized multiple times during the deployment.

Now actively engaged in a full-scale war, Yatch and the rest of the SEALs with Team Three expected to find themselves deep in the mix. However, following those initial ops that helped enable the invasion, the reality was very different. The deployment was generally one of disappointment—if not outright embarrassment—for the SEALs.

"It was a very frustrating deployment for most of us," Yatch admitted. "All the platoons did a lot of stuff, but none of it was what we thought of as combat or what we thought war was going to be like. All of our leadership 'grew up' in peace time. All of our commanders . . . they had never done anything because nothing had gone on for so long—since Panama."

ST3's commanding officer in 2003 was Adam Curtis. Curtis had, in fact, played a pivotal role in Panama but not in a way he would fondly remember.

In late December of 1989, as a young Lieutenant, Curtis and his wife were taken captive at a Panamanian roadblock and subsequently tortured by Manuel Noriega's PDF goons. The following day, Operation Just Cause— the invasion of Panama—was given the go-ahead by President George H. W. Bush.

While Commander Curtis had suffered horribly in Panama, the rest of the Team's top brass was almost entirely without combat experience of any sort. General Norman Schwarzkopf's antipathy for special operations in general seemed to hold particularly true in the case of Navy SEALs, and the CENTCOM Commander-in-Chief forced them into a minimal role during the Gulf War.

"[Schwarzkopf] wouldn't allow the SEALs back in Desert Storm because of his ego—that's just a fact," said Howard Wasdin, who was still with SEAL Team Two during the early '90s engagement. "Norman Schwarzkopf didn't like the SEALs period. He basically made us nonplayers."

Expounding on the lack of wartime experience residing inside Team Three's leadership when it came time to return to Iraq a decade later, Yatch said, "That's not anything negative on them—there was nothing to do. But they had existed in a peacetime environment where if a SEAL got hurt, their career was ended."

As a result, the officers were conditioned throughout the entirety of their careers to be exceedingly risk averse. And even when presented with a wartime environment, they continued to be hesitant in subjecting their sailors to any sort of risk.

The Team's planning methodology was also painfully slow and unrealistic. As such, it proved unable to keep pace with a rapidly shifting situation on the ground.

Yatch said, "Things were happening so fast. In the [nonwartime] environment we existed in prior to that, we would spend a week planning for an op. And so, that environment of being risk averse as well as being conditioned that there are very specific SEAL missions and there are very specific ways to plan for them—well, that wasn't the environment we were in after the opening night."

Opportunities were continually passed up. And a pack of hungry SEALs were helpless to do little more than watch the war transpire around them.

◈

Making matters more problematic, even if a situation happened to allow this outdated mentality enough time to approve an operation, the intelligence provided to the platoons was often woefully inadequate.

DEVGRU, for example, had its missions fueled by a massive intelligence network that combined the efforts of external agencies, supporting units owned by JSOC, and SEAL Team Six's own recce operators, all of which were specifically aimed at locking down their next target.

SEAL Team Three lacked all of these, forced instead to rely heavily on Naval Intelligence personnel who were better suited to support destroyer captains at sea than SOF on land.

ST3 was assigned an ambitious multipart operation that served as the opening salvo of the Iraq War. Given adequate time to effectively coordinate what would be the largest single operation in Naval Special Warfare history, the SEALs partnered with other coalition special operations forces to secure the Al Basrah and Khawr Al Amaya Oil Terminal platforms, their related onshore pumping locks, and the Al Faw refinery.

While later hailed as a historic success—and one that kicked off the broader Operation Iraqi Freedom—all three objectives were threatened with disaster due to faulty intel. As a result, literal and figurative bullets were dodged.

At the Al Faw manifold and metering station, the mission plan called for helicopters to ferry SEALs into location, at which point they would launch from the back of the aircraft aboard DPVs (Desert Patrol Vehicles)—basically armed dune buggies. The SEALs would race their vehicles to strategic locations and then prevent enemy forces from coming through the facility's front gate.

The insertion team planned to release the DPVs on nearby roads but intelligence personnel insisted they land in the nearby fields instead.

"The fields were solid mud and the DPVs are horrible in those conditions," Yatch said. "Some of them didn't even make it a foot off the ramp. The farthest one made it less than twenty-five yards."

That meant they couldn't use the heavy guns mounted on the DPVs to guard the gates. It also meant the stranded SEALs were forced to advance on foot in full MOPP gear (chemical-resistant suits with gas masks) in knee-deep mud. "It was a mess."

It was a similar story at the second target, where the SEALs were provided with another less-than-optimal LZ. Yatch said, "As soon as the gate opened the guys ran out of the back of the helicopter and into ten feet of concertina wire on top of a bunker."

The third objective was an oil platform, which offered significantly more resistance than expected.

The SEAL Lieutenant, whose platoon took part in the oil platform hit, said, "We were told to expect three people—a cook, a maintenance guy, and one soldier. Instead, we ended up facing twenty-four Iraqi Republican Guard, multiple antiaircraft positions, two machine-gun positions, and a thousand pounds of explosives.

"They were completely wrong. And that continued throughout the war."

◈

Two ST3 platoons operated in Nasiriya one week after the invasion opened and just days ahead of the DEVGRU-led Jessica Lynch rescue mission. While there were plenty of targets in the area, the SEALs were handcuffed from actively pursuing them.

"We weren't allowed to go anywhere near where they were during the day out of the risk that we might get into a firefight and someone might get shot," the SEAL officer said.

Meanwhile, USMC Force Reconnaissance platoons were in the area too and operating under considerably greater freedom. In fact, they'd drive directly into town, just daring someone to shoot at them, and then they'd take the fight to anyone who took the bait.

The frustrated Yatch asked, "We're more valuable than Marines? We can't be exposed to that kind of risk and they can? At my level—the officer level—I didn't see much tactical thinking going on at the level above me. We didn't get a lot of direction and no one was coming up with a battle plan. You've got these resources . . . use them. And that wasn't the case.

"The whole environment was very frustrating. You know there are bad guys out there. You know you're better than they are. And yet, we were sitting around or going out on these silly ops to just go sit on a corner and hope someone drives by in the middle of the night."

According to Yatch, throughout the lengthy deployment only two members of SEAL Team Three so much as fired a shot at an enemy combatant, totaling three kills in all.

"It was this feeling of, 'That was pathetic. That's the best we've got?' One of the British SBS guys said we were lions being led by lambs."

◈

Among the Team Three SEALs demoralized and disillusioned by his first brush with combat was a big, broad-shouldered new guy the rest of the platoon called "Tex." The nickname was not in any way ironic—he was Texan to the core, almost to the point of being a caricature of the stereotype.

The son of hardworking, religious parents, Christopher Scott Kyle was born in Odessa, Texas. He grew up on a ranch with his parents and younger brother near Midlothian, a small town with a population of less than ten thousand some thirty miles southeast of Fort Worth.

Larger than life like his home state itself, Kyle earned his "real deal" credentials before ever brandishing the SEAL Trident. While he played football and baseball as a Midlothian Panther before graduating in 1992, he found his (first) calling in the rodeo. When he wasn't competing he paid the bills by working as a ranch hand.

These days an accent marked by a drawl combined with a tendency to play dress-up year-round is enough to earn someone the title "cowboy." But, in certain parts of the country, the genuine article is not yet extinct and Kyle was indeed a true-blue cowboy, the first of several existences he lived that most only dare to dream of.

Kyle's eventual path to a military life was forced when his rodeo career came to an abrupt ending.

He was crushed and pinned in the chute when a bronco flipped over on top of him and pressed up against the gate so the latch wouldn't release. The horse rolled on top of him again and the gate finally swung open. The bronco bucked out with the cowboy hopelessly dragged along for the ride.

"I still had a foot in the stirrup," Kyle explained. "He kicked me in the kidneys, and that's finally what kicked me out of the stirrup. I woke up being Life Flighted to the hospital."

Adding insult to injury, Kyle jokingly lamented that there wasn't even video evidence of the incident to cash in on (*"America's Funniest Home Videos*—I could have won some money").

Years later Kyle was back home from his first deployment, trying to figure out his next move in life. He had specifically requested Team Three because of its reputation as the place to be in the Teams if you wanted action. He even requested it despite the perceived indignity of having to live in Southern California to do so.

However, now back from war and still not satisfied, the 60 gunner contemplated his future. He wasn't beaten down when confronted with the harsh realities of war. Quite the opposite, in fact; he had gotten his first taste of combat and discovered it agreed with him. Instead he was left sickened by what he considered to be cowardice and political maneuvering by his own leaders in search of "bullshit glory."

ST3's potential had been squandered by what Kyle saw as a commanding officer more concerned with career advancement than the effectiveness of his Team. Avoiding catastrophic failure rather than seeking overwhelming success was the most certain way to pad the brass's resume.

He later admitted that if he hadn't been locked in to a contract, he might have left the Teams at that point, perhaps even made good on his initial thoughts of joining the USMC and becoming one of those Force Recon Marines himself.

But he was and he didn't. Instead, Chris Kyle was about to answer his true calling.

◈

"New guy" taint removed, Kyle was granted his wish following his first deployment: a slot at the U.S. Navy SEAL Sniper Course.

Today, the school is considered among the best basic sniper training programs in the world—if not *the* best. That reputation is based on its forward-thinking instruction and supported by the undeniable results of its alumni in the field. However, it wasn't always that way—in fact, it's a relatively recent development.

Kyle did not know it at the time, but he was to become one of the very first of a new breed of SEAL snipers, trained to exacting standards via a thoroughly modernized course.

Prior to the introduction of this pilot program, the reputation of SEAL sniper training had been decidedly mixed.

While SEALs have formally existed since the '60s, the internal sniper program wasn't developed for some time after that. A former SEAL sniper instructor with an expansive knowledge of the program explained, "It wasn't until '86 or so that the SEALs developed their own course. Before that, most of the guys were sent to the Marine Scout Sniper Course, and a few were sent to the Army's."

Even after the introduction of the SEAL program, the esteemed USMC Scout Sniper Basic Course (SSBC) remained the preferred destination for most. As aspiring SEAL Team Six snipers in the early '90s, Howard Wasdin and Homer Nearpass were given their choices of three schools: the SEAL sniper school, USMC Scout Sniper Course, or the Army's SOTIC (Special Operations Target Interdiction Course).

Due to its long history, tradition, and prestige, they both elected to train at the USMC program, a near-unanimous choice among new DEVGRU snipers at the time. In fact, the Red Squadron's sniper team room sports an autographed poster of Carlos Hathcock to this day.

Wasdin vividly recalled his time at the Marine Corps Scout Sniper Course nearly a quarter of a century after the fact. He said, "When I went through, the SEAL sniper program was still considered . . . well, let's say when I talked to my SEAL buddies who had been to sniper school, every single one of them had chosen to go to Marine Corps sniper school. Back then they were saying, 'Hey, you can go through [SOTIC or the SEAL training], or you can *chance* it and go to Quantico.'

"At that time, the reason it was so vaunted was because of the just nut-dragging stalks you had to do there. Quantico in the summertime is like hell on earth. It's hot, you've got to do those stalks in full ghillie suits, and you have a minimum number you've got to pass. I had a buddy who went to Quantico and he'd write us a letter every week: 'Hey man, don't know if I chose the right school or not, but I haven't busted my ass like this since BUD/S.'"

The U.S. Navy SEAL Sniper Course received a much-needed overhaul beginning in 2003. After returning from a combat deployment as a SEAL sniper for Team Three under Task Force K-Bar in Afghanistan, Brandon Webb joined NSWG-1 Training Detachment (TRADET) as an instructor at the West Coast TRADET Sniper Cell.

There he already started rethinking the approach to sniper training when he and fellow TRADET instructor and SEAL sniper Eric Davis were invited to join a pair of decorated DEVGRU snipers in a total redesign of the basic SEAL Sniper Course. A short while later, both men were recruited to join full-time and Webb would eventually be promoted to Course Manager.

The refreshed U.S. Navy SEAL Sniper Course was exacting and extensive. At thirteen weeks, it was almost twice as long as the U.S. Army Sniper School and weeks longer than either SOTIC or USMC SSBC.

While based very much on the template laid out by the Scout Sniper Basic Course, the SEAL program was also designed to be more intuitive, applicable, and modernized. Historical holdovers were rethought or discarded and a major emphasis was made to incorporate any and all relevant emerging technologies that might provide its students a critical edge on the battlefield.

The use of advanced photographic and ballistic software was dissected and perfected, new weapons systems and attachments were integrated, and the students were now expected to master the science that determines how a bullet gets from point A to point B when traveling hundreds, if not thousands, of yards.

And the Marine course wasn't the only model that inspired its design. Leading foreign programs also served as inspiration, as did the training methods of world-class athletes, leading to the development of progressive mental heuristic and observation methodologies.

USMC Scout Sniper Basic Course graduate Wasdin is a believer. "People like Brandon brought it to the next level. The way the SEAL sniper program is now—their program with different weapons and different targets—that's cutting edge."

◈

One of the key developments that differentiates modern SEAL sniper training from other top schools is the emphasis on learning to effectively operate as an independent smart shooter. That is, they are no longer reliant on working as part of a traditional two-man shooter/spotter pair. This not only doubles up the number of guns in the field at any given moment—allowing the small SEAL community to get the most out of their limited number of snipers—it also makes for a more capable, more well-rounded marksman.

"We do this because we started looking at real-world case studies and the way we were employing our snipers," Webb said. "We went, 'Wait a minute—if our guys are being employed in a helicopter as a sniper overwatch, or they're a single sniper overwatch on an assault element that's going into a village, why aren't we focusing more on making sure we're training them to that standard?' "

The snipers are taught to understand the fundamentals of ballistics, allowing them to quickly self-evaluate and zero in on the target in short order.

Webb said, "Without a spotter, that's what you need—you need somebody who can do it themselves. You don't have the luxury of having some guy on a spotting scope saying, 'Oh man, you're ten minutes high,' and give them those corrections. Let's say we're in Iraq and you're shooting someone at close range. You shot and you missed. If you didn't see it impact on the scope, you know you're high. And if the wind isn't a factor, you know you have an elevation problem. Now you need to dial down the correct amount of minutes and you need to do it really quickly and get on target."

This addition also prevented a strong spotter from dragging along a weaker student with whom he was paired. In the Marine and Army courses, shooter/spotters share a grade. This was formerly true with the SEALs as well.

"If you can make a good shot, great, but being a sniper is such a big responsibility and so much more than being able to break a clean shot," Webb said, "If shit goes wrong, you need someone who can figure it out real quick."

◈

Another major change to the U.S. Navy SEAL Sniper Course was the inclusion of its mentor program. It's not that the old sniper course wasn't difficult—in fact, its attrition rates were painfully high. However, the redesigned course was made even more challenging, and yet a much higher percentage of students successfully passed due to a modification in the way they were instructed.

Davis, one of the key architects behind the modernization of the course, explained, "A lot of guys who were already SEALs were failing out. One of the core things we did to address that was instead of just having them go through the course as students, we assigned them individual mentors. At any given sniper course, I would have three or four who were my students. I would watch their test scores, talk with them individually, and debrief them. It was my responsibility for them to succeed."

One of Eric Davis's very first students—a student who would be among the first SEALs trained to this next-generation sniper standard—was Chris Kyle.

Webb singled out Davis for his teaching prowess—an instructor capable of both transfixing pupils with illuminating lectures and dazzling them with prodigious feats of learned memory.

Davis and Kyle came to the Teams hailing from considerably different backgrounds and were naturally drawn to contrasting aspects of SEAL operations. But as a mentor-protégé pairing, they made a tremendous team.

Davis was as Californian as Kyle was Texan. He grew up in the Bay Area where his father was a sheriff in San Mateo County. His father's father was a special agent for the FBI, and his father's father's father was a law-man, too.

Becoming a SEAL seems like a natural extension of that impressive family tradition. But whatever his bloodlines may have predicted, Eric simply describes himself as the fan who grew up to live out his boyhood dreams. Tales of superheroes, secret agents, and special operators fueled his child-hood. And even after experiencing the hardships and dark realities generally scrubbed from the comics and movies, Eric feels he's that same fan to this day, just a few decades older and wiser.

Now Kyle, he just was. He was born to be the guy those stories were stories about.

Davis was immediately impressed with his new student. He also quickly recognized their dialogue could go in both directions. "He didn't hold any-thing back—he told it how it was. But he was able to do that in a very Texan way where you actually wanted to hear it. When a lot of other people speak their mind, it's generally an idiotic thing to do. Frankly, most people's opinion is crap and you don't want to hear it. But not with Chris—it was more than an opinion. He wouldn't speak it if he didn't believe in it and it wasn't grounded in something. Now that doesn't mean he was perfect. He wasn't. But it meant there was something to it."

The former SEAL sniper continued, "You know how he had that swag-ger but was still humble? Well, there's two things—there's arrogance and there's confidence. Arrogance is someone walking around who has all the answers but they have nothing in their experience to back it up. Now some-one who is confident, there's a big, big difference. They are going to seem down to earth and still able to tell you how it is, because they are not speak-ing to produce a peacock effect; they are not posturing. They are speaking because they truly want to help you. They are speaking out of love—not out of some sort of obligation."

◈

Another former SEAL sniper instructor said, "SEAL snipers do things a bit differently—Nightforce Optics and all that. But the main thing is the training—it's ultrahard. We had some Army guys come over and they said this is just crazy. At one point the hours were so intense that we were doing 97-93-91 for the first three weeks of training.

"With the new curriculum—'05, '06, '07—around then we had the best guys to have ever come through here. We had the money to train them and they had the talent and motivation to take advantage. These guys were so well trained, once they were sent overseas, they just crushed it."

By all accounts, U.S. Navy SEAL Sniper Course *is* hard, but it's a different kind of hard than BUD/S. It's more analogous to Green Team, the pressure cooker in which experienced SEALs screen for admission into DEVGRU. It's not simply a matter of pushing your mind and body to the limit and not giving in. You either meet the standard or you don't.

"If you send three guys in a platoon to sniper school, you are only expecting one or two of them to pass," Davis said. "Guys have said they'd rather do BUD/S again than this. Here's the thing with sniper school: BUD/S you can try your hardest and for most people that will work. Now with sniper school, you can try as hard as you want not to get caught, but if you're not figuring it out, you're going to get caught.

"You can't 'try' a bullet into a bullseye. There's no way to just really want a bullet to go where it needs to go."

There's a skill set and a certain set of scientific realities that must be met for a bullet to hit its mark. One needs to either know them academically and be capable of repeating them or somehow embody them as part of his intuition.

Davis explained, "You're working under a certain set of mechanisms that are indifferent to how much you want something. *And that is a son of a bitch*. It's much like life. Life does not care that you need to make $100,000 a year. It does not care if your baby is sick and you can't pay the hospital bills. Life does not care. And that's why sniper training, if understood and applied correctly, is the ultimate formula for success in life."

◈

The U.S. Navy SEAL Sniper Course takes approximately three months to complete. It opens with two weeks of training that might catch prospective snipers off guard as they learn to pull the trigger on a different kind of shot.

"Believe it or not, sniper school starts off with a digital photography class," said Davis. "The first thing we teach them to do is use these twenty-five-thousand-dollar camera kits. I used to take the cameras to the zoo with my family and people thought I worked for National Geographic. It's the absolute best equipment you can get your hands on."

The primary job for a sniper is recon and surveillance. They are the eyes and ears. In the first phase the prospective snipers learn to camouflage a camera, take pictures through items, touch up the photos, and condense and transmit them via satellite or radio.

Following the comms and digital photo phase, SEAL snipers-in-training transition to the month-long scout phase. Here they do four weeks of stalking under direct observation. The students attempt to crawl eight hundred yards or more unseen on their bellies to the location of two highly trained sniper instructors who have years of experience spotting even the slightest sign of movement.

"There's something called a strategic checklist, which is like what a pilot uses," Davis said. "And if you don't have the mental fortitude and discipline to be continually going over your checklist and hold all the items in your head, you'll fail. And you know the deal—you start off for an hour, and you tell yourself, 'Okay, check your camouflage. Before you move make sure you're not getting shadows on your face. Make sure your background matches. Make sure your foreground matches. Make sure you're moving directly at the target instead of laterally.' All of these things. But then you get tired and that stuff starts to go away. 'Crap, I've just got to move,' and that's when you get busted. So there's an incredible amount of discipline required along with the ability to execute a strategy over and over again that goes into stalking."

Initially, students must sneak up and take an identifiable picture of the instructors' faces without being caught. Once the picture is taken, a "walker" will point out their exact location. They must be so perfectly blended into the environment as to remain invisible from the instructors' vantage point.

Later, the requirements progress to firing a rifle with blanks while avoiding observation. Once fired, they must be able to shoot a second time without being seen as the instructors scan for disrupted foliage and the like.

"They are taught to move as if we are looking directly at them the whole time," Davis explained. "The idea is to train them for the worst-case scenario. If you are stalking an enemy, you don't know when that enemy might take his binos and look right at you. That means 100 percent you have to be moving as if he's staring right at you."

The former SEAL sniper mentor also added that while many real-world stalks take place under conditions very different from one in which a ghillie-suited sniper patiently inches his way into location in the brush, the skills readily translate. "A lot of people ask, 'Oh, we're in an urban environment now, why are you teaching these guys out in the bush?' It's because the fundamentals at their core are the fundamentals of performance. It doesn't matter if you're in a mall following someone or if you're in the field. Either way you need to think about your background, your movements, dead space, cover and concealment, and blending into the environment."

Scout phase provides the sniper with the mental tools to juggle these requirements even as they are constantly in flux.

Davis said, "This is where you also start all the sniper games. We have observation drills where we hide objects in a field and give them a certain amount of time to find ten items. They have to get incredibly good at systematically scanning their environment to pick out whatever they are looking for."

Among the observation drills are KIM—Keep-in-Memory—games. Davis is a master at these, capable of memorizing thirty students' phone and social security numbers after reading the list just once. To show them what will soon be expected of them, Davis asked classrooms filled with new students for their names and in return he rattled off their personal information.

"We teach these guys the skill sets to remember anything," Davis explained. "I could teach them to remember a deck of cards in order if that's what I wanted them to do."

While it might seem strange to some that the first month and a half of the course is focused on skills other than sending bullets at targets from great distances, former DEVGRU sniper Wasdin confirmed the importance of the less violent aspects of being a sniper.

"The thing about a sniper is that we are trained observers," he said. "Way more times than not, when I went on an op I didn't shoot anybody. But I damn sure got a lot of information, whether it was terrain, how many stories a building is, or a guard patrol routine.

"If I see a guard patrol routine on a building, I know when to send my assault team in to avoid that patrol. The big thing about being a sniper is playing KIM games. That way all the stuff you observe, you can go back and relay it. You might be pulling the trigger 10 percent of the time, but you're observing 100 percent of the time.

"You can't take most average people and just train them to be a SEAL sniper. Most people just don't possess that attention to detail. First of all, most people don't want it. People think they want it but don't have the intestinal fortitude to get it. Many times I was there freezing, baking, getting mobbed by mosquitos, snakes crawling across me, or whatever, and you're observing the entire time."

The final seven weeks are the sniper phase, where the sweet science of shooting is finally mastered. The finer points of ballistics are drilled into students as they learn how to practically apply them in the field.

Among the drills used to train the sniper students are unknown distance shooting with targets located on hills at various ranges. The students are not told the distance, forcing them to measure it using the Mil-Dots inside their reticles. They accomplish this by utilizing the trigonometric milliradian to calculate the distance to an object—such as an average-sized human—based on its assumed height or width.

Davis said, "They're using their eyeballs with something very far and fuzzy. That's a skill set in and of itself. When they shoot the target, they have to determine whether they missed high, low, left, or right, and that's another philosophical conversation right there. They then make corrections. They typically make corrections that are too small. If you really sit back and do the math, if you missed, you had to have missed by a certain amount."

Another category of shooting drill is called "snaps and movers." Set at a known distance range, targets ranging from the size of a human head to a full E-size target snap into place or move from one side of the range to the other.

"We go out to eight hundred yards in that and they're hitting moving, man-sized targets," Davis said. "Again, they calculate the math based on the speed they're moving and the distance and then they have to pull the shot off at the right moment so that the bullet meets up with a moving target."

◈

Upon graduation, Kyle was among the very first SEAL snipers sent to combat where this modernized training course and its products would be field-tested. The results would be convincing.

He was a natural in the role and the course provided him with the tools to provide a devastating protection presence for his countrymen downrange.

Kyle jokingly referred to himself as an "L" rather than a SEAL. He wasn't particularly fond of time spent underwater or parachuting. Soon that "L" would be just as applicable in reference to his lethality, and eventually, in reference to his forthcoming status as a legend.

Interestingly, in the same way that Chris Kyle developed into a standout SEAL despite his aversion to diving and jumping, both Brandon Webb and Eric Davis admitted that they became SEAL snipers and, later, chief architects of the redevelopment of the SEAL sniper program despite being somewhat less than hard-core shooting enthusiasts.

Davis said, "Chris was from Texas. He hunted and did rodeo. He lived his life the way a lot of people believe you should. He was able to self-sustain, care for himself, change a tire, skin a deer . . . stuff like that. That's a really good attribute for a sniper—that's really their element—the gun range, the dirt, the dust. Where I was like, I don't really like shooting. I mean, I enjoy shooting a little bit, but the other sniper instructors, they would hunt. I was clearly different than them."

However, Kyle's preference would prove perfectly matched to the war at hand in Iraq just as SEAL leadership was allowing its men to contribute at the level they themselves knew they could.

"It was a perfect time for him to be a SEAL and the perfect place for him to operate," Davis said. "I'd rather be growing my hair out long, wearing civilian clothes, and using surveillance equipment or diving with rebreathers and stuff like that. But Chris was like, 'No, no, put me on the ground and let me shoot some folks here.'"

Both would happen soon enough.

7

Kingpin

With Hussein's forces soundly routed, the remnants of his Ba'athist regime were rooted out from their holes just as Saddam himself had been, and, with the deposed dictator's cronies largely rounded up, the Iraq War was effectively nearing its conclusion.

Unfortunately, a different, far uglier Iraq War was restocking the battlefield even faster than the old pieces could be removed.

The coalition was initially in denial over what was transpiring as it focused its sights on the Fedayeen paramilitary force and other FREs (Former Regime Elements). But while few Iraqis shed tears over the end of Hussein's oppressive reign, his removal did create a void that wasn't completely sealed by the occupying forces.

As hoped, the swift and decisive victory set the conditions to create a new land of freedom and opportunity. However, that new freedom provided a multitude of diverse groups the opportunity to reshape Iraq to suit their desires, and many of them proved willing to do so by the most depraved and macabre means imaginable.

Following a near-instantaneous victory over the Iraqi Army, the coalition attempted to impose order while harried by small but persistent pockets of resistance. Initially thought to be largely composed of guerrilla fighters who either remained loyal to the nation's former ruler or were disenchanted nationalists struggling to scratch out an existence as the country was re-shaped, the makeup of the insurgency shifted to something darker, hidden beneath a veneer of overly optimistic situational reports.

New players emerged. Power in country was no longer exclusive to the likes of CENTCOM Commander General John P. Abizad, Ambassador Paul Bremer, or JSOC Commander Stanley McChrystal. Its splintered shards were also being wielded by the likes of radical cleric Muqtada al-Sadr, who sensed opportunity as he had a ready audience composed of the nation's Shia majority. They had long suffered under Hussein's former regime, and now he saw a new enemy in the occupying force to galvanize his forces against.

Another name was increasingly whispered among the militant Sunni opposition—Abu Musab al-Zarqawi—a Jordanian terrorist thug whose shockingly brutal methods saw him rapidly increase his profile while transforming this new Iraq War into the centralized battleground of a truly global conflict.

The nation slowly devolved into a confusing and chaotic mire of unrelenting violence, as each successive vicious strike begat its response, escalating an array of intersecting wars. The nation was spiraling into a near-unstoppable feedback loop of carnage.

In early 2004, the coalition struggled to get a handle on exactly what was occurring. A mass of motivated, militant actors were operating, but they had not yet merged into more identifiable, organized groups. Many had shared motivations but differed in terms of tactics. Others were in direct ideological conflict but willing to stoop to the same inhuman practices as they traded blows. Still others existed only to pull the strings of one side or the other in order to enflame the hell that was formulating.

However, to the American-led coalition, this vast collection of disparate combatants looked practically identical to one another (and even more problematically, identical to the larger, benign populace they were attempting to secure and protect). Whatever their separations, they all posed a lethal threat to Westerners in country, whether they were military, contractors, journalists, or aid workers.

This new, disturbing reality was brought into sharp focus in the spring of 2004.

◈

Tensions between the coalition and Muqtada al-Sadr's Shia Mahdi Army erupted in late March, setting off a series of battles between the two forces in Baghdad and southern Iraq.

At the same time, a diverse and nebulous collection of fighters, ranging from emboldened nationalist groups, Sunni insurgents, and a flood of foreign Salafi jihadists headlined by the aforementioned Zarqawi, bunkered down in Fallujah, a city of some 320,000 in Anbar Province, forty-five miles west of Baghdad.

Initially viewed as a relatively minor concern, the city grew increasingly unwelcoming throughout 2003 and into 2004. Protests turned into sporadic hit-and-run attacks, which in turn matured into coordinated assaults.

These guerrilla strikes intensified alongside the city's widespread anti-American sentiments. This ultimately took the form of a horrific display of protest and violence that changed the face of the war.

◈

On March 31, four Blackwater USA contractors—Jerry Zovko, Wesley Batalona, Michael Teague, and Scott Helvenston—were ambushed as they attempted a shortcut through the volatile city. They were stopped on Highway 10 and murdered in the streets of Fallujah. Their bodies were desecrated and dismembered. A pair of burnt corpses hung from a bridge that straddled the Euphrates River while the other two remained in the streets, put on display as a gleeful mob mugged for the cameras.

The 1st Marine Expeditionary Force (I MEF) had only recently taken ownership of Anbar Province from the Army's 82nd Airborne Division. Prior to the attack on the contractors, they merely contained Fallujah rather than engaged it.

Bremer—the man who effectively ran Iraq at the time—promised an unequivocal response, announcing in threatening terms that the deaths "will not go unpunished."

I MEF was given its orders to conduct an overwhelming offensive on the city dubbed Operation Vigilant Resolve. Fallujah's inhabitants were given advance warning, as leaflets were dispersed that instructed them to leave, stay inside, or prepare to meet their end.

The city was encircled by a force of more than two thousand Marines and masses of concertina wire. Meanwhile, the insurgents actively prepared their defenses, making an already determined enemy that much more difficult to root out.

It's estimated that a flock of residents totaling more than 100,000 fled the city as a bloody showdown loomed. A series of air strikes and devastatingly precise fire from Scout Snipers allowed the Marines to tighten their grip during the battle's opening week in early April.

Following concerns of mass civilian casualties, a tenuous (and largely one-sided) cease-fire was called on April 9, which only allowed both sides to further entrench their positions in anticipation of an inevitable resumption.

The northern half of the city had been assigned to 2nd Battalion, 1st Marines. During its short time in the province, one of its subcomponents—Echo Company—earned itself an enviable reputation as an unusually fierce fighting force—even among Marine infantrymen. It was also one seemingly destined for what laid ahead, its men having crossed paths with the four Blackwater contractors while out on patrol only days prior to their grisly slaughter.

Echo 2/1 was an extension of its charismatic yet uncompromising leader, Captain Douglass Zembiec. Zembiec's skills were unquestioned—he had been a two-time New Mexico state champion wrestler and then a two-time All-American at the Naval Academy. And he was among the first into Kosovo in the late '90s during Operation Joint Guardian while serving as an officer with the fabled 2nd Force Reconnaissance Company.

His bravery seemingly knew no bounds; Zembiec was never so comfortable or in his element as when he was leading his men into battle under withering gunfire. He enthusiastically executed his duties when tasked with killing the enemy. And when the enemy killed his Marines—as they inevitably would during the campaign—he wouldn't allow their brethren to wallow in sorrow. And ultimately, more than fifty of the Marines from Echo 2/1 were wounded during Operation Vigilant Resolve.

His fiery motivational speeches came directly from his soul as evidenced by his actions—words that may have seemed rehearsed or artificial coming from a lesser warrior. Under Zembiec's watch, Echo Company took to battle—to use his preferred terminology—like a pride of lions.

This became evident even prior to the wider offensive. One of Captain Zembiec's Scout Sniper team leaders with 2/1's H&S Company, Corporal Ethan Place, demonstrated his measured skill on multiple occasions. In two separate incidents in late March, Place stitched a pair of insurgents with effective fire, the first action neutralizing an attempted ambush of a convoy and the second while out on patrol.

As the battle set into motion, Place again cut down the enemy, delivering lethally accurate rounds downrange during a pitched April 7 firefight that involved two Marine companies and hundreds of insurgents, just two days ahead of the cease-fire.

◈

Of course, the Marines weren't in this fight alone and neither was Echo Company. While I MEF spearheaded the assault and gave it a face, it was supported by a variety of close air support platforms (including an Air Force AC-130 Spectre Gunship, call sign "Slayer," F-15Es, F-16s, and Navy F/A-18s).

Additionally, it was backed by some of the more shrouded concerns of America's presence in Iraq—including the CIA, NSA, 5th Special Forces Group, and SOCOM's Psychological Operations Group.

Most valuable of these as far as E/2/1 was concerned was the inclusion of a small Task Force 6-26 sniper element from a Delta Force Sabre Squadron's recce troop. The team that arrived was just seven men deep, but collectively they brought around a century of tactical experience to go with their exceptionally rare capabilities.

The recce operators had already shown their ability to penetrate Fallujah. In the weeks prior, they had operated deep inside the city limits to conduct extreme-risk clandestine vehicle recons.

However, rather than turn up in the modest Iraqi sedans that served as their cover on those ops, they now arrived with the newest and shiniest toys in the arsenal. The Delta snipers came bearing a most precious gift—thermobaric munitions—ranging from SMAW-NEs to modified AT4s and grenades. These are weapons that ignite the air's oxygen, creating intensely high-temperature explosions marked by an immense blast overpressure. Utilized in confined spaces, such as building interiors, the effects are magnified and can result in the incineration of any occupants—if not the outright destruction of the targeted structure.

Insurgent marksmen had perched on the roofs and in the minarets that dotted the angular pale brown and gray cityscape leading into the heart of the contested city. It was hoped these munitions would provide a novel solution for countering the demoralizing fire of these enemy snipers.

Every last particle of that extraordinary talent, savvy, and firepower would prove critical on April 26, 2004.

It was actually a little more than a week earlier that the Unit team had first delivered the weapons and brought the Echo Company up to speed in their application. Satisfied that the infantrymen now had the means to "eliminate the [enemy] snipers, or at least let them know that, 'Wow, you are going to get thumped if you shoot,'" the Delta team disappeared, off to execute whatever high-speed, high-risk mission required their attention next.

However, the Marines requested a follow-up round of assistance as they struggled to get a handle on the new weapons. The call was answered and the experienced soldiers returned to establish positions alongside the men of Echo 2/1 at the FLOT—the forward line of troops—directed toward Fallujah from its northwest corner.

The Delta snipers immediately went to work, rotating in and out of guns to capitalize on the insurgent activity in the area, which presented the proficient marksmen with an abundance of "targets of opportunity" down several lanes.

However, over time the enemy fighters learned from the deadly mistakes of their comrades and figured out where they could and could not maneuver. All the while, they continued to harry the front line with sporadic small arms, RPG, and mortar attacks.

Hoping to catch their quarry by surprise in the dead of night and claim new sniper lanes, a combined ground element consisting of thirty-nine Marines (Echo 2/1's 2nd Platoon and a Fire Support Team) commanded by Captain Zembiec, and augmented by seven masterfully skilled SOF soldiers, went on the hunt in the early hours.

The makeshift strike force, which was later described as "an unusual arrangement for sure," paired up the company's infantrymen with some of the nation's most experienced warfighters. The Delta men were not only twice as old as a number of the younger Marines, but had actually served in the military longer than some of their impressionable compatriots had existed on this Earth.

Despite the stark disparity of time and training, respect freely flowed both ways as the special mission unit soldiers appreciated the eager nature of the young Marines and took them under their wing.

The force streamed out into the blackness of 3:30 a.m. and proceeded down through a cemetery, heading southeast into Fallujah. The details of their surroundings were still masked in utter darkness; however, the first hints of the arriving daylight could just be perceived above. Heavily armed shadows of friendly forces were visible in all directions in silhouette against the night sky.

During the movement, the early-hour silence was pierced by the prayers of a nearby mosque.

One of the Delta snipers, Master Sergeant Don Hollenbaugh, turned to Staff Sergeant Dan Briggs—a highly trained Special Forces medic—and spoke in a hushed voice.

"That is eerie. It's not going to be a good day."
"Yeah, I'm afraid you might be right."

◈

The E/2/1 Marines and Delta recce team emerged from the cemetery. They then cleared and seized a pair of buildings in a tightly packed neighborhood in the Jolan District—the alleged Iraqi headquarters of al-Zarqawi. The two structures faced one another on opposite sides of the street—one to the north and the other to the south of an east-west road that led directly into the center of Fallujah.

The buildings were large homes of similar design and layout. Surrounded by six-foot-high walls ringing their courtyards, both pale houses had two interior floors with an accessible, flat roof surrounded by three-foot-high walls, effectively rendering them three-story fighting positions.

The stairs that led to the roof were exposed to the elements, leading up from a walled outdoor terrace on the second floor to the middle of the roof, where it was lined on three sides by another three-foot-high wall to prevent clumsy guests from toppling down by accident.

The Marines split up and filtered into both buildings. The north house was under the watch of Lieutenant Dan Wagner while Zembiec held down a position in the south house. The Unit element joined the captain in the southern structure, assembling on the roof to secure sniper lanes.

Back at the FLOT, observers noticed that armed fighters were egressing the same mosque from which the earlier prayers had resonated. Captain Zembiec led a small team to investigate but found nothing other than a handful of shell casings in the minaret's windowsill.

Meanwhile, back at the houses, the contrasting levels of training and divergent tactics of the Marines and the Unit snipers became evident. The grunts improvised to create covered firing positions but also loudly signaled their location to any nearby insurgents.

Hollenbaugh explained, "When we got up on the roof . . . I had never seen this technique before (well, yeah I have), but the Marines started to . . . it was unnerving. The Marines were basically knocking holes in walls, so there was no more quiet anymore. We took sledgehammers and beat holes into the walls. Well, that woke everybody up."

Near first light a handful of shots rang out, along with a couple of RPGs. While less than a full-blown assault, the probing attacks indicated a waking city—one now home to thousands of bloodthirsty adversaries . . . and not much else. And it was well aware of the Americans' presence beyond the front line.

Hollenbaugh and Sergeant Major Larry Boivin—a Delta Force Master Breacher—were on the glass, aiming down the sights of their weapons and covering the south sections of the position.

Another RPG streaked in, this time impacting the south side of the southern house, directly beneath Hollenbaugh. The heat of the blast radiated all around as his face was speckled with dust and debris left from the crude construction that provided his "hole in the wall" sniper position.

The Unit sniper immediately sprinted down through the building and climbed the courtyard wall. The idea was to not merely assess the damage, but also study the blast pattern and resultant shrapnel splash in order to approximate the most likely hiding spot of the insurgent who had fired the rocket-propelled grenade.

Hollenbaugh instinctively calculated the direction and maximum effective range of the weapon and scanned for any likely positions hidden in the distance. He hustled back upstairs, informed the Forward Observer of the attached Marine Fire Support Team where to place a TRP (target reference point), and hit it hard with indirect fire—the 81mm mortars that were covering the team's movement—should the enemy activity pick up.

In addition to the mortars, Captain Zembiec's plan called for a pair of M1A1 Abrams Main Battle Tanks from the 1st Tank Division to await further orders back at the FLOT, enabling the combined force to dole out a substantial amount of hurt should things get desperate.

Hollenbaugh retook his position to the south and dumped a few 5.56mm rounds from his tricked-out M4 into the dark area he had just located and reported. "It was just my way of telling 'em, 'Hey, I know where you are.'"

At that point, it went quiet again. The earlier attack wasn't overly concerning—this was par for the course back at the FLOT, where the occasional, marginally aimed round or two would harass American troops with regularity but never amount to much more than that.

The Delta operators used the break to reconsider their disposition. Around ten a.m., "JN," the recce team leader, broke things down:

"Hey, the snipers have gotten off a couple shots, but not many. The lanes are choked down too tight here to use our long guns properly. Realistically, we can accomplish the exact same thing with assault rifles. . . . The snipers aren't being utilized to the best of our capability. I want to grab a few guys and go back to the FLOT where we can cover you from the rear."

JN gathered up the element's sniper pairs and left. As they melded back into the cemetery and traveled a few hundred meters to the northwest to reclaim their old perches, the Marine platoon now only counted three of the original Delta element among their ranks—Hollenbaugh, Boivin, and Briggs.

And technically, the exit of the two sniper teams left Hollenbaugh the sole remaining Delta Force operator (a term reserved exclusively for the Unit's assaulters and snipers) and in charge of the team on the roof. Although a Unit sniper himself, he was also trained as a breacher, and for this operation he had been paired with Boivin.

Boivin's presence was critical for the larger mission: he was a specialty breacher with advanced knowledge of thermobarics and shoulder-fired weapons. And Briggs's exhaustive medical training was of immense value as well, as would become all too evident in the hours ahead.

At forty years of age and with two decades of Army experience under his belt, Hollenbaugh lent a measured, calming presence to the mixed crew and aptly filled whatever leadership vacuum was created by the other snipers' hasty departure.

Known as "Kingpin" to his teammates, Hollenbaugh hails from small-town Prescott, Washington, where he graduated with just seventeen other kids in his class.

Humble and downright folksy, people might never know they were dealing with one of the planet's foremost warriors if they were to randomly happen across Donald Hollenbaugh on the streets of Boise, Idaho. However, to encounter him in the streets of al-Fallujah would have been a different matter entirely, where his poise, skill, and confidence were most befitting of his Unit code name.

Hollenbaugh drafted two Marines up to the roof to assume the vacated sniper positions. He pointed them in the right direction, assuring all sectors remained covered as the tension continued to ratchet up in lieu of actual enemy engagement.

The lull, it turns out, was not indicative of a disorganized or unmotivated adversary. Quite the opposite.

The first sign they were facing something greater came in the form of a small pack of maneuvering insurgents who were spied advancing toward the north house only minutes after JN and three other Delta snipers had left the immediate vicinity.

In response, Captain Zembiec took up station across the street, joining Lt. Wagner and his larger contingent of Marines in the north house. He hoped to improve his situational awareness and gain command and control as the shifting scene picked up its pace.

◈

Less than five minutes later, "the whole world opened up," Hollenbaugh recalled. "It got so loud, so fast. Mortors, RPGs, gunfire, and grenades. Everything was coming."

The American troops were suddenly hit with a complex assault. An overwhelming enemy force that had silently occupied a host of adjacent buildings was hitting them from multiple directions. A mass of insurgents—estimated to be 150 to 300 strong—flooded the vicinity, hauled to the fight from throughout the interior of Fallujah by bus, taxi, and pickup.

The initial assault was devastating. Dozens of RPGs cascaded on the American positions, fifty or sixty impacting the buildings during the first fifteen minutes. Sniper fire pinned them down and grenades were lobbed from adjacent roofs with a concentrated effort to decisively finish the job.

The open cemetery to the west, along with the repositioned Delta snipers who were now in overwatch behind it, prevented the marauders from closing the loop completely on the two houses. However, the assailants did successfully obtain a three-quarter pinch of the area. They also managed to suppress the FLOT, preventing reinforcements from storming to the Americans' aid.

Hollenbaugh gave those devils their due. "When they opened it up on us, it was coordinated. You could tell it was because they just turned it on full blast like a faucet, which is the way you're supposed to do it.

"Between the first rounds in the morning that came in, to two and a half or three hours later with the whole world blowing up . . . If you know where guys are, that's a lot of time to plan. Plus, they had been waiting for the invasion. Fallujah had been cordoned off and leaflets had been dropped in saying if you are not a fighter, you have this amount of time to leave. So everybody in that place was a fighter. Period. There was no ifs, ands, or buts about it."

Almost immediately, a four-man Marines element on the north roof was hit by a grenade. All were wounded and pulled down from the roof to the relative safety of the second-floor interior. The screams could be heard from across the street in the south building.

Five more Marines would quickly be added to the casualty list in the north house. Delta medic Dan Briggs didn't hesitate.

"Don, I'm going over."

"Roger that. Go execute."

Hollenbaugh described Briggs's subsequent heroism with no shortage of awe in his voice: "Dan grabbed his medical bag and ran down the stairs, which was exposed to the enemy. Very well exposed. Several Marines found that out quickly, as did I. Well, we already know—they just showed us that they knew as well.

"Dan continued down the rest of the house and ran across the open street, which was being riddled with bullets. Rounds were skipping around him."

While Briggs's audacious charge across the street in the face of a literal hail of bullets ended with him unscathed, his predicament was only to become more problematic. Twenty-eight years old and youngest among the

Unit element augmenting the Marines, Briggs would demonstrate his mettle yet again: the casualty collection point was actually located back across the street in the south house.

That location had the advantage of a covered and concealed route through which the wounded could be evacuated back to the FLOT. Of course, Murphy's Law demanded that the north house be hit first and be hit hardest, forcing Briggs to transport injured Marines back across an invisible wall of supersonic lead.

"In my count, Dan exposed himself to enemy fire no less than six times to do his job," Hollenbaugh recounted. "And he did a great job."

◈

The north house's situation soon became even direr. The "40 mike-mike" vest of a wounded grenadier was left on the roof after he was evacuated, there to be used by the next man up. However, an explosion detonated one of the 40mm grenades and set the vest on fire, causing the remainder of the munitions to sympathetically detonate.

Seven more Marines were hit in the following minutes. Nearly half of the infantrymen had been incapacitated in the battle's chaotic opening minutes.

Captain Zembiec joined Briggs in making the impossible dash across the contested street—multiple times. He frantically attempted to call for indirect fire but that request was denied for fear of civilian casualties. He also sought the advance of the M1A1 tanks, along with any way possible of evacuating the wounded—a group that was rapidly multiplying.

With helo extraction out of the question, First Sergeant William Skiles came to the rescue, racing into position in an unarmored Humvee to remove the most serious casualties. He made the three trips under intense fire, his entrances and exits made possible by the relentless suppressive fire provided by Lance Corporal John Flores.

After helping with their downed brothers, Lance Corporals Aaron Austin and Carlos Gomez-Perez reinforced the north roof, which simultaneously existed as a strategic strongpoint and an all-too-easy target.

Both men attempted to lob grenades at the hordes of amassing fighters. Austin was hit multiple times in the chest in the act but still managed to release his grenade as he spun to the ground and slumped down the open staircase.

A onetime illegal immigrant who moved to the States from Mexico City at the age of nine, Gomez-Perez pulled his fellow American behind cover but was struck while in the act. Despite being hit in the cheek and having his right shoulder torn open by heavy machine-gun fire as he pulled Austin to the relative safety of the roof's surrounding wall, he managed to stay in the fight, throwing grenades and firing his weapon with his off hand.

Gomez-Perez attempted to perform CPR on Austin before the twenty-one-year-old Texan was attended to by Briggs and a Navy corpsman. The two dragged the critically wounded Marine down the exposed staircase and into the interior of the second floor of the north building, where they performed a tracheotomy in a desperate attempt to save the young Marine's life.

Lance Corporal Craig Bell chose to fight fire with fire. After being injured by an incoming grenade himself, he launched an estimated one hundred grenades over the next hour from his M203, placing several into windows of enemy-held buildings.

◈

With Briggs, Zembiec, and the Captain's RTO (Radio Telephone Operator) on the move, the south roof was now manned by just Hollenbaugh, Boivin, and the two Marines pulled up to replace the Delta snipers who had returned to the FLOT.

Bear-sized Boivin held down a critical lane while Hollenbaugh bounced back and forth to cover his position as well as that of Briggs and JN. While ducking from spot to spot, Hollenbaugh noticed some insurgents moving in on the north house.

"I threw a grenade, engaged them, but didn't quite know what the results were—they take cover like anybody else," he said. "Another guy rounded the corner with an RPG. By the time I got up to shoot, he had launched it. I still shot even though by then he was already gone. I just shot to say, 'I know you're there—don't do that again.'"

While Hollenbaugh was keeping the swarm off the other house—which was increasingly undefended due to the rapid attrition—his roof was in turn hit with a grenade. Both Marines suffered serious injuries in the blast. One stood up in a daze, holding his hand over his face, covered in gore.

The Delta sniper yanked the staggering Marine down to cover. ("In a fight you don't stand up—you stay down. There are rounds going everywhere. The enemy is on roofs also, so if you stand up, you just expose yourself.")

Hollenbaugh then forced the young Marine down the stairs and directed him into the building, at which point he returned to aid the other wounded infantryman.

The Marine was moving backward in a low crawl, leaving a streak of blood. Hollenbaugh grabbed his belt to help move him to safety.

"Let's go!"

"No, no . . . Take him first! Take him first!"

"I already got him!"

Hollenbaugh yanked the Marine up by his belt and muscled him over to the stairwell.

"I'll always give that guy credit," Hollenbaugh said. "You could tell he was in pain—just hurtin'. But he shook his head and pointed his finger at where he thought the other guy still was.

"I would have rendered aid to them but I knew they were hurt really bad and they needed to get out of there; we had too much work to do. It was not a time to treat casualties, it was a time to work."

Now Hollenbaugh's frantic life-and-death game of rooftop Whac-a-Mole had been expanded from three positions to five, plus the exposed area to the north he recently discovered. "I looked over at Larry and I rolled my eyes and just started covering the other avenues. Once again, all I was doing was going from hole to hole to hole, just kind of covering where we're at.

"Larry had the south flank, so we couldn't take him out of his position.

He couldn't be bouncing around. These other positions had help from other positions. But that south flank, there was a tall wall downstairs, so nobody else could cover it. Even guys on the second story couldn't cover into that south flank."

As Hollenbaugh was covering the north house, yet another explosion rocked the south roof just behind the sniper's back. He heard Boivin call out.

"Don, I'm hit!"

Hollenbaugh continued to cover multiple positions as the situation rapidly plummeted downward.

"Can you make it over here?"

"Yeah . . ."

"All right—get over here."

Boivin had been struck by shrapnel behind his left ear and arm, and his head was bleeding heavily. As Hollenbaugh was gauging the big soldier's wounds, another grenade landed nearby, rolling across some blankets the wounded Marines had been using to provide shade as the penetrating midday sun began to deliver punishment from yet another direction.

The two men looked at the grenade ("It looked like a mouse running under the blanket"), looked at one another, and then both shouted, *"Grenade!"*

Boivin dove into the stairwell, while Hollenbaugh took cover behind the stairwell's wall. After the grenade went off, Hollenbaugh grabbed a grenade of his own and walked over to the wall near where the offending explosive had just appeared. He cooked it off.

"One . . . two . . . three . . . I better get rid of this."

"Tit for tat."

The Master Sergeant then raked his gun alongside the wall, pushing it out to guide his rounds to the bordering home that sheltered aggressors less than twenty meters away.

With no one else available to man the roof of the south house—or the north house's roof for that matter—Hollenbaugh went back to work, covering each position by himself. Ducking in and out of position, firing a round here and a round there, the Delta operator made himself appear to be several defenders at once in the opposition's eyes. By doing so, he hoped to mask the effectiveness of the insurgent assault and deter a mad rush that could have easily finished off the reeling Americans.

Hollenbaugh explained, "At that point, I was covering all the holes. It was no longer a matter of really sitting there and effectively keeping each position at bay and properly covered. It had become going to each position, identifying likely spots where the enemy might be, putting a couple of rounds in each one of those.

"I just kept things busy and alive from our point, so they don't feel they are attriting us. That was the whole point. Our positions were not unoccupied. I did not want them to think that because if they did, they could have established maneuver and executed on it. Pretty straightforward."

After a couple more rounds of "work," Hollenbaugh noticed that Boivin was still sitting in the stairwell, now in a ghostly pale white daze.

"Larry, you okay?"

He wasn't. A New Hampshire native born four decades earlier to two Canadian immigrants, Boivin also brought a wealth of military and special operations experience to the fight.

However, now he appeared to be on the verge of passing out from blood loss, and his large, muscular frame would not have made for an easy carry down the fatal funnel the second-floor stairway had become. He was transitioning from force multiplier to force divider before his team leader's eyes.

"Oh, great."

"There was nobody in the stairwell and nobody on that deck," Hollenbaugh reflected. "Larry was just sitting there and I couldn't have him as a casualty. I couldn't take him out of there. If he passed out, he might have passed out half-sprawled on that stairwell, which means I would have had to go down the stairwell, drag him down, pick him up, and get him inside the house. And that also would have meant that all the positions went unoccupied."

Hollenbaugh decided to take a timeout. He sat down on the staircase with Boivin sitting a step lower. The sniper grabbed the go-bag and pulled out some medical supplies. The gauze fell off his leg and picked up some sand—a tiny moment in an overwhelming day that still sticks in Hollenbaugh's head.

"I don't know why that sticks in my memory, but I've talked to a lot of guys and they were like, 'Yeah, there's some dumb stuff that just sticks in your memory.' "

He immediately composed himself after fighting with the gauze ("It was probably two seconds, but it felt like an eternity"), prepared a new bandage, and put a drive-on rag over Boivin's head to hold it in place. He then cranked it on tight with the knot tails hanging down low.

Boivin put his helmet back on and turned around to face Hollenbaugh. The side of the breacher's face was caked in blood, which had also gushed down over his uniform. The bloody helmet and drive-on rag combo lent him a truly menacing appearance. Hollenbaugh couldn't help but admire the visage.

"Man . . . you look really cool."

That fleeting moment of levity breathed new life into Boivin, the color rushing back to his face almost instantly. Satisfied, Hollenbaugh didn't have time to witness the miraculous comeback any longer.

"You should be good. . . . I've got to go back to work."

Hollenbaugh resumed his series of rapid transitions and engagements, putting rounds, grenades, or rockets into any suspected position—anywhere he saw a muzzle flash or gases escaping a window.

Lacking angles of fire or any means of calling in artillery or close air support, he intentionally ricocheted rounds off walls, banking shots to reach otherwise inaccessible enemy positions.

"There was a narrow, long horizontal window and I could see where the gases from that gun were coming out of that building," he explained. "I couldn't directly engage him and I couldn't put anything through his window, but through this little narrow window, I could. I skipped a few rounds off of the sill up into his area.

"You learn over time that rounds keep moving after they hit something.

It was improvising . . . 'I can't get to you, but just maybe' . . . kind of like playing pool.

"And then I launched an AT4 over there. And his fire stopped."

Eventually, he noticed that Boivin was gone from the roof as well, along with several magazines of ammo from his opened go-bag. Encouraged that the veteran Unit breacher was back in the fight, Hollenbaugh just went back to plugging holes in the dam, successfully keeping the flood of insurgents at bay.

Boivin, it turns out, had moved down to the second-floor landing area, which had also gone unoccupied by that point. His courageous stand could only last so long, as the wall behind him was getting peppered by RPGs and he was eventually forced to abandon the position and head down through the house.

That constant barrage of rocket-propelled grenades shook the entire building nonstop, creating conditions so deafening it was impossible to communicate verbally even across the road to the other house.

"I remember seeing two enemy maneuvering on their building," Hollenbaugh said. "And out of the corner of my eye, I caught a Marine running up that stairwell exposed to them. I was going to try to yell and I couldn't. I just stood up and started putting down fire and they scurried.

"That's just how it was."

◉

Hollenbaugh faced an impossible task. There was only so long he could fend off an entire army before he ran out of ammunition or the other side finally realized they were battling a solitary warrior.

"I was alone on the roof, but I just knew I could not leave. We were getting attrited, I knew we were getting attrited. I had three casualties just on my roof and I knew there was a bunch more across the street because I had heard the yelling and screaming."

He continued bouncing from hole to hole, throwing grenades and launching AT4s. After a few more rounds, a critical enemy gun position that had been suppressing the FLOT screamed into action again. Making matters worse, it wasn't only preventing the arrival of reinforcements; it was also in a prime location to cut down any attempted retreat back to the FLOT.

Hollenbaugh grabbed a thermobaric AT4 and lined up his shot.

Just then Captain Zembiec reemerged on the south house roof.

"Don, it's time to go!"

"All right . . . just let me shoot this thing first."

Despite having been engaged in hours of frenzied gun-battling, Hollenbaugh placed the rocket with pinpoint accuracy. "The gun shut up and we left."

The Delta recce operator followed the USMC officer as they ran down the stairs. As they arrived on the second-floor deck, Hollenbaugh looked around for the Marine pulling security for them so that he could yell, "Last man!"

While "peeling"—a simple but effective technique utilized to systematically move troops to the flank or to the rear—an individual on the move will inform the man covering the maneuver that he's become the last man. The new last man will then be the next to move and he'll in turn inform his awaiting security that they have become the last man as he moves past.

When Hollenbaugh hit the second-floor terrace, that last man was nowhere to be found. When he and the Captain darted into the building on its second floor, again, there was no last man.

The same was true of the interior stairway, the first-floor hallway, and the main-floor living quarters.

As they exited the house and ran into the courtyard, there was still no last man in sight. Nor was there one guarding the hole that had been knocked through the courtyard wall in the middle of the night to hasten an escape.

Only then did it dawn on Delta Force Master Sergeant Don Hollenbaugh how genuinely he earned the title of "last man" on that day.

◈

Hollenbaugh had shown himself to be the ultimate expression of the advanced assaulter—yet another JSOC sniper who turned the tide of battle without a sniper weapon in hand. He fended off a determined and coordinated enemy force armed with his assault rifle, a borrowed M203 grenade launcher, multiple AT4s, numerous grenades of various types (fragmentation, smoke, and thermobaric), exceptional proficiency, and immeasurable valor.

His actions directly enabled an escape that saved the lives of dozens of U.S. heroes.

Although he and Zembiec had cleared the courtyard, they weren't home free just yet. They still had several hundred meters on foot to cover to get back to the relative safety of the FLOT.

As Hollenbaugh came through the hole, he was struck by the image of Lance Corporal Thomas Adametz, who was armed with a light machine gun he had retrieved from one of the many wounded E/2/1 Marines.

"When we finally get through the hole, there was Larry Boivin and a Marine," Hollenbaugh said. "It's another Marine I'll always give credit to. He was shooting at a gun position that I couldn't get to. He had that M249 SAW and he was just waylaying in there.

"He had himself exposed, standing up on a mound of bricks. I just remember standing there for a moment, just taking in some pride—'Now that's a Marine.' I was watching the brass coming out of his gun. For a moment I was thinking, 'That's pretty cool,' but then I kind of snapped out of it."

"Dude, you're exposed, get down! Oh, and good work. . . . That was awesome."

With Boivin accounted for and Briggs helping to evacuate the wounded, Hollenbaugh and Zembiec bought up the rear as the crippled force made its way back to the front line as quickly as it could under those conditions.

"We went running down the street and I was literally the last guy. I let everybody go, and I pulled cover for everyone, and as we got out of that little area where that Marine was shooting on top of those bricks, I turned around and started shooting back up at that machine-gun station.

"Everybody went and I just kept shooting. I remember off to my right-hand side, I saw one of the Marine tanks had actually made it down into the area. And then I noticed there were some helos above—strafing the streets. It was a significant fight."

One of the M1A1s destroyed the minaret that had been scouted before the attack and had served as a sniper hide for the insurgents. Meanwhile, a pair of USMC AH-1W Cobra attack helicopters pounded the enemy combatants. E/2/1's 3rd Platoon advanced with the tanks to provide additional support.

Included among the reinforcements was Place, the Scout Sniper who had proven so effective during Echo Company's opening days in Fallujah. Following the three actions mentioned earlier, Place continued to excel, racking up thirty-two confirmed sniper kills during a two-week period in the middle of April. On the twenty-sixth, he again performed with skill and heroism, as he "disregarded his own safety and left the cover of his defensive position to close with and destroy the enemy." The Corporal was awarded a Silver Star for his combined action during the months of March and April.

◈

More than half of the forty-odd men who went out in the dead of night to advance beyond the front lines were wounded. A third of them were evacuated on stretchers.

Austin, too, earned a Silver Star, albeit posthumously. He ultimately succumbed to his injuries, the only American to die in the frenetic battle that nearly claimed dozens more.

Marines Perez-Gomez and Adametz also were awarded the Silver Star while numerous others earned Bronze Stars for their actions that day.

For his selfless actions, disregarding his own safety in order to save others, Briggs was awarded the Distinguished Service Cross. The DSC is the second highest military award available to a member of the Army, and one reserved for acts of extreme gallantry.

In later reflection, Hollenbaugh feels it should have been even higher.

"Dan was well deserving of the DSC. And knowing what I know now, I probably should have put him in for the Medal of Honor, quite honestly."

Hollenbaugh, too, was awarded the Distinguished Service Cross. He said, "Everybody always asks me, 'Were you scared? Did you feel anything?' No, I was just working. It's training. I was forty years old, I had been in the Army for almost twenty years, and was a senior NCO. Not my first gunfight sort of thing . . . although definitely the largest.

"If you only knew the events of all the Marines and everyone else. A few people's stories tend to stand out because of who knows what. Those are the guys who get much of the credit for doing what they did, but I always see the awards as representing all those who were in that fight."

He continued with a small sampling of the heroism he observed that day, stating, "It was Larry continuing to fight once we got him bandaged properly. It was Dan who went across and exposed himself to fire I don't know how many times. It was the selflessness of the Marine who was shaking his hand saying, 'Take him first,' and then the other Marine up on the bricks, exposing himself to suppress the enemy.

"It was Captain Zembiec and his poor RTO who had to go everywhere with him. He came into an empty building and exposed himself up that stairwell under heavy fire after everybody else was already off the objective. There was no one providing suppressive fire. He ran up that stairwell to come back and get me and drag me back down.

"It was pretty selfless. It was a lot of guys doing a lot of hard work."

There was one final act of courage from that day that sticks in Hollenbaugh's mind. As the platoon was heading back to the FLOT a Marine was shot as he negotiated the chokepoint. The shot knocked him off course and he fell into the concertina wire that lined a hole separating inner and outer Fallujah. Another Marine and an embedded reporter ran to his aid and pulled him to safety.

Amazed at what he had witnessed, Hollenbaugh later wrote the reporter's editor, stating that he was deserving of an award in his own right.

While Austin was the only American to die in that battle, he was not the last of the day's heroes to sacrifice their lives for those of others.

Douglass Zembiec later referred to April 26, 2004, as "the greatest day of [his] life." His legend quickly spread, earning him the apt moniker, "the Lion of Fallujah." He was promoted to Major but had no desire to continue his meteoric rise up the officer ranks with the Marine Corps.

Rather than be promoted off the battlefield, he sought an elusive slot at Ground Branch, a key element of the CIA's enigmatic Special Activities Division/Special Operations Group.

Ground Branch is the Agency's premier black ops unit, capable of tackling unconventional warfare and counterterror operations of the greatest sensitivity. Typically, experienced Delta Force operators and their ilk are their prime targets for recruitment as Ground Branch usually requires a decade of SOF experience for consideration. It's been claimed that only one Marine officer every few years makes the cut.

Zembiec was that one.

He was later killed while performing a high-risk snatch-and-grab operation in Sadr City in May of 2007, the domain of Muqtada al-Sadr's Mahdi Army. Sensing something was amiss, Zembiec yelled for his men to take cover moments before being gunned down himself.

At the time, his death was reported as occurring while he was still on active duty with the Marine Corps, and Zembiec was posthumously awarded a Silver Star for his actions. However, unknown until several years later, he was also honored with an anonymous star on the Central Intelligence Agency Memorial Wall.

Sergeant Major Larry Boivin, who was awarded a Silver Star and Purple Heart for his part in the First Battle of Fallujah, later retired from Delta Force following twenty-four years of military service. Tragically, he and three other decorated servicemen were killed while riding on a float during the Hunt for Heroes parade in Midland, Texas, in November of 2012.

The float was struck by a freight train. Boivin died as he lived—a hero. He pushed his wife, Angela, to safety fractions of a second before he was killed by the impact.

Hollenbaugh said, "Larry was very disciplined—very motivated and tough as nails. He always wanted to do more. He *always* wanted to do more. He was a great soldier."

The mission in Fallujah would be Hollenbaugh's last as a sniper with the Unit. He retired in 2005 following twenty years of service.

"I am very proud to have served with the [Unit] guys," he said. "I wouldn't want to have been in it with anybody else. And those Marines . . . I don't take anything away from those Marines. They worked and they worked hard and they sacrificed.

"I'm just sad that all of our work that day was for naught."

The First Battle of Fallujah ended just days after the Jolan stand. The United States withdrew from the city, handing operations over to the newly constituted Fallujah Brigade as the coalition attempted to put a local face on an increasingly desperate war.

That decision proved to be disastrous. The Fallujah Brigade not only collapsed almost immediately, it also served to furnish the entrenched extremists with American-made arms and equipment. This development set the conditions for an even bloodier, more brutal battle that would be waged for the city later that year.

8

Making of a Legend

A newcomer—at least officially—to the murky world of special operations hit the ground on its first combat deployment in April of 2004, just as Iraq was set to erupt in unbridled carnage.

That the United States Marine Corps did not previously field a spec ops unit was more a question of semantics, mantras, and bureaucratic decision making than ground truth. Its Force Reconnaissance platoons—trained to freefall or dive behind enemy lines to conduct special reconnaissance and direct action raids—certainly passed any reasonable common-sense test.

Even the infantry battalions' Scout Sniper Platoons (SSP)—highly trained marksmen who operate in small teams and ply their trade relying on stealth—checked a handful of key boxes, at least in terms of how the general public tends to imagine special operations.

However, the USMC chose to keep Force Recon off the table when SOCOM was formed in the mid-'80s, preferring to retain control over its forces rather than fund and train a unit that would partially "belong" to what felt suspiciously like an emerging fifth service.

While Marine leadership may have been prescient in that sense, what they did not anticipate was a fundamental shift in geopolitics, nor the related exponential increase in the prominence of (and budget for) special operations forces.

As a result, the motto "first to fight" had become less and less accurate; the Marine Corps was initially sidelined and then given less critical taskings in the immediate response to 9/11—a humbling lesson for the proud service concerning the new age of warfare.

A second chance at a slice of the expanding SOF pie was forced down the Marine Corps's throat when SOF-enamored Rumsfeld insisted on closer USMC/SOCOM collaboration.

Lieutenant Colonel Giles Kyser made it his mission to transform that mandate into a full-time Marine component to SOCOM, although he encountered considerable resistance on both sides of the table. Many inside the USMC held on to their pre-9/11 beliefs. Meanwhile, a number of key figures inside SOCOM were reluctant to share the mission, money, or glory with the Marine Corps, whom they felt had already chosen their fate two decades earlier, while also questioning the USMC's ability to field a force with the right qualities to excel in real-world special operations.

Despite the reluctance, a proof-of-concept pilot program with an eye on establishing a permanent Marine presence in SOCOM was realized in 2003 with the activation of Marine Corps Special Operations Command Detachment One (MCSOCOM Det One).

Among the detractors of the initiative within SOCOM, Naval Special Warfare was viewed as the most determined to block any permanent commitment. When NSW offered to serve as SOCOM's executive agent—and thus be given operational control of Det One—it was a move viewed with considerable suspicion. Some inside the fledgling unit thought NSW merely accepted the role so that it would be better positioned to kill it rather than foster its growth.

Det One stacked the odds in its favor by drawing its personnel from a talent pool consisting of only the most veteran and talented Force Recon Marines. It then outfitted them with higher-spec gear and weaponry, and provided them with intensive training—including whirlwind CQB instruction from a former Delta Force operator, who made them completely re-think how they fought in tight spaces.

Their average age was greater than thirty. All had deployed multiples times and the bulk of the men had previously held leadership positions in Force Recon platoons, while a number had been seconded to foreign units or worked as instructors at the Mountain Warfare School or a Special Operations Training Group.

And well representative of both the experience in its ranks and the immense importance that has historically been placed by the Corps on the role of the sniper, more than half of Det One's thirty Recon Marines were trained Scout Snipers.

In a forward-thinking architecture, Det One took this supercharged Force Recon element and complemented it with a full-service integral intelligence component. This consisted of a Radio Reconnaissance Team and Signals Intelligence Support Team to secure SIGINT as well as a Counterintelligence Section to focus on HUMINT.

Det One was now ready for war. Placed under the watch of Naval Special Warfare Group One, it was slotted for a tour in Iraq, alongside the SEAL Task Units contained within Naval Special Warfare Task Group-Arabian Peninsula, itself a subcomponent of CJSOTF-AP.

Dubbed "Task Unit Raider" in recognition of its heritage as the spiritual successors of the Marine Raiders of WWII fame, it found itself a frequent collaborator and "kindred soul" in another CJSOTF-AP element—Task Unit Thunder.

While UKSF—most prominently the Special Air Service (SAS) and Special Boat Service (SBS)—lived and operated alongside (and existed *as* de facto) JSOC SMUs in Iraq and Afghanistan, Task Unit Thunder provided CJSOTF-AP with its own Tier 1–level counterterrorism unit in the vein of a Delta or DEVGRU.

Task Unit Thunder was built around the Polish Military Unit 2305, better known as GROM. Following its formative training at the hands of Larry Freedman and other Delta operators, this hard-core unit had since blossomed into one of the most aggressive, dedicated, and revered CT out-fits in existence. In the world of special operations, Poland punches well above its weight.

As the deployment took shape, the operators of Task Unit Raider and Task Unit Thunder stepped up and became the task force's primary direct action assets, operating in conjunction on multiple occasions.

Det One was aided in its first real mission—a close target reconnaissance op—by a female GROM sniper. And the sniper ultimately apprehended the target—a suspected insurgent sympathizer code named "Rachel."

Task Unit Raider first operated in and around Baghdad before being directed to the developing snake pit that was al-Najaf in August 2004.

Located one hundred miles south of Baghdad, Najaf was an important stronghold of al-Sadr's Shia militia, the Mahdi Army. These insurgents had rocked the 11th MEU (SOC), and in turn CJSOTF-AP gave orders to Det One to send its snipers to Najaf to relieve that pressure.

They proceeded to utterly demoralize the Shia militiamen, wiping out dozens of combatants while the terrified enemy force remained confused as to the point of origin of the unrelenting lethal fire.

The unit's deep sniper core paid dividends, as it was able to keep marks-men on their suppressed SR-25s around the clock, providing no respite for the militia.

Twice the Det One Scout Snipers successfully engaged in countersniper ops. Both times they identified Shia sniper positions, and then obliterated the hides and the shooters hidden behind them with an onslaught of .50-caliber Barrett M82 fire.

Ultimately, the Mahdi Army was forced to cease operations and aban-don Najaf altogether.

Det One departed Iraq in the fall of '04, having flashed its potential despite never being allowed to operate in the fashion that was originally envisioned. Almost as soon as it had arrived in Iraq, Naval Special War-fare Group One sectioned up its organic intelligence component into smaller pieces and farmed them out across its other task units to make up for their deficiencies in that area.

And despite its outstanding debut, Det One returned home facing an uncertain future.

◉

Between deployments, Chris Kyle attended one course that felt like a gift—sniper school—and another that he saw more akin to a curse. Despite his desires to the contrary, after completing sniper training, the Texan was sent to navigator school.

The advanced schooling taught him how to plan routes to objectives, hasten rapid exfils, use GPS and satellite maps, and the like, which was all well and good. However, he was less thrilled by the fact that the training could potentially confine him to the vehicle while the rest of the fire team actually does the door kicking and gun slinging when they went out raiding.

But in a bit of serendipity, those skills actually got Kyle thrown into the fight ahead of his platoon. The rest of CHARLIE was sent off to the Philippines to pull some foreign internal defense duty before heading back to the war. However, Kyle was recalled early to flex those newly acquired PowerPoint and map-reading muscles.

Awaiting him in Baghdad in September of '04 was a temporary assignment with Task Unit Thunder. GROM's early success in Iraq had made it a valued contributor to CJSOTF-AP and a popular dance partner for coalition special operation units.

Retired GROM operator Naval said, "Modern war requires more precision and special units are the answers. The level of engagement has increased, obviously. It wasn't only the counterterrorism, but also to combat the most important enemies, such as personality identification playing cards [the Deck of 55]—the most-wanted members of Hussein's government. I think GROM became more versatile in that sense."

During this time, GROM also developed a close working relationship with the U.S. Navy SEALs. "I started working with the SEALs during the Second Persian Gulf War in spring of 2002, before the invasion of Iraq," Naval explained. "We were part of the MIF—Multinational Interception

Forces. We were responsible for taking over weapons and oil. At that time both GROM and SEALs had two boarding teams that during one night could take over as many as eleven ships. This was, I feel, the time when a strong kinship between GROM and Navy SEALs was born. That was also great training that enabled both sides to work together smoothly at the start of the Iraq War.

"The next time we worked together was for over a year in Iraq. The GROM and SEALs lived together in Compound Pozzi, named after the oldest SEAL then, and we were one task force."

While Kyle worked alongside GROM on his first deployment, it wasn't until this assignment that he was actually integrated into the unit. He was assigned to Combat Team B—technically the naval section of GROM, although in practice, the distinction that separates Combat Team B from its land-centric counterpart, Combat Team A, is somewhat fluid.

This could have been viewed as an outstanding opportunity to run with some of the most highly trained gunfighters in the world as they took down targets in Mosul and Sadr City—that is, if he wasn't confined to the vehicle, mapping out escape routes while the assault team was crashing through doorways and gunning down terrorists.

After a week on the job, however, the Polish operators invited the big Texan to join the stack. And for the next three weeks, he was clearing rooms as an honorary member of GROM.

"I met Chris briefly in September of 2004," the GROM assaulter said, while noting their interaction was somewhat limited because "snipers prefer their own company."

"He wasn't known then yet as the best American sniper. But like any SEAL operator, Chris was highly professional, and like any good sniper, incredibly precise. From the moment you met him, you had a feeling he could be your best friend and he never let you feel inferior. I think we all had that impression of him."

The fact that he was not just welcomed by GROM to share some post-op vodka, but actually given a spot in their stack during raids, spoke highly of their confidence in the SEAL, as life and death under those conditions are separated by millimeters and milliseconds.

"Only the best were introduced to join the other group," Naval says. "You can say that meant Chris's work was of the highest standard. He wouldn't be asked to join the team otherwise."

◆

In late 2004, even with the nation at large erupting into anarchy and hellish violence, there was no pit worse than Fallujah.

Following the First Battle of Fallujah, it's estimated another 170,000 occupants fled the city as they sought to escape the even more apocalyptic showdown heading in their direction. This reduced its population to around a tenth of the 320,000 who had called the city home some months earlier, leaving only the most ardent and fanatical of the resistance.

After Operation Vigilant Resolve had been halted following a partial advance, a truce was called and the town council agreed to contain and eliminate its population of insurgents. However, the newly erected Fallujah Brigade meant to uphold this promise crumpled almost immediately.

Months later, Fallujah had only grown more foul, which demanded a more definitive conflict to retake the city. Operation Phantom Fury was set to sweep the city, building by building, in an attempt to root out and decimate the city's insurgent presence, which included the suspected headquarters of al-Qaeda in Iraq leader Abu Musab al-Zarqawi.

By this time Zarqawi had become an even more highly prioritized target than Osama bin Laden, tagged with a $25 million bounty on his head.

A total of 13,500 coalition troops, consisting of two USMC Regimental Combat Teams (assembled around the 1st and 7th Marine Regiments), the Army's 2nd Brigade, 1st Cavalry Division and 1st Squadron, 124th Cavalry, 36th Infantry Division, and a collection of British and Iraqi forces encircled the city in late November.

Some four thousand of the most fanatical, self-medicated, and *well-prepared* terrorists imaginable awaited the advance. The city had been rendered little more than a battleground in waiting. With the residents gone, the insurgents transformed the city into a mammoth den of traps, turning entire buildings into remotely detonated IEDs, building rat tunnels between rooms, and generally setting the conditions to kill as many poor Marines and soldiers brave or foolish enough to set foot inside the city.

The result would be the bloodiest battle America has waged since the Vietnam War.

During the First Battle of Fallujah, Marine platoons were augmented by the inclusion of a small number of Delta Force snipers, whose skill and leadership significantly enhanced the team's combat effectiveness.

A similar approach was taken for the Second Battle of Fallujah, this time with SEAL sniper elements. Snipers from Teams Three, Five, and Eight were called upon to integrate with the Marine assault group and were let off the leash at last.

By this time, Kyle had already seen combat. He took part in a handful of notable operations during his first deployment and came to Fallujah fresh off a month of on-the-job training, hitting buildings in Sadr City with some of the world's preeminent practitioners of CQB.

However, he had never seen anything like this. Few had.

◈

As Operation Phantom Fury opened, Kyle and his small joint SEAL/USMC sniper element set up a hide in an apartment tower complex to serve as overwatch for the Marines below.

Looking down from on high, a sniper can influence the outcome of a battle without firing a shot. Kyle explained, "You're their eyes and ears. You're their early warning system. And you're feeding them the intel. There's no embedded intel out there, so you're telling them all the details. When your boys roll up, it's like they've been practicing on it because they know it inside and out. Most times as a sniper you don't take a shot. It's for your boys to come in, do their hit, and get out without a shot being fired and you're just covering them. If they get in and get out, you sneak back out. Your job's been done outstandingly."

Of course, "most times" in Fallujah weren't exactly representative of "most times" elsewhere. Here, plenty of shots would be fired.

As the battle took shape, Kyle and his fellow snipers gradually moved deeper and deeper into the city. First they traded their apartment view outside the city proper for buildings just behind the front lines. And then they started sneaking out in front of the Marine advance.

The SEAL snipers would routinely take down a building in a prime location and then transform it to a combination sniper hide/defensive position.

While considerably more dangerous, this scheme also presented a great deal more opportunities, as they took the insurgents attempting to maneuver into fighting positions completely by surprise.

Unlike his first deployment, Kyle was well and truly in it now. He found himself involved in multiple pitched battles and dropped numerous targets. At one point, he even stood face-to-face with an equally surprised enemy combatant when a wall that had separated them was erased by an explosion. Not surprisingly, the big Texan won the pistol draw at high noon.

On another occasion, in an act of bravery that would seem painfully clichéd by Hollywood standards were it not the real deal, Kyle rushed through a hail of gunfire, laid down cover so two embedded reporters and a Marine could escape, and then dragged a gravely wounded Marine to safety. All the while, bullets and shrapnel tore through the air around them, including a grenade fragment that struck Chris's leg.

For that selfless display he would be awarded one of the five Bronze Stars for valor he would ultimately earn, in addition to two Silver Stars, by the time his SEAL career came to an end.

◉

Left at that, Chris Kyle was a certified hero of the Second Battle of Fallujah. However, in reality, he had barely begun to fight.

With the insurgents digging in—both in order to prepare for the Marine assaults and to avoid the continued sniper onslaught—Kyle offered his room-clearing talents to the Marines.

Without informing his commanding officers, the SEAL pulled himself from overwatch and slotted in with the Marines. The infantrymen had been engaging in some of the most vicious, harrowing urban combat since Operation Gothic Serpent went south in Mogadishu in 1993, and they could use all the help and expertise they could get.

In Iraq, operators from Delta Force had found their calling doggedly hunting down the most dangerous men in the world, men like Abu Musab al-Zarqawi (who, incidentally, had slipped out of Fallujah shortly before the battle and proved an elusive target for some time afterward).

Kyle, meanwhile, found his purpose serving as an unwavering protector of his fellow servicemen no matter the odds. Whether they were SEALs, soldiers, or Marines, the Texan was relentlessly—arguably recklessly—selfless in risking his own life to come to the aid of others. But no matter how ill-conceived it may have seemed in the moment, he proved time and time again that he had the skills to back up that unlimited courage.

He traded his .300 Win Mag for a Marine-issued M16 (and later, an M4 he borrowed from another SEAL), and for weeks, he trained up the Marines whenever they had a breather. And then, when they were back on the clock, he led them through the breach and to the absolutely brutal close quarters combat that awaited them.

When the tide of the battle turned, he placed himself back in overwatch. And he later reinserted himself with the team on the ground when he deemed it the best place to watch over the guys he placed under his care. Wherever he could issue the most damage on the insurgents while best defending the troops—that's where he was going to be.

Considering his experience in the aforementioned Battle of Mogadishu, Howard Wasdin's words carry serious weight on the matter. Reflecting on Kyle's actions in Fallujah, Wasdin said, "Chris pulling himself from overwatch is one of the most selfless things I've ever heard of. My knowledge of the way urban warfare was in Somalia . . . I assume it was every bit as bad in Fallujah. That's definitely going above and beyond, giving up an overwatch position like that. That goes right back to the fact that people don't become SEAL snipers to be tough guys; they do it for love and country. For Chris to do that, that exemplifies exactly who SEALs are.

"He didn't have to do that. That's not just showing love for your country, that's showing love for those guys that need your help."

Eric Davis, Kyle's SEAL sniper mentor, said, "I could have argued, 'Chris, you're risking your life and you're going to take a sniper off the battlefield, and a sniper is much more valuable.' But then you have Chris Kyle going, 'No, this is the way it is.'

"My argument holds up for 99 percent of the population, but for a guy like Chris—again, not arrogant but confident—Chris knows who he is. He knows he's not 99 percent of the SEAL Teams. He is who he is. 'I can do this, therefore, I should do this.' That's out of the box. He's existing on a plane that other people don't exist at.

"I think that's down to him being clear on his ultimate purpose. When you understand why you're doing something, it's different. When he said, 'Yeah, I'll go with you Marines—let's go kick down doors and train together,' he was not there to be famous. He was not there to get the most kills. He was not there because he's bloodthirsty. He was there to save Marines' lives, and he was going to do whatever he needed to do to do that. Most people would have been like, 'Yeah, you guys have got it—I'm out—I'm going to get lunch.' But that's the difference between a story and a legend."

◉

Chris Kyle's exploits during the Second Battle of Fallujah served as the basis for his nickname, "the Legend." It was initially meant in a mocking fashion to keep his ego in check, but he would come to embody it so thoroughly that it stuck.

He wasn't alone in his heroism. During the Second Battle of Fallujah three servicemen were awarded the Navy Cross, the second highest award for military valor.

Delta's snipers were silently back in the hunt. So too were GROM's snipers whom the CIA reportedly found particularly useful for the low-ered threshold their rules of engagement allowed—a mere cell phone and a broken curfew were enough for the Polish marksmen to engage according to Priest and Arkin's *Top Secret America*.

Kyle's Navy SEAL brothers certainly acquitted themselves well, playing a significant role in the victory despite their limited numbers. That sort of courage under fire—especially the unflinching bravery demonstrated by the Texan day after day—is never a certainty until put to the ultimate test.

Even some SEALs fail when their very survival is in doubt. In his memoir, *American Sniper,* Kyle harshly described one such case, a SEAL he refers to as "Runaway." According to Kyle, Runaway fled from combat three times, leaving the Texan in the lurch each time.

American Sniper also tells a very different sort of tale—myriad stories involving hazing inside the Teams. These range from humorous to horrifying—and usually more than a little of both.

While they may seem unrelated, Kyle claimed that while rituals may seem cruel and sophomoric on the surface, they are done for the genuine betterment of the Team. Even if not every "Runaway" can be identified and weeded out before they put their fellow SEALs in jeopardy, the bulk of them are, in fact, run off by a necessarily ruthless pack.

"No matter what unit you're in, there's going to be turds," Chris said. "There's going to be turds in Six. There's going to be turds in Delta. In every unit there's going to be a turd. . . .

"We kicked one out my first deployment. He was a turd. He was a turd all through BUD/S. He was a cocky, arrogant guy, and he struggled. He almost quit several times. He cried during BUD/S but always came off like, 'Oh, BUD/S was easy.' It's like, 'Dude, you're the guy that was crying in the corner. We stopped you from quitting. I should have let you do it.'

"Looking back at BUD/S, they're trying to push teamwork. So you're all like, 'Oh, don't do it, man.' In BUD/S, I should have gone, 'Yeah, go do it. Go right over there. Please.' I should've been pushing him. We kicked him out when we got to the Team because he was an underachiever, couldn't perform. So the platoon kicked him. [Last I heard] he was pumping gas in Norfolk.

"We're all like the sharks in the water. As soon as you smell blood, you find a weakness on somebody. Even if he's a good guy, you find a weakness on him, you're going to harp on it. But if you find a guy who is just weak, then everybody starts circling because you want to get rid of him. He's going to kill you downrange—so shit-can him.

"But it's good because it also makes you tougher. You're not only getting it, but you're giving it. You're part of a tough love family."

◈

A total of 107 coalition troops were killed in the Second Battle of Fallujah and another 613 wounded. Estimates place the number of insurgents killed in the neighborhood of twelve hundred or more.

In his first significant utilization as a sniper, Chris Kyle accounted for forty of those enemy KIAs himself (which doesn't take into account his time spent "in the shit," exchanging lead at high speed across contested living rooms).

While the Iraq War presented warfighters and politicians alike with an impossibly complex reality to suss out, the SEAL had no problem mentally simplifying it. It was beautifully black-and-white as far as he was concerned.

Ba'athists, Salafi jihadists, Sunni nationalists, Shia death squads, what have you—however different their backstories and motivations may have been according to the historians and the politicians, to Kyle, as long as they were actively attempting to kill American troops, they were the enemy. They were *"savages."* And they would all be dealt with in the same manner.

The resolute Texan also had precious little difficulty rationalizing or justifying his actions. Chris fired his weapon with absolute conviction. He not only admitted to being rather good at this grim occupation, he loved it.

He was not without feeling; he felt the losses of friendly forces all too deeply and was plagued by crippling guilt at times. However, that guilt was reserved for those he couldn't save—not for those he sent to the grave. That he did with an unclouded conscience.

It's nearly impossible for most—especially those who have not been in combat—to put themselves in the place of a man who has taken so many human lives—guilty, innocent, good, evil, or otherwise—and gauge how they'd deal.

The daily struggles of those who have endured the horrors of combat are painfully apparent in today's society. Post-traumatic stress is increasingly recognized as a crisis reaching epidemic proportions—the fallout absorbed by those who have served a nation that has now been at war for nearly fifteen years in succession. On any given day, an average of twenty-two veterans take their own lives, irrevocably destroyed by their time spent in combat.

Eric Davis has studied human performance intensively and he credits Kyle with rare psychological strength. He explained, "Sometimes people ask how he was able to live with himself after killing that many people. Here's the thing—psychologically speaking—human beings can't do something that's disagreeable with their senses or their morals. That's where PTSD can come from. You could kill a bunch of people but then all the guilt and the remorse and all that stuff will just wake your ass up at night."

Another former SEAL sniper instructor also explained the mind-set of a sniper. He said, "You have to find a way to justify your actions in your mind. These guys are able to compartmentalize it. Some guys, like Chris, see themselves as saving lives. Other guys see it as a profession: 'I'm just doing my job.' And some guys are just there to hunt."

Davis elaborated, "What's going on is, you told yourself some sort of story in the moment to make yourself feel okay about what happened, but that story will not stand up over time because at the end of the day, it was just a story.

"Now everything inside a human's life is a story, but some are better than others. Chris's confidence can come off like he's just some redneck running his mouth. But he's one of those tough guys where if you were able to unpeel the layers of the brain, you'd discover an incredible amount of intelligence. This 'redneck bull-riding dude' probably gave some pretty serious thought to it all. It was not the first time he thought about it.

"So when he was out there operating and killing people, his brain had already processed the justification for doing so, at least to some degree. And when you can justify something, that's when you can execute aggressively and violently. You're already good to go."

Davis provided a specific example to illustrate this single-minded justification at work. The story may actually serve to confirm to Kyle's detractors their suspicions of some sort of mental disorder. Davis would argue to the contrary considering what was at stake.

A stray dog was adopted and kept around the camp where Kyle's SEAL sniper element was resting between operations. Unfortunately for all concerned, the animal barked through the night, one evening after the next.

"I've got to fucking go to sleep. I've got to wake up and go on a mission tomorrow. You get that dog to shut up."

When the owner proved unable to do so, the Texan took matters into his own hands and gutted the dog.

"A lot of people were like, 'Holy shit! We need to give this guy a psych evaluation,'" Davis said. "Chris admitted that people freaked out about it. But I would say, no, that is simply someone who is 100 percent mission focused. His job is to go out and save the lives of other Americans and he knew that this dog could stop him from doing that.

"He was able to put his feelings and conscience aside to do what needed to be done. There are not a lot of people that can do that anymore."

3/75 Ranger snipers training ahead of deployment at Fort Campbell in 2005. *Courtesy of Jack Murphy.*

Isaiah Burkhart on the range with a .300 Win Mag. *Courtesy of Isaiah Burkhart.*

3/75 Ranger snipers on a 160th SOAR MH-6 Little Bird at Fort Campbell. *Courtesy of Isaiah Burkhart.*

Jack Murphy sporting a pakol hat in the mountains of Afghanistan in 2004. *Courtesy of Jack Murphy.*

Jack poses with some locals. *Courtesy of Jack Murphy.*

Jack minutes ahead of an aerial platform support mission in Khowst, Afghanistan, in late 2004/early 2005. *Courtesy of Jack Murphy.*

A 3/75 Ranger sniper in Mosul, Iraq. *Courtesy of Isaiah Burkhart.*

3/75 Ranger snipers Isaiah Burkhart and Jack Murphy. *Courtesy of Jack Murphy.*

The glory boys of 1st platoon, A/co, 3/75 with Platoon Sergeant Jared Van Aalst in Mosul. *Courtesy of Isaiah Burkhart.*

MACV-SOG's Don Martin and Timothy Kephart pose with Colonel Ho Tieu upon receiving their Gallantry Cross medals. *Courtesy of Donald Martin.*

```
                                        Republic of Viet-Nam
                                        Department of Defence
                                        Joint General Staff
                                        Armed Forces of Republic VN
        C I T A T I O N                 -----++++++++------
                                        Liaison Service
                                        APO  3.562


T o  be awarded the Gallantry Cross Medal with Bronze Star


To   :  Sgt. Donald C. Martin

RA   :  19876906



            A gallent NCO, volunteered in every difficult missions at
the Border.

            Special in the operation Echo 60 dated 20th Dec. 1967, when
the friendly unit was besieged by enemy. Under the horrible situation, he
was very bravely to xkpqm stop many time of the enemy's assaultings in order
to support the friendly who were in danger.

            By his brave action is distinguished the gallent combat moral
of the VN and US personnels.

            He is worthy to be awarded the Gallentry Cross Medal of Regt. Leve
```

The Gallantry Cross medal citation. Note the citation's decided lack of command of the English language as well as the actual facts of the mission. *Courtesy of Donald Martin.*

Navy SEAL joint training. *Courtesy of Brandon Webb.*

Navy SEAL sniper on the grass and on the glass. *Courtesy of Brandon Webb.*

A Navy SEAL sniper in Afghanistan. *Courtesy of Brandon Webb.*

Navy SEAL snipers take position in Afghanistan. *Courtesy of Brandon Webb.*

.50 cal sticking out of a Navy SEAL sniper hide. *Courtesy of Brandon Webb.*

Thai SEALs training with U.S. Navy SEALs. *Courtesy of Brandon Webb.*

Isaiah Burkhart and his 3/75 sniper shooting partner in Tikrit, Iraq. *Courtesy of Isaiah Burkhart.*

3/75 Ranger snipers and recon tasked with foreign internal defense, training Khowst SWAT. *Courtesy of Jack Murphy.*

A Navy SEAL sniper at the office in Afghanistan. *Courtesy of Brandon Webb.*

9

Industrial Revolution

As JSOC adapted to the situation and developed increasingly accurate intelligence, the chaotic violence following the initial toppling of Hussein's regime slowly came into focus despite its nuanced and evolving nature.

A multifaceted insurgency composed of nationalist and jihadist elements was compounded by the escalation of an ugly sectarian conflict that cascaded into a full-blown civil war.

What had been loose and disparate armed groups congealed into larger forces as tens of thousands were killed in an ever-ratcheting series of attacks. Sunni suicide bombings compelled equally repugnant executions carried out by Shia death squads, which sparked the next round of the cycle.

Foreign influences driven by their own larger goals not only encouraged this intensification, they compelled it by pulling strings on either side of the equation.

While the United States cited dubious ties connecting Hussein and al-Qaeda ahead of the invasion as a motivating factor, the presence of American troops on the ground made the fear of al-Qaeda in Iraq (AQI) a reality. AQI solidified into a monstrously bloodthirsty faction, fanning the flames of civil war.

Superficially supporting the nation's Sunni population, AQI exploited the conflict to bring about more bloodshed and recruit new terrorists to wage jihad against the "infidels."

The profile of AQI's leader, Abu Musab al-Zarqawi, continued its stratospheric ascension. His notoriety was marked both by his boundless brutality (at a level that left even Osama bin Laden and Ayman al-Zawahiri uncomfortable) and his ability to continually slip free from the net as JSOC attempted to hunt him down.

Meanwhile, Iran quietly backed the Shia population. This was done as much to conduct a veiled war against the United States as it was to support their ideological allies and shape the future of Iraq to its long-term benefit.

The Iranian presence generally came in the form of intelligence, training, and armament that effectively transformed the extremist Shia militias into a proxy paramilitary army, but the Iranian Revolutionary Guard's elite Quds Force was heavily suspected of playing a more direct role as well.

With AQI and Iran dumping gasoline on an already volatile situation, matters were made even more complicated by the staging and smuggling of men and munitions across the border. This was not only in Iran, but also Syria, and, to a lesser extent, Jordan and Saudi Arabia.

Despite their fanatical differences, all sides with bad intentions viewed the coalition—and the Americans in particular—as enemy number one.

The tactics utilized were among the most vile and gruesome imaginable. Wide-scale bombings of public markets, videotaped beheadings, mass executions in the systematic slaughter of innocents, and improvised explosive devices (IEDs) became the standard operating procedures of the rival factions in play.

Genuinely at risk of losing control of the situation in Iraq beyond repair, JSOC responded to this unique and extremely challenging set of circumstances by undertaking the most ambitious and revolutionary special operations campaign the world had ever witnessed.

◈

Then-Secretary of Defense Rumsfeld leveraged loosened restrictions to provide the Joint Special Operations Command with an open-ended mandate, unlimited funds, and a bolstered intelligence capability.

Meanwhile, he also shielded it from oversight, with the idea of transforming it into a proactive, standalone counterterrorism powerhouse. Continually frustrated with interagency feuding and the CIA's consistent inability to provide actionable intelligence to JSOC's special mission units in the early stages of the Iraq War, Rumsfeld hoped to free up the Pentagon's premier CT forces so that they might operate more freely and effectively.

However, shortly after taking command of JSOC, General Stanley McChrystal seized the reins handed off to him by the Secretary of Defense and did an about-face: he took "the Command" in the opposite direction Rumsfeld expected in order to complete the radical transformation he desired.

Rather than cut off ties and make the augmented command even more insular, McChrystal embraced the input of outside agencies and emphasized open lines of communication. This was done in an effort to slash through layers of bureaucracy, both inside JSOC and throughout its wider support network. Minimizing lost opportunities, JSOC radically ramped up its ability to collect, analyze, and act on intelligence.

Along with a dramatically enhanced internal capability as JSOC created new units and strengthened preexisting ones, McChrystal's inclusive approach also resulted in significantly improved relations with—and product from—the CIA, NSA, FBI, MI6, DIA, and other military intelligence units, conventional military forces, civilian contractors, etc. Anyone who could play a role in turning JSOC into a more effective machine was welcomed and empowered to do so.

The combined efforts of these entities, along with JSOC's authority to dominate ISR resources in country, eventually resulted in an "unblinking eye" of 24/7 surveillance provided by a fusion of imagery from satellites, UAVs, and manned aircraft in constant rotation. This allowed the Command to perform complex movement analysis, such as rewinding truck bombs or death squads to their point of origin, pinpointing the objective for the next direct action mission.

Now spurred on by unprecedented intelligence, Delta's gunfighters were truly unleashed. As this process was continually refined and perfected, the Unit slowly ratcheted up its operations tempo (OPTEMPO) to previously uncharted levels. By 2005, JSOC was executing multiple raids per night and hundreds per month in a relentless campaign to chart and dismantle webs of insurgents with Zarqawi's AQI network serving as its primary target and victim.

This effort was fueled by a system known as F3EA—Find, Fix, Finish, Exploit, Analyze—in which each subsequent raid was rapidly processed in order to secure new intelligence with which to initiate the next series of direct action raids.

Operators in the field communicated directly with a wide range of intelligence personnel and leadership on a daily basis. Operations and intelligence (O&I) video teleconferences (VTCs) connected the warfighters to their enablers both back at the JOC (Joint Operations Center) and Stateside six times a week. This ritual connected and united a dispersed effort (dispersed both by its globally distributed personnel and their widely varied skill sets and experience) and encouraged decentralized decision making, further quickening the pace.

Collectively, this allowed JSOC and Delta Force to increasingly outpace and outmaneuver the adaptable terrorist groups that had proven such elusive targets prior to this transformation.

A retired Unit recce operator summed it up: "You know why we won in Iraq? And you know why Stanley McChrystal was the greatest general we've ever seen? The Internet and global real-time video conferences."

In the words of McChrystal himself, "It takes a network to defeat a network."

It must be noted that the early phases of this effort certainly encountered growing pains—to say the least. There are troubling stories of detainee abuse and questionable interrogation practices in secret detention centers.

It's been reported that frustrated task force members attempted to wring out the vast amounts of intelligence necessary to ramp up operations to the desired level. However, gradually the larger process built up its own momentum, lessening a sense of need to regularly engage in these sorts of objectionable activities.

◈

While McChrystal and his chief intelligence officer (or J2) General Michael Flynn have widely been credited as being the primary architects behind this "industrial-scale counterterrorism" approach, in reality much of the innovation was driven from the ground up.

In 2004, when McChrystal was in the earliest stages of conceiving this network, he was approached by then-Delta Force commander Bennet Sacolick, who presented the F3EA solution to the general.

This idea built and capitalized upon the tagging, tracking, and locating techniques the Unit had developed internally while hunting down the scattered fragments of Hussein's Ba'athist regime, including the dictator himself, along with its pioneering use of unblinking ISR.

John McPhee, a sniper with the Unit at the time, explained, "The government inherently does not know how to harness technology. We really got things working in Iraq when JSOC got out of the way and we ran the show."

Long championed for its creative problem solving—from dreaming up the modern spike strip to capture PIFWCs (Persons Indicted for War Crimes) in Bosnia to contemplating bicycle-mounted, cross-border offset infils—the Unit continued to deliver operational breakthroughs that helped fast-track the success of the new initiative. A pair of operators suggested a modification to an existing technology that, when utilized with specialized ISR aircraft, allowed for real-time target tracking. This also made possible the deep mapping of the target's network of associates and eventually the enemy organization as a whole.

◈

Both Delta's tactical and its research and development influence tend to trickle down and spread out wide over time.

The Heckler & Koch HK416 carbine was originally developed for, and in collaboration with, the Unit. It was widely adopted by Delta Force in 2004 and quickly subjected to an extensive trial by fire as JSOC had just started to cut a wide swath through Iraq's terrorist factions. It's since become established as the preferred assault rifle among elite military and law enforcement units across the globe.

Similarly, variants of the Knights Armament SR-25 have largely proven to be the weapon of choice among special operations snipers during the Global War on Terror. A semi-automatic sniper rifle that doesn't feel altogether unfamiliar to those trained on M4/M16 platforms, the SR-25 delivers a heavier 7.62×51mm NATO caliber round versus the former's 5.56x44mm.

This makes the SR-25 useful to spec ops snipers both at a considerable distance and in more confined spaces, capable of dropping targets whether they're eight or eight hundred meters away.

However, the SR-25 didn't always have such a sterling reputation. And without the weight of Delta's influence forcing improvements along, it may have never come into such wide use by the nation's SOF marksmen.

The SR-25 was originally developed by Eugene Stoner in the early '90s as an improved version of his '50s AR-10 design. However, according to a former Unit operator, "It took a long time to get that gun sorted out. By all accounts now, though, it's a pretty damn good gun and you can thank Delta for that because they held Knights's feet to the fire. Knights was smart enough to know that if Delta no longer used their gun, that would have a horrendous effect on them. They were about the only organization that could really leverage Knights to fix the gun."

The realities of the Iraq War whittled the rifle down into a shorter, more maneuverable weapon better suited to tight engagements. "It's really kind of your benchmark now. And what you're also seeing is—due to the different kind of conflicts you have going on and the urban activities—hey, we don't need this twenty-inch gas gun. We can get by with a sixteen-incher and make the shots we need to make in an urban environment out to four hundred meters or so. And then if we have to do CQB, it's an easier gun to manage."

The former operator continued, explaining, "The Mk 11 Mod 0 was the big turning point for that gun, which was really around post-9/11. That had a lot of upgrades and a lot of stuff that was really ramrodded on Knights to do.

"Delta bought a number of them. Previously, they were using M14s and they liked what the SR-25 brought to the table. But they had to have a big sit-down and create a list that said, 'You've got to fix this shit and we're going to give you X amount of time to do it. If you don't, we're getting rid of your guns.'

"That would have been the death knell of that gun."

◈

Once fully up and running, JSOC's industrial operations dealt with its adversaries with all the regularity of a mass production line.

With a constant flow of intelligence guiding direct action elements, and JSOC's pull ensuring they were supported by close air support at all times, AQI found itself under an unrelenting assault of brass and lead, bombs and missiles, and ones and zeroes.

For Tier 1 CT units such as Delta Force, extreme proficiency in close quarters combat is considered a core competency, not to mention a source of pride and an area of distinction. In Iraq, the assaulters (and advanced assaulters) of the Unit were given the opportunity to demonstrate that capability on a scale previously unimagined. A staggering body count resulted.

If you ask them, operators from DEVGRU, the UKSF's Special Air Service, Polish GROM, and other leading units will insist that their respective outfit represents the global standard bearer in this particularly exacting and deadly arena.

The same, of course, is true with operators from Delta Force. Their claim is made with complete and utter conviction, confident that their counterparts know this deep in their souls as well even if they are unwilling to make the admission public.

While they would likely appear identical to the untrained eye, JSOC's special mission units take contrasting approaches to CQB. A former Delta officer described the Unit's style as "instinctive" and "explosive" while terming SEAL Team Six as "more controlled and rigid" when things get kinetic in tight spaces.

Think of Delta as jazz improvisation to DEVGRU's classical score.

John McPhee, a former Unit advanced assaulter said, "No one does free flow like the Unit. Why? No one else trains the right way. Effective training focuses on mind-set, lessons learned, and absolutely no ego. Plus there's no myth or sacred cows. If it sucks let's call it that and move on to better stuff. I could teach a SWAT team to do it in a couple weeks but they don't have the right mindset. They see it as 'too fast, too loose, too dangerous.' Well, what happens if you don't do it and the adrenaline is flowing when you're out on a target? You get shot."

As the campaign against al-Qaeda in Iraq and other enemy forces lifted off, the Unit took its trademark speed, surprise, and violence of action out from the controlled conditions of the training kill house and into the wilds of Sadr City, Fallujah, and other extremist lairs.

In mid-2004, A Squadron rescued multiple hostages while the Unit as a whole began the systematic decimation of AQI. By May of 2005, the Delta-spearheaded campaign had resulted in the deaths of Zarqawi's top twenty-one lieutenants while capturing another thirteen, leaving just one unaccounted for. Three months later, some two hundred of AQI's leaders had been eliminated.

◈

While Delta's Task Force Green took the fight to AQI in the areas surrounding Baghdad, the Rangers of Task Force Red operated to the north in much the same manner—and with equal ferocity and frequency.

That actuality might have come as something of a surprise to those not paying full attention. Call it the Black Hawk Down effect.

Too often when outsiders (including those in other spec ops units) think of the 75th Ranger Regiment, they envision a sort of supercharged version of a conventional infantry unit, filled with eighteen-year-old Privates who get the honor of playing "blocking force to the stars"—pulling security for Delta Force and SEAL Team Six.

And in fact, the Rangers of a slightly earlier generation were somewhat more "conventional" in their approach—hard-charging and disciplined infantrymen to which the rest of the Army could look to set an example. And they'd be called in to back up their big brothers from Bragg on occasion, too. This was the case in Mogadishu in '93, and subsequently this image became the defining one for a generation whose primary source of Ranger knowledge is *Black Hawk Down*.

But the accelerating pace of operations required that the Rangers both evolve and step up in a major way. Before long, the 75th Ranger Regiment assumed responsibilities not massively far removed from those of JSOC's special mission units, at least in a pure DA capacity.

The days of holding down street corners while CAG (the unit designation most often used by Rangers in reference to Delta Force) goes to work have largely become a relic of an older world. Post-9/11 Rangers are eager to dispel the fallacy when presented with the opportunity to do so.

"That's the great myth," former 3/75 Ranger sniper Jack Murphy said. "As far as the operations I did in Ranger Battalion—the amount of times we did security or support for any other unit—I could probably count on one hand."

Isaiah Burkhart, a former 3rd Battalion sniper team leader, added, "It's a poor misconception that all we do is block positions or whatever. That's not true. I think in my four deployments as a sniper, on three of them, I worked with CAG at some time. And in all that time, in the hundreds and hundreds of missions that I did, I know one for sure, and maybe two, where I was actually ever on a blocking position. That's a pretty low percentage."

GM, another ex-3/75 sniper, opined that while the Regiment—even the very active, very lethal Regiment that has emerged over the past decade— has been slow to capture attention in the way its more celebrated SOCOM counterparts have, people are finally starting to catch on.

He said, "Vietnam made SF and SEALs look like gods. They rode that forever. And when you really look at it, between Vietnam and GWOT, there's really been nothing. I mean, there's been a few things here and there, but nothing crazy like 'Nam or like this. Not too long ago I used to hear, "[Rangers] don't do anything; they just do blocking positions for the guys at Bragg.' That was the reputation. 'You all don't do anything, y'all just pretty much carry their water.' Nobody says that now. *Nobody.*"

A major reason no one says that now is due to the heavy influence of Stanley McChrystal, who thrust his former unit into the spotlight when he ascended to the very top of the black spec ops world.

"I think if McChrystal were wounded on the battlefield, he would bleed red, black, and white—the official colors of the 75th Ranger Regiment," wrote former Ranger and Delta officer Dalton Fury. "He is 110 percent U.S. Army Ranger. As the Ranger Regimental commander, McChrystal was considered a Tier 2 subordinate commander under the Joint Special Operations functioning command structure. The highest level, Tier 1, was reserved exclusively for Delta Force and Seal Team Six. This always seemed to bother McChrystal. His nature isn't to be second fiddle to anyone, nor for his Rangers to be considered second-class citizens to the Tier 1 special mission units."

McChrystal became the tenth consecutive Army general running the Joint Special Operations Command, a stretch of Army leadership that dated back to JSOC's inception. However, he wasn't so much just another Army "daddy" as he was the Rangers' "daddy." And he made sure the 75th Ranger Regiment would play a lead role in this new age of special warfare.

◈

The Regiment largely planned and executed its own operations in Iraq, supported by JSOC's intelligence fusion and complete with access to the

160th Special Operations Aviation Regiment. Bolstered by top-flight gear and weaponry paid for by inflated budgets, sporting relaxed grooming standards, and executing surgical raids on myriad high-value targets, the GWOT-era 75th Ranger Regiment more closely resembles an outsider's (similarly misguided) idea of Delta or DEVGRU than it does the tired BHD image.

"I'd say that people have this conception that SEAL Team Six is saving the world," Burkhart lamented. "I really don't have anything bad to say about those guys. They are an amazing unit in their own right. But they've been so publicized and everything, I don't think people realize the Regiment . . . we had our set of targets we went after all the time. We were getting bad guys all the time. And we were not just going after these little small guys."

In Iraq, Task Force Red's JOC (Joint Operation Center) prominently displayed a large graphic featuring images of the top HVTs in the task force's sights. Arranged like a pyramid, Zarqawi sat at the very top, with a spiderweb of connections linking the remainder of the most wanted terrorists on JSOC's target deck beneath him.

Burkhart said, "As the deployment would go on it was like, 'Check this guy off, check that guy off, check this guy off. . . .' "

Once JSOC's industrial counterterrorism campaign was put into full effect, the 3rd Battalion alone was responsible for eliminating multiple HVTs who held down places near the very top of that chart. "These guys were top ten guys in the whole country," Burkhart said. "They were on Delta's top ten list, the CIA's top ten list. These were the dudes that we really want to get. We were doing big things. We were getting big guys."

In the summer of 2005, the blistering pace required that 3/75 put two platoons into rotation near Mosul so that they could press the initiative twenty-four hours a day.

"One platoon would do day ops for two weeks straight while the other platoon was doing night ops," Burkhart explained. "We generally didn't do day ops that much, but we were up there because there was so much going on. It was such a big hub for guys coming in from Syria; it was a major meeting point and from there they spread out to the rest of the country."

Fortunately, the battalion arrived at FOB (Forward Operating Base) Marez in Mosul in July 2005 armed with an extremely potent, dedicated sniper capability. Unfortunately, the line companies did not fully appreciate that fact, at least not initially. While 3/75's sniper platoon had enjoyed considerable success at the Haditha Dam during the initial invasion of Iraq and in its previous deployment to Afghanistan, the rifle platoons still did not understand how to fully exploit their organic force multipliers nor did they necessarily recognize their value.

As a result, the snipers were forced to sell themselves to secure work. GM said, "Half the job in Battalion of a sniper was being a sniper. The other half was being a businessman. You had to build relationships with the platoon sergeant and the PL [platoon leader].

"If you have a bad relationship with the platoon sergeant or anybody there, they are going to shut you down. They are not going to put you on manifest. They're going to cut you at every turn. I saw that with one guy. He was an asshole. They wouldn't put him on missions. They didn't want to bring him out. They just thought about him as a liability. He ended up getting fired from the [sniper] platoon."

❖

While the rifle companies still needed to be convinced, 3rd Battalion's sniper platoon was hitting on all cylinders and just waiting to be set loose.

Jared Van Aalst had only returned from the Army Marksmanship Unit to serve as the section's platoon sergeant. And just prior to the battalion's Mosul deployment, he showcased his skills by scoring a blowout victory in the 2005 U.S. Army Rifle Individual Championship.

While the advantage inherent with being based at Fort Benning and in proximity to the AMU provided 3/75 was a factor, that alone did not account for the section's sharpened edge. That had been instilled by Van Aalst's management style and the resultant environment that had been fostered. Snipers were forced to perform under constant stress or risk being jettisoned back to the line with little warning.

"Sniper section guys were different," said GM, a former 3/75 sniper team leader. "It was just kind of the personality profile. They were quiet, they were into guns, they were kinda into themselves, they were secluded, and they didn't like to talk to people. They kind of do their own thing, you know? And all of them are extremely competitive alpha males.

"It was a shark tank essentially. They ate the weakest one. If a weak guy came in, he didn't last long. And we're talking about Ranger team leaders. You could go at any time. They could fire at will. It was stressful."

In fact, it was so stressful that established snipers in the section (and some stayed in their position for several years) welcomed the introduction of new blood to the platoon . . . simply so that the blood most likely to be spilled in the water was not their own.

"You wanted a bunch of new guys because it would take heat off you," GM continued. "It was so stressful because they're constantly looking to fire guys. They even said, 'We're going to put someone's head on the chopping block because that's how we get the best out of people.' The 'Hey, he's a good guy—he's my drinking buddy . . . '—that didn't work there. You performed or you didn't. When I was there, it was like twelve guys and nobody was safe. It's what you want—that culture of fear to get the best out of people."

The uncompromising approach evoked Jack Welch's vitality model in which the bottom 10 percent of a company are slated to be fired each year. "You want it to be competitive and it was. That's why it became so good."

◈

3/75 Sniper Platoon leaders Van Aalst and Robby Johnson demanded a certain degree of experience in potential candidates for the section—one had to be an E-4 and have already earned their Ranger Tab. (Around that time the other battalions' sniper platoons experimented with accepting much less experienced Rangers.)

But beyond that, the right mind-set was all that mattered. There was no extensive selection process, simply an interview ("You never knew what was going to get asked, never. They'd feel you out. And then, 'Okay thanks' and they'd send you out"), an internal background check, and a psych evaluation to determine if someone could succeed in the role.

GM said, "They needed guys who were thinkers who you could send out in the middle of nowhere and he could do his own thing. He's fire and forget; you don't have to worry about babysitting him."

The personable Isaiah Burkhart is enthusiastic and welcoming. Despite his four deployments as a 3/75 sniper in which he played a decisive role in some of the more intense combat operations American SOF has conducted since 9/11, he doesn't exactly fit the profile (in fact, one sniper got his walking papers simply because even Burkhart couldn't find a positive thing to say about him).

Now an Oregon State grad living back in Oregon with his wife and their young daughter, Burkhart admitted that he had to, in a sense, fake it to make it in Sniper Platoon. To do so, he first had to identify the traits that were most coveted.

"I don't know if I necessarily had *it,* but I did a good job of not standing out," he said. "I think *it* is a mentality of believing that you are the best maybe even if you're not all the time, but still being humble enough to know when you've screwed up. They have that mentality of, 'We're better than you' type of thing. And I honestly do believe at one point in time the 3rd Battalion had the greatest sniper section in the entire military."

◉

Prior to the battalion's 2005 deployment to Mosul, Jack Murphy became one of the victims of the notorious 3/75 Sniper Platoon shark tank. While others credited Van Aalst's leadership style and the pressurized atmosphere it produced with elevating the section to new heights, Murphy felt the corporate approach reeked of insecurity and was too often petty and counterproductive.

"Jared was an interesting cat," he said. "I had a strange relationship with him to say the least."

While Van Aalst was assigned to AMU, "the entire Ranger Regiment had deployed multiple times and guys had combat jumps and CIBs [Combat Infantry Badges] and VA [Van Aalst] hadn't done anything. It's a fucked up way of thinking but that's the way the military works and it's the way soldiers think."

Murphy earned his Ranger Tab and then joined the sniper platoon shortly following Van Aalst's first (rather quiet) combat deployment. He quickly found his lifelong dream of becoming a special operations sniper to be a nightmare in reality.

"VA became a guy who became well known for breaking balls and he had a trail of figurative dead bodies behind him," Murphy explained. "It was definitely my worst year in the military if not the worst year of my adult life, period. It was like junior high. It was like a popularity contest. VA and RJ were like the cool guys in the secret tree fort.

"I think it was out of insecurity. Because those guys had done all the shooting competitions and stuff, but now you have these other dudes come in and they already have like six deployments under their belts."

Murphy recalls a sniper platoon run with an iron fist, complete with power plays to remind subordinates who ran things. "There were just childish displays of power. When VA would shake my hand, he would hold his hand out, but not extend it so I had to bend over and submit to him to shake his hand. That's how it went with me and VA. I'd come into work and say, 'Good morning, Sergeant,' and he'd would walk right past me and not say anything. That's the type of shit I was dealing with. And the attitude that persisted there rolled down hill to the squad leaders who were under pressure to behave the same way.

"That was VA's style of leadership. He read all these corporate self-help books about how to be the ruthless, cut-throat CEO that destroys everyone in their career conquest, and he'd actually use that stuff."

While on his first deployment as a Ranger sniper, Murphy found himself in deep due to an undisclosed situation ("nothing illegal, unethical, or immoral. But it was really fucking bad shit overseas in Afghanistan").

That would quickly result in the end of his career in Sniper Platoon.

Murphy was just the latest in a long line of snipers to get their walking papers courtesy of Jared Van Aalst.

Even the manner in which it went down rubbed Murphy the wrong way. He was first clued in by a Ranger from outside the section.

"Hey, Murph, I see you're coming back to the company."

"Wait—what? No, I'm not."

"Yeah, you are. Your name's up on the whiteboard."

"What the fuck is going on?"

Murphy tracked down the sniper platoon sergeant to suss out the validity of the rumors. "I was fucking pissed at VA. I talked to him and he just had this cold—I feel fucked up—attitude."

"I won't apologize to you for how this happened. I won't apologize for something I did not do."

"That said, it all went very civilly. We weren't screaming or anything, and in the end we shook hands. In my mind, I was accepting that we were parting ways and would go our own separate ways and do the best we could."

Murphy was sent back to the line and made a team leader at Alpha Company's 1st Platoon.

"I get there, and I am there for—I am not fucking kidding you—twenty-four hours, and the platoon sergeant gets fired," he said. "He gets the can and the new platoon sergeant who gets brought in to take over 1st Platoon, A/co, 3/75? Who is that? *Jared Van Aalst.*

"Holy shit. Do I have the worst fucking luck in the world?"

It turns out Murphy's new home had a reputation that went all the way up to USASOC, and it wasn't exactly a sterling one at that. The "Glory Boys" of 1st Platoon were widely considered cowboys and Van Aalst had been rewarded with a coveted position as a platoon sergeant of a rifle platoon—even though it meant leaving the sniper platoon he had nurtured just as it was poised to truly live up to its potential. However, the promotion came with the expectation that he would rein the wayward platoon back in check, and his history as an exacting taskmaster made him the ideal candidate to do exactly that.

According to Murphy, "The platoon always had a reputation for being out of control, so who do you send to take over for an inept platoon sergeant? Someone who is a fucking Nazi like VA who will dig into every little detail of every goddamn thing. He'd get pissed off at you for the way you filled up a water can."

As it turns out, the two proceeded to work together in a highly productive, professional manner when removed from the 3/75 Sniper Platoon pressure cooker. And it's a good thing too because their subsequent deployment in Iraq would prove intense.

"That antagonism wasn't there like it was before. Professionally, we worked together well. But personally, I never forgave him and I always fucking hated him."

◈

As the operations stacked up during the summer of 2005, so too did the kill count for 3rd Battalion's sniper platoon, and in turn, the number of believers it had inside battalion.

During Burkhart's first deployment as a sniper, Task Force Red captured more than six hundred insurgents and killed well over a hundred during their three-month deployment in the Mosul region of the country.

"Approximately 75 percent of those kills came from just our two sniper teams," he said. "It was just crazy. It was Wild West shit.

"That deployment really set the bar for how everybody else perceived our sniper platoon. Before that, it was, 'Oh, whatever. Snipers, we don't really need them. We can take care of all the stuff ourselves.' I think they really realized how much of an asset we were and how much of a ground force multiplier we were. It set the tone for the next few years I was there."

Subsequently, Ranger officers actively sought the snipers' input during mission workups rather than simply directing (or outright dismissing) them.

"It's funny—as soon as you kill a few people for them they totally change their tune," Burkhart added with a laugh. "It was bullshit that it took that, but yeah, it was really good. I see that as the turning point for us and that was when Iraq was really ramping up. Really, *really* ramping up. It was nuts there. It was just craziness."

❖

While the 3/75 sniper platoon played a somewhat more robust—or at least varied—role during the prior deployment to Afghanistan, that was the product of a less-than-scorching pace and a desire to find a niche in which they could effectively contribute. However, in Iraq the platoons were constantly hitting objectives and the snipers' capabilities were now very much in demand.

As a result, over the next few years, they would serve purely as direct action snipers. Recon ops would have to be shelved until another time and another AO.

"Nah, man—you're not ISR," a former 3/75 sniper said. "You already have other elements out there doing that stuff, you know what I mean? If you did that, you could burn the target and then it was over. The thing was, we were rolling out every night and it was time sensitive. You didn't have time to go out there and do your thing. [The platoons] were constantly on the move."

❖

"When the war first started out, nobody knew what to do with the augmentees, like the snipers and stuff," former 3/75 sniper team leader GM said. "Now everyone knows what to do with them—the dogs, the snipers . . . everyone knows the job."

Burkhart added, "I learned the way from my first team leader and I took that and ran with it. It kind of evolved a little bit. They gave us a lot of freedom after those first couple of deployments. Everything was going so well that most people kind of stayed off our backs."

The 3/75 Ranger snipers had hundreds upon hundreds of raids with which to perfect their methodology and practices in a sort of twisted, death-dealing take on *Groundhog Day*.

The snipers had to quickly absorb intel on their next objective and plan accordingly. After the team leaders and squad leaders were paged ahead of an operation, the sniper team leader would report to the Joint Operations Center to be brought up to speed.

"Okay, this guy's cell phone is locked," Burkhart said, providing an example. "I would talk to my F2—the intelligence guys at the JOC who could print out the GRG [grid reference graphic, a black-and-white satellite overview of the target area superimposed on a numbered grid]."

The GRG was then used to study shadows to determine the heights of potential overwatch perches. "Okay, here's the target house. . . . Where do we want to go? Do we want to go on the back side or do we want to go on the front side?"

The sniper team leader would generally confer with the platoon sergeant he was supporting, offer suggestions, and then take the assault team's preference into account.

GM said, "After a while, when you're working with a platoon, you know how they act and you can brief it in a split second. I'll do this and this. You look at a map and know instantly, I'll go on this roof right here."

Initially, the snipers leaned toward setting up on the back side of target buildings ("that's where the insurgents always ran to escape"). However, that all changed when a 3/75 Ranger platoon was ambushed during the '05 deployment in Tal Afar, a city located fifty kilometers west of Mosul.

A terrorist training complex had been established in Tal Afar to train the foreign fighters pouring in from Syria, and thus became a primary hunting ground for the 75th Ranger Regiment.

When an unsuspecting assault force approached their target house, they were greeted in the courtyard by a bombardment of grenades from awaiting insurgents.

"These guys had chutes built almost like rain gutters and they snuck up on the rooftop and started hammering them with grenades," Burkhart said. "They came popping out in the courtyard where you had a whole platoon of guys. They got pretty messed up."

After that, the rooftops became a heightened priority. "Even though we had ISR flying above us, those guys are fast enough that they can act before you have a chance to communicate, 'Hey, there's dudes up there.'"

Once a workable overwatch location was identified, the snipers would typically head out toward the target with the assault team in vehicles only to be dropped off a kilometer or so short in order to maneuver into position on foot.

GM explained, "They'd let you out first, and you'd run up first and set up before the element. Call up and tell them you're set and they'd move up. You had to be quick because if anybody gets wind, they call each other and it's all lost."

Actually getting into position occasionally required its own special tools and skill set. For direct action snipers in an urban environment, the ability to scale buildings is every bit as vital as their talents as a marksman.

"We had these backpack ladders with hooks on them," Burkhart said. "We'd climb some random building. I'd even carry a climbing aider in my pocket so I could climb ledges and terraces. It was kind of sketchy, now that I think back on it. There would be a lot of times you'd be like forty feet off the ground and if you fell you'd just land on the pavement below."

Working almost exclusively at night forced the Ranger snipers to make heavy use of Mil-Dot range estimation—the process of acquiring distance utilizing the milliradian reticles found on their optics, the known height or width of an object in the distance, and a simple trigonometric equation.

"We really worked on not having to dial in our scopes," Burkhart said. "We didn't have night-vision rangefinders and everything we did was at night so I couldn't look at something and go, 'Oh, that's five hundred meters away.' I had to estimate and hopefully hit the guy when I put a round downrange.

"I think that's why guys in Ranger Battalion had such an advantage and were so much more effective than a lot of units. We shot so much and we were always on the range. We put in an amazing amount of time just getting that feel, that muscle memory."

During training, 3/75 snipers would practice this skill by first estimating the range with their eyes and their Mil-Dots and then confirm the actual distance with a laser rangefinder.

Experience operating in Iraq proved crucial too because markers back home didn't necessarily translate. "I went to Iraq so much, I got really used to certain things," Burkhart explained. "How big certain things are and how they should look from a certain distance away. Cars over there are smaller than in the USA, especially like the full-size pickup trucks. When you're looking at vehicles, you kind of have to judge like what does a little Toyota pickup truck look like compared to a full-size pickup truck."

Once in position, the platoon would be notified and begin their advance while the snipers trained their SR-25s on the target in anticipation of whatever was to follow.

GM explained, "The assault element would go do their thing, and we'd be overwatch making sure nobody climbed up on a roof to do anything or run out the back side. It was an evolution. You would call up too. I was constantly looking through windows with my scope. 'Hey, you've got people moving around.'"

"A lot of times nothing would happen," Burkhart added. "Most of the time, nothing would happen. But when it did, it was generally pretty chaotic."

◈

Late in their 2005 deployment to Mosul, 3rd Battalion located and eliminated Abu Zayd, al-Qaeda's emir of Mosul.

Just a month earlier, he made headlines when a Task Force Red raid intercepted a scathing letter penned by Zayd and intended for Abu al-Zarqawi. Zayd's growing desperation in the wake of the Rangers' nonstop assaults was obvious, as he complained of the local insurgents' lessened ability to carry out meaningful attacks while warning that Mosul could soon be lost too.

In early September, the Rangers raided a safe house in Zanazil. Four terrorists were rounded up in the hit while Zayd was gunned down in a nearby field.

The following spring 3/75 was back in country and operating north of

Baghdad, albeit this time in the Samarra/Tikrit area. And again, they dispatched another of the ten most wanted terrorists in country.

In late April 2006, Hamadi 'Abd al-Tahki al-Nissani, the emir of Samarra and Tikrit, was tracked to a location some fifteen kilometers north of Samarra.

The Rangers hit the compound in two MH-60 Black Hawks, rushing in low and landing on the "X"—less than one hundred meters from the target—in an L-shaped formation to isolate and contain the area.

The assault team breached the compound and immediately engaged in a heated firefight. Two terrorists inside the house were quickly killed, including one as he attempted to lob a grenade at the Rangers.

"And this other guy pops outside of a window," Burkhart recalled. "My sniper buddy, Jake, and I were the first guys off the Black Hawk. It was this crazy brownout with dust everywhere."

A tall and rotund figure emerged from the building and charged straight for the Black Hawk with his AK-47 in hand. It wasn't some ill-advised but admirable mad charge for the attacking force. Rather, the man was confused and disorientated by the swirling dirt and sounds created by the aircraft. Instead of escaping his fate, he sprinted directly to it.

Burkhart said, "We were moving toward the building. We were going to go set up in cover and secure the building, and the guy happened to be coming right at us. We didn't even use our scopes; we just used the lasers on our SR-25s.

"Jake and I both fired at the exact same time. He aimed the chest. I aimed the head. We both got the guy and he dropped."

The assault element that had dismounted the Black Hawk just behind the snipers followed suit, firing at the fallen man who would later be positively identified as Hamadi Tahki.

"The rest of the guys opened up and popped another twenty rounds into him. Everybody was like, 'We got him. We got him!'"

Burkhart laughed. "It's always a group effort."

◈

While built around rotating Ranger battalions, JSOC's task force in the north of the country also included a small Delta component. As the Rangers pulled off missions and targeted HVTs that previously only would have been tasked to a Tier 1 unit, the Mosul-based Unit operators elevated their operations to the next level yet.

B Squadron's deployment schedule was synced up with that of 3rd Battalion, allowing the two entities to develop enhanced coordination over time.

And while 3/75 was regularly adding X marks to the most wanted poster in the JOC with a succession of violent raids, a five-man recce element was doing the same in a considerably more clandestine fashion.

During the same '05 deployment in which the Rangers took out Abu Zayd, a small Delta sniper element led by "RS"—a B Squadron recce troop Sergeant Major—operated inside Mosul and the surrounding vicinity disguised as locals. Outfitted in Middle Eastern garments called *twabs*—but almost universally referred to by the American servicemen as "man dresses"—RS and his team tracked down their prey utilizing stealth and subterfuge.

"What these Delta guys were doing was basically assassinations," one ex-Ranger said. "They were going out and just whackin' guys left and right. We were there as a QRF just in case they really got into something and we'd be thirty seconds out so we could respond."

Another 3/75 Ranger added, "[RS] has probably killed more guys than cancer. He was doing low-vis target interdictions, vehicle to vehicle. It was basically high-level drive-by shootings."

10

Punishment Due

By the conclusion of his first combat deployment as a U.S. SEAL Sniper Course–trained sniper, Chris Kyle had stacked up enough confirmed kills to solidly establish himself as one of the most lethal snipers in American military history.

Word of his accomplishments had just started filtering through the usual SEAL channels, but Kyle's status as an emerging historical figure was still largely unknown. However, one SEAL officer was keenly aware of what the big Texan had been up to.

The last time Lt. Larry Yatch had seen Kyle he was just another new guy on his first deployment. He wasn't "the Legend" at that point. If anything he had been rather unremarkable, although that was considered a positive in itself because it meant he hadn't done anything terribly boneheaded to draw attention to himself as new guys tend to do.

It's not as if he had many opportunities to stand out either. Their shared deployment back in 2003 just as the Iraq War was kicking off had been disheartening to all of Team Three—and an utter debacle in the eyes of both Yatch and Kyle, who had expected so much more from their first experience in combat.

SEAL Team Three's embarrassing opening in Iraq had been softened somewhat by the deeds of its snipers the following year in the Second

Battle of Fallujah and elsewhere, albeit largely in an augmentee capacity rather than as part of a larger ST3 campaign.

But now the SEAL officer was placed in a position to address the deficiencies that had afflicted the Teams from the ground floor. Following his '03 deployment, Yatch was assigned two senior chiefs, a warrant officer, and a mammoth task: to head up Naval Special Warfare Group One's nascent internal intelligence effort, then known as "NSWG-1 Special Activities."

It also provided him an opportunity to closely monitor Kyle's mounting success in Iraq. He paid closer attention than he normally might due to the fact that the Texan hailed from Team Three's CHARLIE platoon— Yatch's former outfit back when his was a third O. And its OIC, Lt. Leif Babin, was also an old friend. Their connection went back to their very first day at the Naval Academy together, further solidifying his interest.

And what he observed astonished him. "At Group One I spent a lot of time reading the intel traffic," the SEAL officer said. "I remember very vividly reading all of those after-action reports and just being amazed."

The macabre statistics alone were undeniable. "You'd read that he'd had nineteen confirmed kills in a twenty-four-hour period. It was almost unbelievable. It was also neat to read that those guys were finally getting into it. That was a testament to the leadership."

◆

Whereas the Joint Special Operations Command—including SEAL Team Six—had hugely benefited from its amped-up intelligence emphasis, the vanilla SEALs had found themselves handcuffed. Worse than that, they'd even needlessly been put into danger on occasion due to an ill-suited ad hoc intelligence apparatus—one devised for blue water analysis, not commando raids.

JSOC was increasingly able to parlay the efforts of its organic assets into actionable intelligence. The Activity efficiently secured high-tech signals and low-tech human intelligence in order to "prepare the environment." Meanwhile, this effort was further augmented by the AFO capabilities provided by its special mission units' recce snipers.

Without the ability to find and fix, JSOC's much-vaunted finishers would have been relegated nonfactors. And in fact, they too had been largely caged prior to the world-altering strikes on the World Trade Towers and the Pentagon, and even in its immediate wake. But by late in 2004, JSOC's shooters were finishing Iraq's innumerable targets in extraordinary numbers.

However, this capability was virtually nonexistent on the "white" side of American special operations—as evidenced by the inability of the SEALs to operate effectively once the Iraq War set into motion, along with the need for Naval Special Warfare Group One to divvy up the integral intelligence section of Task Unit Raider for use by CJSOTF-AP's SEAL task units.

In an attempt to transform this weakness into a strength, Lt. Yatch precommissioned the SEAL's own "Activity": NSWG-1 Special Activities grew into what officially became known as "Naval Special Warfare Support Activity One."

Support Activity One was designed to provide the regular SEAL Teams with its own Activity/AFO analogue of sorts, which would allow it to develop actionable intelligence internally. And it would, in part, recruit from the ranks of the SEALs to do so.

While clearly influenced by JSOC's more recent successes, its inspiration actually traced back considerably further.

"This was in the effort of what we call preparing the battlefield," Yatch explained. "The philosophy was to go in ahead of time and make sure we were more successful. But really it was going back to our core tactics that allowed the SEALs to be so effective in Vietnam. There, SEALs went out, gathered intelligence, processed that intelligence, got other forms of intelligence where needed, planned the next op, and then executed it. It was a closed loop."

Intelligence developed outside the Teams and later handed off for them to execute too often resulted in missions that went sideways. "It was either not good enough, old, or just plain wrong," Yatch said. "With the SEALs developing their own intelligence, they could actually plan and execute missions very effectively because they knew the degree of reliability of their intel. We got away from that after Vietnam."

Following the humiliation of Team Three's initial foray in the Iraq War, Larry was motivated to bring about change. "We got back from that and learned and said, 'We need to go back to our roots.'"

Initially, a number of hand-picked SEALs would receive specialized training—either ASOT (Advanced Special Operations Techniques) or AFO (the aforementioned Advance Force Operations). Those who trained in ASOT would focus on human intelligence—developing and running sources. Meanwhile, the SEALs with advanced AFO training would learn to use technology to support the ASOT operations, along with individual platoons, by gathering and collecting intelligence through tracking and tagging items by means of technical surveillance.

Having recently tracked Kyle's exploits in Fallujah and elsewhere, when it came time to select an all-star team of operators to provide Naval Special Warfare with this enhanced capability, Yatch was quick to recruit the Texan to complete the three-month AFO pipeline.

"After Chris's platoon got back [in 2005], I was ramping up the Support Activity," he said. "When we're looking to pull people into this—which is a very sensitive group—of course I'm going to pick Chris."

Kyle was sent to New Orleans where he learned basic electronics and the finer points of building and utilizing covert camera systems. He was taught how to conduct countersurveillance, both on foot and in vehicles, along with surreptitious entry—picking locks and "borrowing" other people's cars when necessary (for example, to successfully complete his training).

Just as he added sniper and navigation skills to his toolset following his first deployment, Kyle learned to operate in a manner closer to a DEVGRU Black Team sniper following his second. His training was now loosely akin to what the real-world realization of the Hollywood fantasy that is James Bond or Jason Bourne might be—well, with a thick Texas drawl anyway.

Despite the new assortment of skills, Kyle's focus immediately snapped back into sniper mode when he redeployed in 2006. And he was presented with what can only be described as a target-rich environment in the city of Ramadi.

The reverberations of the remarkably violent offensive that unhinged AQI from its booby-trapped stronghold of Fallujah were felt some twenty-five miles west in Ramadi.

The capital of Anbar Province and home to a half-million residents, Ramadi replaced Fallujah as the most dangerous city on the planet in '05 and '06. This was no coincidence—following the dedicated campaign to rip Zarqawi's forces from Fallujah, al-Qaeda in Iraq regrouped, picked up shop, and reestablished their business of dealing out widespread slaughter from a new central location.

Ramadi now stood as the destination point for foreign jihadists who flooded into the nation, driven by a confused notion of achieving paradise by bringing about hell.

In April 2006, Zarqawi's men launched multiple simultaneous attacks in the city, setting about the conditions for another coalition/insurgent showdown.

Contrary to the unrestrained leveling of Fallujah, a combined American-Iraqi force of nearly eight thousand soldiers planned a more deliberate attack on Ramadi. The brunt of the fire and manpower would be delivered by conventional Marine and big Army forces—the 1st Armored Division; I MEF; the 1st, 2nd, and 3rd Infantry Divisions; and the 101st Airborne Division chief among them. However, mobile SEAL sniper elements would provide precision fire and overwatch throughout.

◈

It was at the Battle of Ramadi that Chris Kyle became more than just an accomplished sniper; he established himself a transcendent warrior—a symbol to friend and foe alike.

Seemingly more at ease on the two-way range than he was back in the nation he risked his life to defend, Kyle took pleasure and pride in removing unprecedented numbers of enemies from the fight.

Kyle slaughtered leagues of insurgents in Ramadi. His accumulating confirmed kill tally not only quickly surpassed that of Carlos Hathcock, but also Hathcock's USMC contemporaries Eric England and Chuck Mawhinney, along with that of Vietnam-era Army sniper Adelbert Waldron III. The SEAL had established himself the most lethal sniper in American military history and showed no signs of relenting.

And it wasn't just the prolific kill count that was reminiscent of Hathcock—it was also the stories that came along with each successive notch.

The Texan first earned his "Legend" tag back at Fallujah in 2004 when he delivered a kill shot from his .300 Win Mag from sixteen hundred yards away. Later, he would one-up that. To prevent the ambush of an Army convoy, he eliminated an RPG-armed terrorist from a distance of twenty-one hundred yards with a .338 Lapua.

Reflecting on Kyle's long-distance kills, former Black Team sniper Howard Wasdin just shook his head. "There was a point I was arrogant enough to say you don't need any luck. But a sixteen-hundred-yard shot? Okay, you've got to be good—you really need to refine your breathing and squeezing skills, eye relief, shoulder placement, all that. But you still have to have a little bit of luck."

Kyle's mentor, Davis, added, "There are a lot of variables involved in making shots at those sorts of distances. That speaks to the skill set, meaning the hard-set scientific skills that go into shooting. He embodied that through practice and experience and with an intellect that I think was probably superior than we know."

In Fallujah, Kyle also creatively (and merrily) dispatched more than a dozen heavily armored targets. To do so, he shot their makeshift amphibious personnel carrier (read: beach balls) out from underneath them.

And in Ramadi, Kyle added another to the oddity column by scoring a double moped kill.

Following an eight-hour firefight alongside the Marines, Kyle noticed that the appearance of scooters was all too frequently a sign of impending danger. "Five minutes after that scooter disappeared, indirect fire was coming in—mortars and rockets. After the fires were done, the scooter would come back. He was redirecting their fires."

The SEAL requested permission to be cleared hot to engage anybody on a scooter, which was promptly denied by the JAG.

"Forty-eight hours after we made that request—they'd already denied it, so there's no way in hell you can do it—we're back out," Kyle later explained. "I see these two guys on a moped, which first of all, if you see two guys on a moped, that right there should be grounds to shoot. . . ."

The scooter slowed and its passenger dropped a backpack into a hole in the road along a major supply route.

"Ooh—that's within my rules of engagement. That's an IED."

Kyle woke up the rest of the house and invited them to the impromptu show.

"Watch this—I'm fixing to get two with one."

Unaware they had a .300 Win Mag trained on them, the scooter duo headed directly toward the awaiting sniper. When they got within two hundred yards, Kyle pulled the trigger.

He said, "It looked like *Dumb and Dumber*. The guy's dead, but his hands are still on the handlebars. And he smacks into a wall. It was hilarious."

Apparently, the Navy's legal representative didn't share Kyle's sense of humor. Kyle said, "Soon as I got back the JAG investigated me."

"What? No . . . he dropped that. I have all these witnesses. I woke everybody up in the house."

Six hours later the pothole was examined and nothing was found. However, Kyle was ultimately cleared of any wrongdoing, thanks in large part to the eyewitness account of a Marine element at a neighboring OP.

◈

Besides the kills and the anecdotes, Chris Kyle earned himself a serious reputation in the same way Carlos Hathcock had before him—and not only among those his rifle protected.

To the Americans, he was "the Legend"—a moniker that was used less and less ironically with each successive kill.

And to those on the other side of the battle lines—at least among those who survived to spread their warnings of oncoming dread—he was "Shaitan Ar-Ramadi"—the Devil of Ramadi.

Along with that honor came another sign of respect for his architecture of aggression: a bounty on his head large enough ($80,000) that Kyle joked it might just tempt his wife to cash in.

He and the rest of his platoon embraced the notoriety. They played it up and actively instilled fear in their adversaries by adopting the demonic skull logo of the comic book vigilante "the Punisher" as their own.

"We put it on our body armor, our helmets, we'd put it on everything," Kyle explained. "I mean, if you look back at the Punisher, he was going back to right a wrong. He was going back for vengeance, to get rid of the bad guys. We were going back to right a wrong. We're going to get rid of these bad guys, and that was the symbol."

After the platoon killed enemy insurgents, they'd stencil the logo in the immediate vicinity to let their enemies know who was responsible. They even dared further attacks by adorning their Humvees with the symbol.

Kyle said, "PSYOPS . . . 'We were here. We're the guys that are going to fuck you up. You mess with us and you mess with America, we're the guys coming in and take you out.' We wore it on us so that they would know, 'Oh, shit, those guys are in our area.'"

At the Battle of Ramadi, Kyle stood as a combatant at the peak of his existence. He lived for the fight and was thoroughly convinced of his invincibility. This unique combination of talent, training, experience, and boundless confidence made him the rare example of a man on the ground with the ability to singlehandedly turn the tide of battles.

Lt. Yatch reflected, "What Chris was able to do was unique to him. . . . It's very rare in modern times that you have an individual who is able to make contributions that are unique, and without them, those contributions would not be possible. The end results would not have been the same. The right scenario was in place so that the right culmination of skills, mentality, and raw ability existed in the man that was in a position to do so."

Former U.S. SEAL Sniper Course Manager Brandon Webb added, "The stars aligned and he was in the right place at the right time."

◉

Kyle was one of the first graduates of the modernized program to field test its lessons. He would soon be joined by a host of marksmen with similar abilities.

"Chris would want to point out that there are probably twenty guys in the SEAL community who have almost as many kills as he did," Webb said. "These guys are deadly. It doesn't matter if you're a DEVGRU guy or at a regular SEAL team, the main training course is the NSW course. They've all got to go through the SEAL sniper program. And these guys are out there and just lethal.

"The proof is in the pudding, right? It's like someone graduating from an MBA program and going out and building a billion-dollar company. We've got guys like Chris and other guys you don't hear about just wasting guys overseas."

Soon the SEAL Sniper Course schoolhouse would be receiving calls from the Army and the Marine Corps asking for their secrets of success.

"Man, what the fuck are you teaching these dudes? They are over here just fricking laying waste."

"Then we started getting foreign spec ops units. The Danes and Norwegians started sending guys over and the Germans were calling us. Everyone wanted to know how we were training these guys."

Even though Kyle was actually in a tight race to claim the top spot in the all-time American sniper kill category during his run in Ramadi, his unique presence made him a natural to serve as an unofficial ambassador for those sailors sending rounds downrange with deadly accuracy during the Global War on Terror. As his celebrity grew—first inside the SOF community and later in the wider public—Kyle would come to represent SEAL snipers as a whole.

In the same way Hathcock put the Marine Scout Sniper program on the map, Kyle forced the sniper world to wake up and recognize the effectiveness of the radically overhauled SEAL training. His exploits put a face on what was actually a much wider trend.

Webb said, "Now, I think because Chris was this big, friendly Texan and a personality among personalities, that's how he got elevated into the spotlight. They called him the Legend and that got out to his friends and family. But he was a widely known personality in the SEAL community. We get guys like that who come along every so often. Chris was definitely that guy of his era.

"The same way Hathcock was that guy for the Marine Corps back in his day. You had a lot of Marine snipers in Vietnam, but Hathcock was the guy that stood out because he had a little bit of a swagger behind him, he had the competitive shooting team background, and he did a lot to elevate the tradecraft."

Webb furthered the comparison: "Hathcock had a really big influence on the Marine Corps course and it's a solid program. He had all these confirmed kills and that book, *Marine Sniper,* came out, which was like *American Sniper* in the '80s. I think there's a lot of similarities there. The way that Hathcock brought awareness to the Marine Corps Scout Sniper program, I think Chris Kyle has really raised awareness of the SEAL program. Before him a lot of people didn't even realize that the SEALs have their own sniper course and it's one of the best in the world.

"Hathcock became this cult figure among the sniper community. And now Chris Kyle has done the same in his time."

◈

A longtime East Coast SEAL sniper instructor first got word about Kyle's exploits from one of his former students. "One of the East Coast guys told me they heard one of our snipers had 150 kills. *"Holy shit."* I did the math— that meant he was getting one guy every third day . . . unbelievable. It was such a target-rich environment.

"He was an above-average shooter, he had the right mind-set, and he was in the right place at the right time. But he was nowhere near our best."

The instructor compared the situation in Iraq as comparable to what snipers faced during WWII in the Battle of Stalingrad ("very aggressive—you see a bad guy, you shoot").

He added that for every Chris Kyle there were several others with similar accomplishments who went unrecognized. "There are lots of guys you'll never hear about. There's one guy in particular who is very, very professional. Others are still out there doing it—they just keep going back. One is an absolute ass kicker. He's extra-prepared, patient, and has all the shot solutions in his head."

The instructor said he knows of one SEAL sniper who racked up more than Kyle's combined total ("and not just a little more") over the course of just a few days by directing in air strikes.

The Second Battle of Fallujah marked the beginning of a shift, and this new breed of SEAL snipers were prepared and in position to rise to the occasion.

"This is how it happened—the ROE [rules of engagement] changed overnight," the former instructor explained. "Those bad guys thought they were safe and were just out there walking around. But our guys knew ROE was going to change and were gearing up for it. As soon as it happened, they were dropping them like flies. The insurgents were getting their asses kicked so bad, they were literally crawling into cemeteries and digging graves to hide in. That's some badass shit right there.

"It was unprecedented sniping in military history. And these guys were incredibly well trained. The guys from the '90s and early 2000s stepped up and made sure the new generation coming through the program would be ready to go."

He added, "Chris Kyle is representative of an amazing generation of truly dedicated guys. I know one who was making $450,000 on Wall Street—his dad told me—and after 9/11 he joined the Navy, went through

BUD/S, and then came to the sniper school in 2005. Just think of all he sacrificed."

◈

"The Punishers" gradually developed an SOP (standard operating practice) that invited regular, extended firefights. They would take down a building and then transform it into a sniper hide. Once a target was identified, Kyle or another of the element's snipers, such as Kevin "Dauber" Lacz, would pull the trigger, transforming their hide into a defensive position in an instant.

At that point, they would bunker down and fend off the resultant counterattack. Well positioned—usually on the roof or behind an upper-story window—Kyle and his crew would pick off reinforcements as they attempted to rally to their location. Once the battle was won, they would head back out, find a new prime location, and repeat the process.

CHARLIE's confidence bordered on arrogance but the results backed up their belief. They considered themselves untouchable to the point of amusement, intentionally adding to the level of difficulty. For instance, they'd swap through their weapons just to chalk up a kill with each one— simply for the entertainment value.

"Hey, new guy . . . film this!"

"Combat was a daily event," Kyle recalled. "It starts happening, your training takes over. You start telling jokes to each other. Guys are laughing, high-fiving, saying, 'Hey, watch this one.' You're cool under fire. It's when the fire stops and when everything is done that your heartbeat starts to spike."

When he was back in the States, Kyle was subjected to virtual reality testing in an attempt to unlock the secrets of his, arguably, irrational calm when confronted with such remarkable violence and peril.

He explained, "They wanted to do this experimental type stuff to figure out the mind-set, heart rate, and all this other stuff of SEALs. They basically put us in this video game. It was a virtual thing. . . . It puts you right back into some scenarios you're in."

As it turned out, at that point, Kyle only felt vulnerable when subjected to virtual combat. After his platoon would come back to camp following a number of days in the field, the rest of the guys would immediately crash in bed. The Texan, however, would instead fire up his PC and play games long into the night (or day).

While typically more a connoisseur of sports titles like *Tiger Woods PGA Tour* or *Madden NFL*, he tried his hand at digitized warfare as well.

"The new *Call of Duty* came out and we had the headsets and we hooked up our whole camp so we could be playing each other from our rooms," Kyle explained. "We were going online with satellites and every-thing. I had a headset that one of my guys gave me and I'm sitting there playing. And the same kid keeps killing me and he was talking mad junk to me. I'm sitting there, and I'm getting *pissed*.

"He's cussing and everything. Come to find out, he's like a twelve-year-old kid back in America. He kept killing me, and he's like, 'I'm going to slay you.'

"*Motherfucker—when I get home, I'm going to sneak into your bedroom and I am taking you out. I'm a Navy SEAL!*"

"*Whatever. You're in your mama's basement.*"

Kyle laughed as he considered the surrealism of it all: "Oh, God—I couldn't handle the war games anymore. I just wanted to take that little kid out."

◈

In Kyle's eyes, his apparent invulnerability bordered on divine right. After fighting back an attempted assault on their hide, the SEAL moved through the building and into another room.

Just as he entered, a bullet aimed in his direction came straight through the window. At that moment, he fell back and slumped onto the floor as the round soared safely—albeit inches—over his head.

"*Chris is dead! Chris has been shot!*"

"*What? No—I'm good. I'm good!*"

"Holy shit."

"Well, I don't think I fell back," Kyle admitted. "I honestly think I had a guardian angel; I think I was pushed down. When you're being shot at, when would you ever just fall straight back? You don't do it. If you're going to fall down to avoid it, you go to the side. . . . That's the only time where I just went straight back."

However, that illusion of invincibility would be shattered in Ramadi, replaced by a sense of inevitability that hung over the sniper for the remainder of his career.

After taking control of a four-story building to set up an overwatch for an Army infantry platoon, one of the Punishers—60 gunner Ryan "Biggles" Job—was gravely injured. Joking only moments earlier, the sniper team came under heavy fire and a bullet ricocheted off Job's rifle and struck his face.

After transporting Job back to Shark Base but fearing he had been mortally wounded, CHARLIE immediately went back out into the field in search of payback. Instead, they had taken the bait and stepped into a trap. Another of Kyle's closest friends, Marc Lee, was ambushed—shot through the head and killed in action.

Though left blind, Job survived his wounds. However, he died years later due to complications from surgery.

◉

Though Kyle had honestly believed he had a guardian angel watching over him, what the SEAL perhaps failed to recognize was that he *was* the guardian angel for so many others.

While outsiders sometimes look at snipers with morbid fascination, the shooters frequently see themselves as instruments of preserving life more than taking it.

Kyle served as a prime example of this motivation—perhaps better described as a compulsion. He channeled his dysfunction into something heroic and was both reckless and unrelenting in his efforts to save his fellow servicemen. He was merciless in their protection and repeatedly disregarded his own safety repeatedly to defend American troops.

Thomas "Drago" Dzieran grew up in Poland and spent time locked up in the Russian gulag before immigrating to the United States. There he became a SEAL while in his thirties and served from '91 to 2011.

Drago, who describes himself as "just American," reflected on Kyle's ability to use his extreme lethality in order to save the lives of others. He said, "We all know Chris's prowess as a SEAL, as an operator. But there is one aspect of Chris that seems to me is somewhat overlooked. Chris saved lives. People need to understand this.

"Chris saved lives while we were conducting our operations. When we were patrolling neighborhoods, he was the angel watching over our shoulders, watching over our heads, making sure that nobody could sneak up on us and take a shot at us. I see him as a great protector of coalition forces."

Black Team sniper Howard Wasdin understands the drive to protect. In the opening of his memoir, *SEAL Team Six,* Wasdin quoted Gunnery Sergeant Carlos Hathcock himself to get this mentality across.

Hathcock once said, "I like shooting, and I love hunting. But I never did enjoy killing anybody. It's my job. If I don't get those bastards, then they're gonna kill a lot of these kids dressed up like Marines."

Wasdin said, "People don't become a SEAL because they want to prove they're tough guys or say look at me I've got this trident on my chest. People get in because they have a special kind of love for their country that most people can't fathom.

"Before any op I ever went on, I never asked anyone's race, color, sexual preference . . . you know, all those things that divide groups. The only thing I ever asked was, 'Are these people Americans who need our help?' or 'Is this going to help the United States of America?' And if that was the case, okay, sign me up, I'm ready to go and I'm definitely ready to die if necessary."

Wasdin spoke directly about Kyle's contributions: "Anybody that looks at that man's career . . . anybody that really gets it knows it's not just about putting notches on your rifle butt. It's about that love and that compassion.

I heard that before you kill somebody, you're not supposed to think of what you're killing; you're supposed to think of what you're allowing to live. If you think of it in those terms, every time Chris pulled that trigger, he was not only allowing other Americans to live who could have potentially been killed by one of those booger-eaters, he was allowing the American way of life to go on."

◈

Kyle never did show any signs of disturbance or regret when contemplating the scores of men he killed—his conscience was clear as polished glass. However, he was endlessly haunted by those he was unable to save.

Following his breakthrough first deployment as a sniper in which he registered nearly one hundred kills, Kyle opened up to Larry Yatch after the two became close while together in New Orleans.

Yatch expressed an overriding sense of frustration with his career to that point. Their shared combat early in the Iraq War had been demoralizing. And even as he was precommissioning Support Activity One, Yatch strove for more.

The officer explained, "At that point I felt like I needed to get to the next thing; I needed to go to Dam Neck [SEAL Team Six]. If I could go to Dam Neck maybe I could finally do what a SEAL does and feel like I'm accomplished or that I've proven myself."

However, he was shocked to discover echoes of those same sentiments expressed by Kyle.

"*What about you?*"

"*I feel like a failure. Guys got hurt that I couldn't protect. There were all these times I wasn't able to—*"

"*Man, what the hell are you talking about? Of anyone, you're one of the few of us that can actually say you did something. . . .*"

"He said it wasn't about the success," Yatch recalled. "It wasn't about the kills. It wasn't about killing bad guys. It was about all the Marines, the Army guys, and his own SEALs that he couldn't keep from being killed or injured.

"He wasn't a taker of life. He was a giver of life. He judged his worth not on the number of people that he killed. He didn't even judge it on the number of people that he saved. He saw it as his duty to save everyone. He judged his worth on the number of people he was not able to save. And that's why it ate at him on being unsuccessful—on being a failure."

The conversation altered the direction of Yatch's career. He realized that even if Chris Kyle—the SEAL he could point to who had lived up to what it means to be a SEAL and executed it beyond any other—could not be satisfied with his accomplishments, that was something he needed to accept about himself as well.

"Chris not only changed the tide of battles and saved hundreds, if not thousands of lives, he took thousands of enemy combatants off the battlefield," Yatch said. "Yeah, there's two or three hundred actual dead but there's also four to five for every one that gets killed, between dealing with their dead or just going, 'You know what? I'm not going to do this anymore because I just saw my friend's head explode.' Chris had taken thousands off the battlefield within a couple month period and that changed the tide of battle. He was the only person who could have done that—it's not like he was in a jet dropping a bomb that anyone could have dropped.

"And yet he viewed himself as a failure. That gave me the permission to accept that I will never be fulfilled and that's okay. I had to accept that and stop worrying about it.

"He was not unique among SEALs—but he was one of the best among SEALs. He was a great sniper. There are many other snipers who can and would have done what he did. He just did it better. Every SEAL has a mentality of feeling like a failure even though there's perfect execution. He just took it to the extreme."

◈

By the conclusion of the Battle of Ramadi more than a hundred coalition and Iraqi troops had been killed with multiple more wounded. Estimates placed the number of insurgents dead at 750 or more.

Ramadi was made considerably safer in the process, and the battle showed hints of a larger shift in the conflict. While the sectarian civil war had once appeared to be an unstoppable, self-perpetuating tidal wave of bloodshed, an "awakening" of sorts was taking place that would play a pivotal role in reestablishing some semblance of order in the war-torn nation.

The Anbar Awakening first came about in 2005 as the Sunni nationalists found themselves increasingly at odds with their alleged associates—the foreign radical Sunnis of al-Qaeda in Iraq. Realizing they had been coopted by AQI and their motivations were not actually, intrinsically linked, the Sunni militias turned on their allies.

The movement picked up momentum as the Battle of Ramadi raged, fueled by what was seen as an attempt by the AQI terrorists to pivot the might of coalition forces toward the indigenous Sunni tribes.

SEAL Team Three's Task Unit Bruiser had provided a disproportionate contribution to the victory as well, winding up the most decorated unit in CJSOTF-AP.

In addition to the achievements of Kyle and CHARLIE platoon—along with the untold success of the nameless SEAL snipers who performed at a similar level during the battle—one SEAL was posthumously awarded the Medal of Honor.

Michael Monsoor, a member of Kyle's sister platoon, had previously earned a Silver Star dragging a wounded comrade to safety, along with a Bronze Star.

On September 29, 2006, he threw himself on a grenade to save the lives of two SEAL snipers who were holding down overwatch for a Delta platoon assault element. Monsoor, who was pulling security duty for the snipers, was the only man positioned to escape the hide site but instead he chose to sacrifice himself to save them.

11

The Bullet Does Not Lie

With JSOC's Find-Fix-Finish-Exploit-Analyze war plan in full effect, Delta Force took a bloody fight to al-Qaeda's doorsteps—literally—with nearly immeasurable violence and intensity, night after night, for months on end.

In 2005, many viewed the Iraq War as unwinnable. Besides an endless stream of reinforcements on either side of the civil war that could be drawn from the local populace, there was a continuous flood of foreign fighters into Iraq who came simply to wage jihad against the Americans.

JSOC embraced the impossible challenge. The plan was not so much to disrupt al-Qaeda's multithreaded networks as it was to disintegrate them, cutting down the amorphous organization quicker than it could be repopulated.

However, the brutal reality is what that required could not be accomplished without considerable sacrifice. The most highly trained warfighters the nation had ever produced put their lives on the line repeatedly—some operators exceeded one thousand combat operations—in order to execute the radically ambitious campaign.

And despite their overwhelming advantage in terms of training and technology, sooner or later, significant losses were inevitable. And Delta Force paid a heavy toll indeed for its collective heroism.

A former 3/75 Ranger who was in country at the time said, "East Iraq was going crazy in 2005. And CAG got their ass handed to them one deployment."

The situation was so dire that DEVGRU assaulters were redirected from Afghanistan to help augment Delta troops and serve as substitute Unit assaulters. Meanwhile, the British SAS put together a collection to donate to the widows and orphans of Unit KIA.

It's been reported that the Unit's casualty rate was near 20 percent during this time, with more than half being wounded in action.

Every successive "eagle down" represented the loss of an epic warrior. Each loss was as damaging as the last . . . and the next.

But one in particular seemed to reverberate with an added sense of despair. And it bit painfully deep inside both the 75th Ranger Regiment's 3rd Battalion and Delta's B Squadron recce troop.

◈

Robert Horrigan—who had played such a pivotal role in Operation Anaconda in early 2002—was widely considered the quintessential Delta Force recce operator.

He was a gifted tracker, remarkably fit, and mentally unbreakable. His endurance and dedication were legendary in the community, but so too was his kind, gregarious nature—a laid-back Texas boy who actively sought to help others in order ease their burden.

While Horrigan was on his eighth combat deployment in 2005 with nearly two decades of SOF experience under his belt, those years merely represented the finishing touches of an education that had taken place his entire life.

Born in Maine before moving to the Austin area, he grew up in the woods, hunting and fishing alongside his identical twin brother, John.

That's not an uncommon tale among SOF snipers; an inordinate number were shooting rifles and developing their fieldcraft instincts years before they ever joined the service.

Former DEVGRU sniper Craig Sawyer, who grew up in southern Texas himself, explained, "I think it's just part of the culture, growing up hunting and target shooting out in the woods. I guess just being raised in that culture, you're more familiar dealing with all that stuff. Your rifle almost becomes part of you, you know? With the urban hits and quick raids—in and out—it's not such a big deal with the NVGs and lasers and all that. But when you do the slow, deliberate recons and the more traditional sniper roles, those field skills really come out."

Delta sniper Don Hollenbaugh, another country boy from a small town, said, "Maybe because you're bored as a kid, you need some exhilaration in your life. 'I'm going to do something unique.' And snipers, all they are is hunters. They're just hunting a different cat."

As teenagers, the Horrigan brothers even formed their own juvenile "paramilitary" force—the Manchaca Liberation Organization—with some high school friends for the fun it. The MLO was mostly harmless; they would get decked out in fatigues and face paint and hone their budding tracking skills—and successfully avoid the police when a frightened neighbor woman would call 911. They were also just a bit devious. Two years running the MLO pulled off a clandestine operation at Crockett High School in Austin, Texas, rappelling into a courtyard and chopping down the Christmas tree with the declaration "MLO was here." And again, they avoided capture as the principal desperately sought the identities of the culprits.

After graduating high school in 1984, Bob and John Horrigan joined the Army where they would serve alongside one another in A Company of the 75th Ranger Regiment's 3rd Battalion, under the command of a young officer by the name of Stanley McChrystal.

In 1991, Horrigan joined Special Forces as an 18B (Weapons Sergeant) with the 7th Special Forces Group's ODA 721.

Ten years later, he was already a seasoned member of Delta's B Squadron recce troop and one of the men Lt. Col. Pete Blaber tasked with the most demanding and perilous missions in the wake of 9/11.

Horrigan would execute hundreds of additional missions following Operation Anaconda, transitioning from calling down air strikes upon snowy mountain peaks of Afghanistan to leading fellow heroes in the vicious alley and hallway gunfights of Iraq.

In June of 2005, Master Sergeant Horrigan was forty years old and only weeks away from returning home. Once back in the States, he was set to file his retirement papers, move back to Texas with his wife and daughter. There he would focus full-time on his passion as a bladesmith, making knives with his brother. He might even find the time to earn himself another Texas fishing state record or participate in some Iron Man Triathlons.

However, until then, he was still doggedly in pursuit of Zarqawi. Living up to his advanced assaulter tag, Horrigan was the first man through the door of a building in Al Qaim—a known Zarqawi compound.

As he burst through the room, he was shot and killed instantly. Another Delta operator, Michael L. McNulty (who also had an identical twin), was gunned down as well and would die hours later.

Retired Unit assaulter Larry Vickers said, "Bob went in and the dude was hiding in a corner. It was the last building in a compound and the guy was there waiting for them. Bob went in and didn't see him. The guy had zeroed in on him. They went in and the guy shot him and the other guy from the corner.

"And the saddest thing of the whole deal is he was two weeks from coming home and starting his retirement paperwork. Everybody was disturbed that he got killed the way he did. That would have made it sad in any case but he was such a well-liked guy."

Horrigan was awarded his third Bronze Star posthumously. His loss was a crushing blow inside the Unit as he had helped to shape its newer generation of operators serving as an OTC instructor and had a wide base of admirers inside Delta Force, among both its younger and more experienced soldiers.

Vickers added, "I don't know a single person who didn't like Bob Horrigan—extremely well-liked guy. Honestly, I don't know anybody who didn't. He was a really just engaging guy. He just seemed like one of those guys who could click with anybody. He was thoroughly likeable and very well respected operator."

◈

Following the deaths of Horrigan and McNulty—which came just over two weeks after fellow Delta solider, Sergeant First Class Steven Langmark, was killed in action in Al Qaim—McChrystal formally requested the aid of the UKSF's Task Force Black.

The UKSF declined due to contrasting rules of engagement and ongoing detention and interrogation concerns. This was to the dismay of SAS commander Richard Williams, who wanted the Special Air Service and Special Boat Service to redirect their focus and join JSOC's fight against AQI rather than continue to pick at the carcass of Hussein's defeated Ba'athist regime.

However, SBS's M Squadron was thrown into the fire a month later when JSOC shared critical intelligence relating to an al-Qaeda network as its forces were already overcommitted elsewhere.

In Operation Marlborough—which was executed jointly with the 75th Ranger Regiment and the ISA—SBS operators approached the target building both from the air and from the ground, with SBS snipers loaded in Puma helicopters in an aerial overwatch.

Immediately, a suicide bomber ran out of the compound and detonated himself just outside the target. The explosion very nearly caused one of the Pumas to crash into the rooftops below. Another Puma spotted a suicide-vest-laden squirter attempting a mad dash out the back. However, a heliborne SBS sharpshooter took him down with clutch accuracy.

The SBS assault team then proceeded to take down the objective, neutralizing a third suicide bomber inside.

The UKSF would continue to work in an increasingly tight fashion with JSOC as the war went on, gradually enmeshing operations to the point that they were essentially de facto JSOC special mission units themselves.

◈

The following year, B Squadron escalated the campaign to wipe out the elusive Zarqawi and acquire a measure of vengeance, blowing doors off hinges and clearing buildings with even greater intensity. Over a six-week span, Operation Arcadia resulted in the killing of more than a hundred AQI fighters. This push demonstrated the expansive powers JSOC had harnessed by 2006, fusing the intelligence obtained on site following each successive raid with that which was collected from the air, backed by the analysis of hundreds of hours of UAV footage.

During one particularly eventful weekend, B Squadron shredded through an entire network in the so-called Triangle of Death located southwest of Baghdad. On a single evening, Delta operators raided four houses in Latifiyah, taking out the gang's leader, Abu Mustafa, and more than a dozen of his men.

Supremely confident following their rolling sequence of assaults, the squadron hit another compound the following day, electing to go in without the cover of darkness in its favor. This proved to be a critical miscalculation that would have lethal consequences.

Under intense fire as quickly as they departed the 160th SOAR Black Hawks that ferried them to the objective, the Delta Force assaulters were pinned down. A Night Stalker AH-6M Little Bird was then knocked out of the sky by enemy fire while attempting to defend the Unit operators on the ground. The helicopter's pilots, Chief Warrant Officer 5 Jamie Week and Major Matthew Worrell, were killed in the crash.

The assault element continued to pursue its objective, killing more than two dozen terrorists and apprehending four more in the process. However, despite scoring a tactical victory in the face of overwhelming odds, B Squadron's top officer was relieved of his command due to the mission plan that was deemed over-the-top even considering the Unit's ultra-aggressive stance.

◈

Meanwhile, the close-knit collaborative relationship that formed between Delta's B Squadron recce snipers and their 3/75 counterparts was forged even stronger after they returned home following the '05 deployment to Mosul.

Multiple Rangers interviewed termed the Delta/Ranger relationship akin to one shared by a big brother and a little brother, and the B Squadron Delta snipers lived up to that unwritten contract, enthusiastically taking the Ranger snipers under their wing.

In '06, RS—the Delta recce Sergeant Major—invited the 3/75 Ranger sniper platoon up to the Unit's expansive, high-tech facility for a two-week advanced sniping master class.

According to one of the ten or so Ranger snipers who attended the session, "It was like drinking from a fire hose; it was the best training of my entire life."

RS and a couple of other snipers from his troop subjected the Rangers to Delta-style drills. They were instructed on the finer points of climbing and various other tricks of the trade. The Ranger snipers trained with shot timers, worked on barricade shooting, firing with both hands, learned unorthodox positions, and were even introduced to the low-vis vehicle interdiction techniques B Squadron's snipers had used with such lethal efficiency in Mosul.

"They treated us like we were one of them," a former Ranger said. "It was really nice. We used their gym and they have a frickin' Olympic-sized pool in their compound with diving platforms and everything. The place is an amazing complex."

The connection carried over to subsequent deployments as the Delta recce operators again took on the role of big brother. In 2007, the B and 3/75 snipers rotated into Baghdad.

A former regime palace in the Green Zone had been transformed into a sort of black SOF village known as Mission Support Fernandez—named after Delta C Squadron Master Sergeant George Andy Fernandez—the first Unit operator killed in the Iraq War.

Adjacent quarters at MSS Fernandez housed not only the Rangers and Delta operators, but also British SAS troops of Task Force Black and an Army Special Force CIF Company, along with a collection of OGA spooks and soldiers from the conventional 1st Armored Division, who "would barely ever go out but were there as a last ditch, 'Come save our ass with your Abrams tanks' capacity."

A minirange was set up for pistol training and zeroing rifles, which encouraged further cross-training. One of the Delta recce troop snipers who had worked with RS to train the Ranger snipers in Fort Bragg pulled aside one of the two-man Ranger sniper teams and said, "Anytime you're not going out, I'm paging you and you're coming out with us."

It was a heady experience for the 3/75 sniper team leader, who found himself in mission briefings surrounded by an abundance of warfighting experience, including the Unit commander along with a bevy of Master Sergeants and Sergeants Major. *"Holy shit—this is crazy."*

Typically, when operating together, the Delta and Ranger snipers would perch on the opposite sides of a 160th SOAR Little Bird's outer benches where they could quickly dismount atop strategically located rooftops to overwatch a raid on a target building.

However, on one occasion, the objective was deemed especially sensitive, with the possibility of escape a genuine concern. As a result, the sniper team was positioned well ahead of the primary raiding party to swat down any potential squirters.

While one Black Hawk loaded up with the primary assault element, another carried just the two Delta snipers, two Ranger snipers, a JTAC (joint terminal attack controller—a soldier trained to direct close air support), and an assaulter armed with a Squad Automatic Weapon, who tagged along in the event things went sideways.

The recce element set down five kilometers from the objective to conduct an offset infil.

"The six of us were on our own," the Ranger recounted. "We had to walk through a couple villages and set up positions around a big complex, overwatch it for an hour before the full complement of CAG guys flew in. It was a fifty-minute flight and we were put down in the middle of fucking nowhere. *'We are in some shit right now.'"*

While it may have seemed like they were on their own, this small six-man sniper team actually had some pretty serious support in the form of the dedicated aerial assets assigned to them—two F/A-18s, an AC-130, and other platforms waiting on standby.

"The assets that were just flying above us the whole time we were out there . . . it was pretty amazing," the former Ranger sniper said. "It was equivalent to the amount of assets a whole conventional Army brigade might get—if they requested it months in advance."

Once the snipers were in position, the larger Delta Force team swooped in and secured the targeted individuals without incident.

While the evening was not punctuated by a chaotic firefight, merely playing in the big leagues alongside their Tier 1 counterparts proved to be an eye-opening experience for the Ranger snipers.

◉

Working with Delta's recce troop could be an eye-opener for those watching from on high as well. In late 2007, 1st Lieutenant Brian "STUFR" Watts (his call sign had been "Flex" before he was "hostilely renamed") was at the stick of one of those dedicated assets.

An F-16 pilot with the 421st Fighter Squadron, Watts belonged to one of the three USAF F-16C squadrons that continually rotated through Iraq and served—along with Navy F/A-18s—as the primary close air support platforms watching over the troops.

JSOC's exceedingly brisk OPTEMPO required the air assets remain flexible just to keep up as missions were nonstop and ever in flux. Watts explained, "What the tasking would start off with versus what actually ended up happening—rarely did they gel. After the briefing, the Army liaison guy would come back and say, 'Okay, here is what you're doing at this time, this time, and this time. . . .' And then you'd get ready to go and he'd come back in again. 'Okay, no. Now you're doing this and this.' And then you'd walk out to the jet and it would change again."

He continued, "I remember my first mission over there. I was getting ready to fly for the first time in a combat zone and the mission literally changed four times before takeoff. It was a kind of surveillance thing for the Tier 1—that's what we classified it over there. They were waiting for a high-value target to come back to a building and they were set to action them, all teed up and ready to go."

The fighter pilot reflected on the experience of being just one small ($20 million) cog in the JSOC counterterrorism machine. He said, "A lot of times we would provide overwatch. Now how many assets they had besides us . . . What we kind of found out was we'd think we'd be on to something but they'd also have two Predators or whatever. You'd be thinking, 'Okay, we're all ready to go,' but, 'Nope, we've got a drone.' 'What the fuck? Why are we sitting here burning holes in the sky?'

"At other times, one guy in the [two F-16C] flight would track the target and the other would track the U.S. guys. There was a code and a relay so the Delta guys—or whoever they were—could sit and watch what we were seeing. They'd take their helicopters and just put them down in the desert and wait until the guy got to where they wanted to roll up on him. We'd just provide security and make sure nobody was sneaking up on them out in the middle of nowhere."

Watts was taken aback by the level of detail JSOC's recce assets were able to provide in advance of an operation, providing an almost prescient degree of intelligence.

When working in support of conventional troops, the F-16C pilots of the 421st Fighter Squadron (call sign "Ninja") would take on the role of subject matter expert, providing in-depth descriptions of their aircraft, munitions, and time-on-station during their check-in. They'd also lend suggestions as to what types of weapons would be of most use and when.

When supporting Rangers, the check-in was of a generally similar sort, although considerably condensed.

However, when tasked with a Delta operation, the fighter pilots simply did as they were told. "It was pretty much check in and just shut up," Watts admitted. "Give them your call sign; tell them you're on station. They'd acknowledged and they knew the drill. They know what's going on. They probably knew what that guy they were targeting was eating for breakfast.

"They would literally say, 'This car is going to go here, and then two guys are going to come up, and then they are going to go there,' and so on. And you'd just sit there and watch it unfold exactly as they said it would. There was obviously a lot of intelligence that was going on. It was just nuts."

The pilot appreciated the opportunity to work amid such refined competence: "You know when you are being utilized properly and when you are not—when a guy knows exactly how to use your asset to help them—and these guys were, as expected, all over it. It was fun to sit back and have a front-row ticket to a lot of the stuff."

◈

While U.S. Army Special Forces primarily concentrate on unconventional warfare and foreign internal defense missions, each SF Group boasts its own specialized direct-action-centric component in the form of a CIF Company. This relatively under-the-radar capability skirts the line between "black" and "white" and "Tier 1" and "Tier 3."

These CIF (Combatant Commanders In-extremis Force) Companies grant each geographic area of responsibility (AOR) of the Unified Combatant Command structure with a dedicated, specially trained unit that is prepositioned and able to immediately respond to highly sensitive operations.

Not surprising considering their SF lineage, combined with their advanced direct action, counterterrorism, and hostage rescue training, these (approximately) forty-man CIF Companies are also utilized to raise and train the Tier 1 CT units of other nations.

These capabilities led to JSOC calling upon them in a time of need: a CIF Company was made part of the larger JSOC equation operating out of Baghdad, allowing the industrial CT campaign to continue unabated even after Delta Force had been hit especially hard.

In 2006, the 7th Special Forces Group's CIF Company (C/3/7), which included a troop led by former Delta recce legend John "Shrek" McPhee, took up shop at MSS Fernandez alongside JSOC's band of U.S. and coalition black SOF and operated as an extension of the Unit.

The following year, SF CIF was given its own quarry and set off the leash in another direction. While the Delta-spearheaded Task Force 16 would continue to hunt down Zarqawi and dismantle AQI, the Special Forces DA specialists would take the lead on the new Counter Iranian Influence (CII) mission with the newly created Task Force 17.

Prior to that, U.S. intelligence had estimated that upward of 150 members of Quds Force—a special unit of the Iranian Revolutionary Guard tasked with "extraterritorial operations"—were operating inside Iraq. Quds Force was there training, directing, and arming Shia militias, known as "Special Groups."

Unwilling to ignore this growing issue any longer, even while the White House deliberated the next step, Delta Force took the initiative and mounted a shock raid on the Iranian Liaison Office in Irbil in northern Iraq in January of '07, storming in from the roof and the ground simultaneously. Five Iranian operatives were captured while attempting to destroy documents, signifying the official commencement of a second major CT campaign in Iraq.

While Delta and JSOC returned their focus to al-Qaeda in Iraq, CIF, along with their newest creation, ICTF (Iraqi Counterterrorism Task Force)—owned the CII mission while still being fueled by JSOC's massive intelligence collection and processing capabilities.

The ICTF had only recently been activated. Recruits were trained by SF in conjunction with Jordanian SOF at the Jordanian Counterterrorism Training Academy in Amman, and then returned to Iraq to operate alongside their American mentors in the field.

This fork of the industrial CT campaign proved as torrid as the one that raged versus AQI. In late 2007, Task Force 17 killed almost fifty Shia militiamen during the course of a daylight raid in Sadr City while suffering no casualties—and causing no known friendly civilian casualties.

The team narrowly escaped a potential *Black Hawk Down* redux as the assault force battled their way through the streets to avoid being surrounded by a gathering swarm of enemy reinforcements.

While some soldiers received specialized marksmanship training, Army Special Forces did not have a formalized sniper program until the creation of the Special Operations Target Interdiction Course (SOTIC) in 1983 (which was rebranded as the Special Forces Sniper Course, SFSC, in March 2007).

SFSC is conducted at Range 37, a 130-acre training facility near Mott Lake at Fort Bragg, and serves as the primary basic training course for prospective SF and Delta snipers, along with a small handful of fortunate snipers from other units.

"That's the one everyone wants to go to but there are not very many slots coming down," former Ranger sniper Jack Murphy said.

As with most 3rd Battalion Ranger snipers, Isaiah Burkhart received his basic qualification through the U.S. Army Sniper School at Fort Benning. However, after serving as a 3/75 sniper for more than two years, he was finally granted the opportunity to attend SOTIC.

"The general rule was, because the battalions don't get that many slots for SOTIC, it was the more senior guys who would go," Burkhart explained.

The slots are so rare, in fact, that Burkhart was the only sniper from the entire regiment in his class. He found the course to be worth the wait. Compared to the U.S. Army Sniper School, he said, "SOTIC was definitely a higher level. The technicality of it is higher. You get a lot more into actually doing more equation stuff, fine-tuning things. The Army one is more of a 'Big Army,' big house, 'You're a dumbass until I tell you otherwise and you do exactly what I tell you' kind of thing."

Burkhart's SOTIC class was loaded up with Sergeants First Class and Master Sergeants (as an E-6, he was the least senior man in attendance) and the students were treated accordingly. "It's definitely more of a gentleman's type course. You're in big boy land."

Students were provided with the training but then expected to follow through on their own, no babysitting or hand-holding included.

As its name suggested, Burkhart also found that SOTIC geared itself more toward teaching spec ops skills. He explained, "I would say that the U.S. Army School was a little more intensive in the stalking department.

They were definitely more of an old-school, conventional warfare approach in the sense of stalking and fieldcraft-type stuff. Whereas with SOTIC, we had an entire week of doing low-vis stuff: following people, sneaking into somewhere to take photographs, and going back to Photoshop to do an overlay over a photo and map out entrance points, cameras, and things like that. They even had a Subaru that was all set up like a low-vis tracking vehicle.

"It was a really good course—the best sniper school that I've ever been to."

A Special Forces soldier who successfully completes the Special Forces Sniper Course is considered a "Level I" sniper. That not only suggests an HR-ready skill set, but also qualifies him to return to his Group and train other Green Berets—generally mimicking the SFSC curriculum, albeit in an abbreviated manner.

Those trained in this fashion are deemed "Level II" and can operate as an ODA sniper as long as they are teamed with a Level I sniper. They are also considered qualified to train partner nation snipers.

Each ODA strives to have at least two Green Berets with sniper training—and sometimes in practice has several more—but generally that's only considered a secondary role, if that. As a former Unit and SF sniper said, "In an A-Team, sniper is a detail not a position, and one guys don't really want. . . . 'Why did I get stuck on the roof for this op?'"

That's not the case with the CIF Companies, which are broken down into assaulter and sniper cells similar to Delta Force or DEVGRU. The CIF snipers are dedicated, full-time sharpshooters in the same way that Ranger snipers are; however, they also have hostage rescue training similar to that of Delta snipers (although they are not tasked with the same advanced reconnaissance role, at least not nearly to that degree).

To gain entrance to a CIF, an SF soldier has to pass more stringent physical requirements and complete the two-month Special Forces Advanced Reconnaissance Target Analysis Exploitation Techniques Course (SFAR-TAETC), which drills its students on surgical direct action and room-clearing techniques necessary for the assignment.

Held four times a year, each SFARTAETC session mirrors an SFSC class. As Murphy explained, "They've been able to combine the final exercise between SFARTAETC and [SFSC]. The assaulters and snipers come together for training operations at the end of the courses, working together the way they would in reality."

◈

The shift from Special Operations Target Interdiction Course to Special Forces Sniper Course was more than just a name change.

Following a similar path previously blazed by the overhauled U.S. Navy SEAL Sniper Course, SFSC was modernized and expanded to reflect the post-9/11 realities of sniper employment in combat.

A glimpse into the effectiveness of the Special Forces Sniper Course was provided by the results of the 2011 International Sniper Competition, which was won by Master Sgt. Kevin Owens and Sgt. 1st Class Terry Gower, snipers from B/2/3—the 3rd Special Forces Group CIF Company.

The year before that, the title was taken by SFSC instructors Sgt. 1st Class Chance Giannelli and Sgt. 1st Class Edward Homeyer, both of Company D, 2nd Battalion, 1st Special Warfare Training Group.

Applying the lessons gleaned on the modern battlefield and marrying them with rapidly developing technologies and an enhanced understanding of the hard science of ballistics (the nuances of which are complex enough to push a Cray supercomputer to its breaking point), the updated SEAL and SF courses represent a larger trend in the training of long-distance shooters.

The U.S. Army Sniper School and even the Marine Scout Sniper Course have been similarly augmented in recent years as well, while a whole host of advanced classes—both inside the military and via third parties—exist to further hone snipers' abilities.

Practical and realistic scenarios are emphasized, as is the total comprehension of a multitude of factors that can affect a bullet's trajectory, from the initial pressure on the trigger to its flight across hundreds, if not thousands, of meters. Today's snipers are instructed on the use of ballistic computers—which come in a variety of forms, including smartphone apps—to help streamline the process of calculating these complex firing solutions.

"The days of Kentucky windage and 'feeling' are over," said Todd Hodnett, the president of Accuracy 1st.

Hodnett is a leading figure in this increasingly rational and digitized sniper age. He also stands as one of the most sought-after instructors among USMC and SOF snipers.

Perhaps surprisingly, the Texan himself doesn't have a background as a military sniper. He was a farmer and a rancher who grew up shooting prairie dogs. He gradually found his way into competitive pistol and sniper competitions and garnered enough success—national championship victory–level success—that the military came to him rather than the other way around.

Hodnett's ballistic engines have changed the way spec op snipers approach the craft and his reticle designs are already in wide use.

"We have taken a very math-driven scientific problem and removed the myths from the equation," he explained. "We did this by making the science work for us. No more shooting every one hundred meters for DOPE— that is laughable nowadays. It's not opinion; it's fact. The math is always right. The bullet doesn't lie and doesn't get to vote. Everything I teach is based off where the bullet hit, not just a standard generic ballistic chart. We can be so much better than that."

And if the results of the 2010 International Sniper Competition served as evidence to the credibility of SFSC, consider that the winning team— SFSC instructors themselves—attributed their victory in large part to receiving instruction from Hodnett prior to the competition.

In fact, the top three teams in both the Open and Service class all trained under Hodnett.

After attending a ten-day session with Accuracy 1st, USMC Scout Sniper Cpl. Ryan Lindner said, "Training with Todd Hodnett has taken our capabilities to a level that I didn't think was possible as a Scout Sniper. Todd has really revolutionary tactics about shooting around, over, and within buildings."

In other words, he knows his stuff.

Hodnett's methodology is based around streamlining extremely complex ideas into equations that allow shooters to determine solutions and send precise fire downrange in a matter of seconds.

"When it is boiled down to the basics of ballistics, you have MV [muzzle velocity], BC [ballistic coefficient], and DA [density altitude], which gives you a TOF [time of flight] to the target," he explained. "Elevation is the easy part; wind is everything—the ability to look at mirage or look at terrain and see the orographic or katabatic effect of winds across terrain. I think that everyone had the same issues with ballistic engines when they started up. Things didn't work out real well. We didn't know why but the bullet didn't always hit where we wanted or thought it should.

"That's when I started truing my ballistics. Really, all I did was take the answer the bullet gave me and made the predictive ballistics match the actual flight path. Then I was able to place my methodology into ballistic engines. This started in the supersonic algorithm and then I worked on the subsonic portion of the algorithm. Now truing is common and everyone has adopted it."

When Hodnett first came onto the scene to train special operations snipers, the community was still largely set in its ways. However, that has changed in recent years. He explained, "At first, most of the POIs [programs of instruction] that were taught in the school houses had not changed in the past thirty years. And like with everything, some don't like change because it takes them off their own self-appointed pedestal. Lucky for me, I don't see much of that now.

"In the past, each group was different and they had their own way of what they thought was correct. But most groups have changed and are now on the same path. That's great to see."

According to Hodnett, the adoption of modern technology has been a major factor driving the various sniper courses in a similar direction or risking being left hopelessly behind. "When you look at all the equipment the guys use today . . . I have watched the change form 10x scopes to 20x plus, and the use of ballistic engines which really takes us of out of the '70s. I have heard snipers tell me they felt cheated by what is being taught at sniper school. The world has changed and most of the military has followed with the new changes."

As a result, SOF snipers in general have stepped up their games considerably. He said, "It's crazy to see how far the skill has progressed in just the last six years. From scopes to ballistic engine usage, lasers, and night vision—the conflicts of the past decade really allowed SOF men to step into the twenty-first century in gear and technology. Second focal to first, reticle changes to maximize speed and accuracy, and so on.

"What is most exciting is the changes are still coming. We are working on new projects all the time. It's a great period to be a part of the long-range community. I am always humbled by the class of individuals that I get to work with on a daily event. And I feel very fortunate and blessed to be a part of the change that has affected the sniper community across the board."

◈

The Iraq War was the definition of a target-rich environment and the special operators were not the only snipers in the thick of it.

A one-time 3/75 Ranger sniper by the name of Staff Sgt. James Gilliland selected and trained a ten-man sniper section at the 2nd Battalion, 69th Armored Regiment, 3rd Infantry Division dubbed "Shadow."

Gilliland's band of conventional snipers produced results that would have to be deemed special, erasing an estimated two hundred enemy fighters during a single five-month deployment in 2005. Gilliland himself accounted for nearly a third of those, including one from 1,250 meters with an M24—among the longest ever recorded by a 7.62mm rifle.

That same year, 1st Battalion, 67th Armored Regiment, 4th Infantry Division sniper section leader Timothy Kellner was credited with 139 confirmed kills—and had another hundred or so that were never formally confirmed.

There was controversy related to the actions of the "Big Army" snipers as well. Three snipers of the 501st Infantry Regiment's 1st Battalion sniper section—the "Painted Demons"—were charged with murder while operating in the so-called Triangle of Death region south of Baghdad in 2007.

They were accused of killing unarmed Iraqi citizens in three separate incidents in cases of either mistaken identity or a compromised hide site, and then planting weapons or bomb-making materials on their victims to make the shootings appear justified.

Two, Staff Sgt. Michael A. Hensley and Spc. Jorge G. Sandoval Jr., were acquitted of murder but found guilty of lesser charges. The third, Sgt. Evan Vela, was found guilty despite Hensley's admission that he ordered Vela to take the shot.

Adding some additional intrigue is their alleged connection to a classified "baiting" program instituted by the Asymmetric Warfare Group—the same unit of which former Delta and Ranger hero Greg Birch served as Command Sergeant Major until retiring in '07.

According to the sworn testimony of then-Lt. Matthew Didier, the platoon leader who oversaw the Painted Demons' sniper operations, AWG provided the unit with items such as fake detonation cords and explosives used to lure potential targets into both the snipers' sights and their acceptable rules of engagement.

Didier's statement claimed, "If someone found the item, picked it up, and attempted to leave with the item, we would engage the individual as I saw this as a sign they would use the item against the U.S. forces."

◈

The torrid pace of operations in Iraq that pit two ever-shifting networks into direct conflict on a daily basis also resulted in a rapid evolution of tactics as both sides adjusted to account for the other.

While JSOC SMUs are expected to achieve the desired results across even the most difficult of scenarios, they do not do so without first stacking the deck in their favor.

Units like Delta Force and DEVGRU are not meant to engage in fair fights.

As a Unit sniper explained, "The only fair fight is the one you just lost."

Delta's operators are always far more talented, better trained, and better equipped than their adversaries. And if that's not enough working in their favor, they always strive to seize the initiative with the element of surprise on their side and then strike decisively, through the use of both overwhelming speed and (relative) numbers.

This philosophy has long been summarized in the Unit's mantra: "surprise, speed, and violence of action."

However, the regularity of the hits of this fashion—as impressive as they may have been with Little Birds dropping in from seemingly nowhere, charging assaulters disembarking and kicking in doors in a fury of concentrated chaos—threatened to make them predictable, and thus vulnerable.

Insurgents could simply lie in wait—as was the case in the deaths of Horrigan and McNulty—to take advantage of any SOF tactics they may have seen and dissected.

To stay ahead of the curve, the Tier 1 assault teams adjusted their tactics. Instead of storming in loud and fast, they began to tiptoe their way into compounds, eliminating or capturing HVTs who were lying in bed rather than lying in wait. They utilized suppressed HK MP7s quiet enough not to stir sleepers separated from the attack by just a couple inches of wall.

The old mantra was supplanted by a new one: "silence, stealth, and decisiveness of action."

However, that approach too is susceptible to booby traps and suicide bombs.

As the war wore on, assault teams became more and more likely to simply stay outside, call the target out, or call in a five-hundred-pound JDAM at the first sign of trouble.

GM, a former 3rd Battalion Ranger, said, "You know, guys want to clear rooms and all this stuff, and guys still do. But they got away from it because it's so dangerous with the suicide bombers and stuff. Guys just started doing call-outs. 'Hey, come out of the house or we blow the house up.'

"It's way easier than trying to go through the door. You're totally in control when you do a call-out."

Brian Watts, the former F-16 pilot, added, "The buildings over there . . . they'd booby-trap everything. If they had any issues and you had somebody on station—whether it was us or an Apache, why send guys in if it's not a guy you're trying to take back and interrogate?"

When JSOC finally cornered Zarqawi in the village of Hibhib in June 2006, the JOC at Balad Air Base instructed an F-16C to put a pair of five-hundred-pound bombs—a laser-guided GBU-12 and a GPS-guided GBU-38—on his roof rather than risk another narrow escape, even with a Delta operator en route via the 160th SOAR express just minutes out.

B Squadron's white-hot pursuit of Zarqawi during Operation Arcadia bore fruit. JSOC's eclectic team of 'gators (interrogators) coaxed critical information from a captured AQI facilitator by playing on his ego. They were tipped on how to decipher the particulars of meets between Sheik Abd Al-Rahman—Zarqawi's spiritual advisor—and the AQI emir himself. The prisoner also passed along the locations of fifteen or so Zarqawi safe houses in the Baqubah vicinity.

While the task force dedicated an inordinate number of highly valuable ISR platforms over an inordinate amount of time—especially considering the pace of this supercharged campaign—to track the movements of a man they believed to be Al-Rahman, they lacked incontrovertible evidence that they were actually following the right guy.

Two recce operators from Delta B Squadron supplied the necessary proof. Yet again, they attempted a perilous clandestine reconnaissance mission through the most unwelcoming parts of Baghdad.

During one of the most heated periods of the war, when civilians were routinely pulled from vehicles and executed at militia checkpoints, the Delta snipers again draped themselves in local attire and negotiated the dangerous city in an unassuming sedan.

Playing Al-Rahman's movements to their advantage perfectly, the vehicles crossed paths in opposite directions and the recce team hit the bullseye with the shot fired from a camera.

This evidence bought the larger plan of tracking Al-Rahman more time, a decision that proved critical in at last finding and fixing Zarqawi.

The bombs that finally finished him triggered fourteen additional raids. Two Delta B Squadron troops, an SAS assault team, a pair of 3/75 Ranger platoons, and a SF CIF element divided the objectives (safe houses and moving vehicles) and unleashed a series of simultaneous killing strikes meant to decapitate al-Qaeda in Iraq in the immediate aftermath of their leader's death.

Zarqawi somehow survived the initial blasts, only to die minutes later after being retrieved off a stretcher and pulled from an ambulance by the Delta operators who leapt off of MH-6 Little Birds moments earlier.

JSOC took no time to celebrate despite at last succeeding in what had become a three-year obsession—one that literally fueled a special operations revolution.

Building upon the first wave of raids that immediately followed the bombing, almost forty more were conducted the following evening. Together, those actions netted twenty-five more captive terrorists and killed another. Those statistics shot up to nearly 150 raids, close to 180 captured, and more than thirty killed in the days that followed.

❖

In the early '80s, the FBI raised an elite counterterrorist capability of its own—the Hostage Rescue Team. HRT was heavily inspired by, and patterned after, the Army's Delta Force. To this day, its operators are split up into assault and sniper troops and trained in similar CQB techniques and held to similar standards, albeit with a civilian, law-enforcement bent as stated by its motto: *Servare Vitas*—"To Save Lives."

While Delta Force and SEAL Team Six racked up scores of HVT kills in Iraq and Afghanistan, the FBI HRT has garnered its own fair share of headlines in recent years.

In February of 2013, the unit successfully breached a bunker and dispatched the kidnapper behind it, downing him with precise fire to rescue a five-year-old hostage in Alabama.

Months later, HRT was at it again, tracking down a fugitive across miles of mountainous Idaho terrain, freeing yet another kidnap victim with the return of accurate and lethal fire.

In April of 2014, the unit's assaulters took down a North Carolina apartment complex at midnight to secure a hostage who was about to be dismembered and apprehended his five captors.

And in July 2014, the HRT saved a South Carolinian, storming a home and apprehending three Mexican drug cartel thugs who had taken him captive.

Almost since its inception, the HRT has been no stranger to perilous high-stakes missions—and occasionally the controversy that can accompany them. The FBI HRT's reputation absorbed serious damage after playing critical roles in the fiascos at Ruby Ridge and Waco. And conversely, it was buoyed by the successful captures of a number of the most wanted men in the world over the years, including Beltway snipers John Allen Muhammad and Lee Boyd Malvo in Maryland, pirate leader Mohammad Saaili Shibin in Somalia, and Boston bombing suspect Dzhokhar Tsarnaev in Massachusetts.

However, until very recently, one thing the Hostage Rescue Team did not do was rescue hostages.

That assessment is not exactly fair, nor precisely accurate. In 1991, the Hostage Rescue Team did successfully retake the Talladega Federal Correctional Institution from 121 rebelling Cuban inmates, freeing nine hostages in the process. However, the HRT's track record of the more traditional sorts of HR missions for which it derives its moniker was rather skimpy, to be generous.

Its first of that sort didn't actually come until the unit had been in existence for a full quarter-century—and actually took place in Iraq with a large portion of the credit going to the 75th Ranger Regiment's 3rd Battalion Sniper Platoon.

Throughout the Global War on Terror, HRT operators have routinely embedded with JSOC task forces; in addition to their world-class gunfighter talents, they lend expert investigative and SSE (sensitive site exploitation) skills to missions that further enable the rapid seizure and processing of intelligence materials to spur subsequent raids.

And in this capacity, a 3/75-attached HRT operator stumbled across the mission for which his unit was originally conceived.

The Rangers were tasked with taking down a compound thought to house some particularly notorious insurgents near Samarra.

"SM," the 3/75 sniper who was in overwatch for the operation, explained, "This was during the surge and everything was hot. We saw these guys driving around in trucks and they even had a DShK in the back of one, which they unloaded and hid under a tree near this little house. We were getting ready to do the hit later that night and we knew we were going to eliminate this threat."

As had become the fashion at that time, rather than attempt to breach the house and take the target unaware, the Rangers simply took up a defensive position and ordered the men out via an interpreter armed with a bullhorn.

"We did the call-out and this guy sticks just one hand out of the door," the sniper said. "He was speaking Arabic, saying, 'I'm a hostage! I'm a hostage!'

"But the thing is, some of these guys have said that before blowing themselves up with a suicide vest or come out spraying an AK. Plus, we knew it was hot and the DShK was under the tree. These guys meant business."

The man in the house continued to insist he was a captive and pleaded for the Rangers to hold their fire.

SM glassed the man and started to believe his story ("We're totally in control. We had the house in an L-shape position where we could just obliterate it"), so he spoke up in his defense:

"Hey, I think this guy actually is a hostage."

The HRT operator was set up alongside SM. The sniper attempted to tell the special agent what to have the interpreter say, but whenever the interpreter followed through, the shrill distortion of his amplified instructions would emit directly into the Ranger's ears at a piercing decibel.

SM explained, "I was trying to tell them what was going on with this guy and I had the interpreter with a bullhorn, screaming into my ear. Honestly, it was comical. It was like something out of a comedy. I had the guy with the bullhorn behind me screaming at me and I was like, 'Shut the fuck up—I can't say anything.'"

The interpreter ordered the man to put both arms out.

(In Arabic) "I can't—I'm handcuffed!"

Despite the fact that he wasn't following through with the instructions, SM still urged the rest of the platoon to hold their fire for the moment.

"Hey, I got it covered. He looks like a hostage. If anything happens, I'll just shoot him."

The assault element proceeded to breach the door.

"All right, now come on out."

"I can't."

"Why not? Now why can't you come out?"

As it so happens, the man was handcuffed to a bed. He did his best to do as he was told, ripping the bed frame apart and running out of the shack with the bed's broken frame dragging behind him.

"Hold up! Hold up!"

The sniper said, "We nearly took him out right there because he was freaking out. He was scared he was about to be killed."

"Take off your man dress!"

The Ranger continued with a sense of exasperation as the scene replayed in his head, "It was cold as shit, but he took off his man dress. He's butt naked, he's handcuffed to one of those metal frame beds that he had just ripped to pieces, and he's freaking out. Our guys were on edge. They wanted to kill somebody because we knew what was going to go down. We already knew there were two guys not far away that we're going to have to deal with, so everybody was already amped."

The man turned out to be the village's mayor who had been stopped at an al-Qaeda checkpoint. He was not only being held captive, he was about to be beheaded.

The Rangers then turned their attention to the captors, who had attempted to hide in an adjacent field with little success. "They were thinking they couldn't be seen because they were under blankets, attempting to hide their heat signature. So we sent the dog out and they started opening up with AKs and we just blasted them. We made Swiss cheese of them and pretty much destroyed these two guys."

The sniper's starring role in that evening's macabre comedy wasn't yet complete.

"*Umm . . . they have suicide vests on.*"

"*Okay, well, just get them out of the ditch. Drag them out just to see if they've got anything on them.*"

As an encore, SM and a Ranger squad leader tied a ten-foot rope around the feet of the corpses and pulled the bodies out of the ditch. "Nobody wanted to do it because of course, the vest is all strapped and ready to blow. Me and the squad leader are like, 'Fuck it.' We would have totally died. It was so stupid. We might as well have just carried them out. But the rope made us feel better. That's all it was."

The rescued mayor was loaded up with the Rangers on the Chinook for extraction and SM sidled up alongside. He put the interpreter to work once again.

"*So, are you going to give me your daughter, since I just saved your life?*"

"*Umm . . . I don't know.*"

"*Come on, man, I look just like Brad Pitt in* Legends of the Fall *with my long flowing locks.*"

"*I don't know . . . I have to talk to her first.*"

"*But isn't it part of your culture? You've got to give me your daughter or something because I saved your life.*"

"*I have to talk to her. I don't know what she's going to think.*"

The Ranger laughed and said, "This guy had just won the lotto. It never happens. His head was going to be on the ground later that day. He should have blown me right there. It was like one big pain in the ass, but the guy is lucky he didn't get killed."

As the team was exfiltrating, they performed gun runs on the bodies. The suicide vests ripped what had remained of the dead insurgents' bodies apart with impressive explosions, confirming the vests had still been very much live.

The HRT operator then spoke up:

"Congratulations. That was the first hostage rescue in HRT history."

The sniper reflected, "Jesus, I thought they had been around for like twenty-five years. I guess he got some big award. We never get awards."

◈

Late in 2007, the 3rd Battalion scored another pivotal victory—and yet again it was almost by happenstance.

Delta's B Squadron was tasked with taking down a house that was deemed a critical target. With the Unit laying claim to the Black Hawks, 3/75 split its platoon in half and took a pair of Chinooks to scout two related houses a few kilometers out in the desert considered a lesser threat.

Former Ranger sniper Isaiah Burkhart explained, "We didn't think there was going to be anything there in this tiny house. We had seen cars go back and forth between them and this main target house a couple times so we figured we'd hit them just in case. Maybe they were storing weapons there or something."

As soon as the Chinook settled down near the objective, an RPG rocketed out of the house and took a serpentine route in the general direction of the bird. A pitched gunfight broke out between the two forces—seventeen Rangers versus a dozen fanatical AQI terrorists—with hundreds of rounds cracking in each direction.

The house was actually teeming with weapons masked behind a hidden wall ("the same number of rifles as in an arms room at a Ranger Battalion") and dedicated fighters willing to use them.

"They had everything," Burkhart said. "There was a U.S. serial-numbered M4. They had night vision. They had a technical with a DShK under a tarp. We were in a major firefight."

The Rangers were in no mood to play around; they called in the big guns: two 160th SOAR MH-60L Direct Action Penetrators (DAP)—a fearsome gunship variant of the Black Hawk bristling with weaponry, including M134mm Miniguns, Hydra-70 Rocket pods, and thermobaric AGM-114N Hellfire II missiles.

"We were in the middle of this field with no cover, and we were only about fifty meters away from this target," Burkhart said. "We just laid down and had the fire support officer call in the DAPs. They came in and fired 2.75-inch rockets right over top of us and lit them up with the miniguns. And then they even fired a thermobaric Hellfire into the building, which collapsed the whole thing."

Unbeknownst to the Rangers, a handful of prisoners were chained to the floor in the makeshift al-Qaeda torture chamber/gun room and were killed in the assault. However, the compound's defenders happened to be the complete courier network of Abu Ayyub al-Masri, the man who succeeded Abu Musab al-Zarqawi as emir of AQI following the latter's slaying.

Initially, it was thought that al-Masri himself might have been present.

"Me and my sniper partner sat overwatch and then they pulled in everybody," Burkhart said. "The CAG team that hit that other target came in and so did the spec ops PJs. They came in and took over."

Inside more than ten computers were discovered, wrapped in plastic and stocked with sensitive intelligence detailing the ins and outs of the entire AQI network.

Meanwhile, the Rangers were saddled with the grisly task of sorting through body parts to speed along the identification process.

While Abu Ayyub al-Masri was not there, the strike killed him in an operational sense. Unable to effectively command AQI without his chief lieutenants, the coalition dropped the bounty on his head from $25 million to $100,000 in 2008.

Abu Ayyub al-Masri was killed for real in April 2010—along with Abu Umar al-Baghdadi, the leader of the Islamic State of Iraq—in a joint American/Iraqi SOF raid conducted southwest of Tikrit.

Kristofar Kosem—the B Squadron recce troop sniper who led the AFO team Juliet at Operation Anaconda for which he was awarded the Silver Star—was forced into retirement in June 2008.

Just one month after leaving Iraq for the final time, he was in Colombia, rehearsing for a potential hostage rescue mission. The rotor blade of a helo he was aboard struck the jungle canopy and Kosem was thrown from the bird, smashing into a tree branch headfirst.

Kosem survived but was later diagnosed with TBI (traumatic brain injury). While he suffers from symptoms commonly associated with TBI (mood swings, short-term memory loss, etc.), he continues to heal and adjust, relying heavily on his faith and with the support of his wife.

Incidentally, just weeks following Kosem's training accident, Colombian presidential candidate Ingrid Betancourt, Americans Marc Gonsalves, Thomas Howes, and Keith Stansell, and eleven others were rescued from the rainforests of Colombia.

In what was coined Operation Jaque, members of a rescue force posed as aid workers, guerrillas, and television journalists and tricked FARC rebels into handing over the hostages. The local FARC leader and another guerrilla were apprehended during the course of the rescue.

Despite Delta ultimately playing a crucial role in the rescue, full credit was given to the Colombians. The nation's defense minister, Juan Manuel Santos, went so far as to claim that the mission was "100 percent Colombian," and that "no foreigners participated in the planning or the execution of the mission"—likely to the Unit's great satisfaction.

12

Reaper

JSOC's Delta-spearheaded campaign in Iraq redefined the possibilities of special operations warfare and what a relatively small group of highly skilled men can accomplish when backed by virtually unlimited support, intelligence, and initiative.

The task force was estimated to have killed three thousand enemy combatants and captured nine thousand more, numbers totaling almost thirty-five hundred and twelve thousand when factoring in the intrinsically linked contributions of the United Kingdom Special Forces.

A confluence of factors—including the troop surge, the Anbar Awakening, and a ceasefire agreement with the Mahdi Army—led to a drastic curbing of the overall level of violence in Iraq by 2008.

However, JSOC's central role is nearly undeniable, as the extraordinary results of its industrial counterterrorism effort devastated AQI. When journalist Bob Woodward later asked President Bush about this in an interview, the president famously replied, "JSOC is awesome."

Gen. McChrystal's influence and reputation swelled alongside JSOC's; he was subsequently named ISAF and USFOR-A Commander, tasked with overseeing the reignited war in Afghanistan just as the nation pivoted its attention back to the Taliban and al-Qaeda proper. (McChrystal's promotion would, of course, end prematurely and controversially following the publication of a semi-scandalous article in *Rolling Stone*.)

In June 2008, the void in the black SOF world created by McChrystal's departure was filled by Navy Adm. William McRaven. McRaven, a onetime ST6 squadron commander Dick Marcinko, became JSOC's first non-Army commander after a run of ten consecutive Army generals that dated back to its inception in 1980.

The articulate and erudite McRaven, a McChrystal protégé, was well versed in the history of special operations. In an earlier life, he wrote about it. Now, he was helping to write it. The Texan had played a critical role in overseeing the tactics, tempo, and technologies of this new age of SOF while serving as McChrystal's chief deputy in Iraq. He not only embraced his predecessor's methods, he strove to refine them and exploit them further, even if Afghanistan's infrastructure was less conducive to the "industrial" approach.

◈

Just as the under-the-radar wrecking crew that is the 75th Ranger Regiment began to slow its dismantling efforts in Iraq, they picked up the pace in Afghanistan.

While not as specialized in some specific and exacting areas, the Rangers had proven a reasonable approximation for JSOC's special mission units for the large majority of their assignments. If not the scalpel, they were certainly no clumsy sledgehammer either. Perhaps a long sword is the more apt analogy.

This fact allowed for the widespread initiation of JSOC's ambitious global strategy, as the Ranger Regiment—while small and elite by almost any practical standard at around two thousand soldiers—was roughly four to five times larger than the combined forces of Delta and DEVGRU.

This allowed the Ranger Regiment to literally be in two places at once and was heavily deployed in both theaters throughout.

McChrystal helped to push his old unit further to the fore. The Ranger

Regiment had rotated commands with SEAL Team Six in Afghanistan, and the units regularly coordinated their efforts, running joint ops and alternating HVT hits. They were not precisely equal partners in this arrangement, but in the majority of circumstances, they were effectively so.

However, a number of Rangers noted that it generally lacked the big brother/little brother dynamic with DEVGRU that it shared with Delta Force (which does, it should be noted, recruit a large percentage of its operators from the Regiment). The SEALs were more likely to treat them like the "blocking force to the stars"—the outdated BHD image that infuriates so many modern Rangers.

One Ranger noted that he'd taken part in high-profile operations in the Afghanistan theater alongside SEAL Team Six ("stuff that made *CNN Headline News*") that ended up getting credited solely to DEVGRU.

The Navy has always shown a rare talent for marrying merit with marketability, and the SEALs have long been a powerful recruitment tool.

So it wasn't all that unusual that a skinny kid raised by a military family in the Northeast wanted nothing more than to become a SEAL someday.

Nick Irving was a schoolyard sniper-in-training: he made his own ghillie suits and practiced stalking the other kids in the playground while in middle school. He devoured all the Carlos Hathcock books and DVDs and read all about Vietnam-era SOF.

But once he saw the Charlie Sheen flick *Navy SEALs,* his future was set.

Irving joined the United States Naval Sea Cadet Corps and went through "baby SEAL" training where teenagers receive coaching from SEAL instructors and even take the actual SEAL PT test.

However, there was one problem that he couldn't see. Literally. He couldn't see—at least not colors the way the armed forces require.

He only discovered this when it was time to sign on the dotted line. Straight out of high school, Irving was ready to take his first official steps toward becoming a career SEAL in 2004.

And then it was time to take the test for color blindness. "The only page I could read in that book was the page you're not supposed to read," Irving said.

A motivated Army nurse heard what happened and pulled the defeated wannabe-SEAL into her office.

"Hey, you want to be in the Army?"

Irving retook the test, only this time he aced it—fourteen out of fourteen. He didn't prove he could differentiate colors so much as he could follow the finger of the nurse as she traced the invisible numbers, but either way, he was now in the Army.

He was then introduced to an Army Sergeant who had also been made aware of Irving's dilemma.

"I heard you wanted to be a SEAL. Well, we have something like that called Rangers."

"What the fuck is that? Is it hard?"

"Yeah."

"Do they have snipers?"

"Yeah."

"Okay, sign me up."

◉

Despite his obvious desire, Irving not only struggled to get into the military, he also struggled to even make it through Basic Training. He wasn't in BUD/S, he wasn't yet in RIP, but he was shocked to find himself pushed mentally and physically right from the very start.

It was a dilemma of his own making. Irving had overtrained prior to joining up in anticipation of the strain that awaited him and suffered from stress fractures to his tibia and fibula.

It didn't help that he came to the Army with the nickname "Stick Figure"—which at five seven and 110 pounds he well deserved.

However, he gritted it out. He made it through Basic, and then Airborne. Next up—RIP—the Ranger Indoctrination Program. He kept on fighting and in the end he was one of just seven out of an original eighty to be standing at the end.

Oh well, that just left more food for Irving. "I went into Ranger Battalion and our chow hall was just fucking epic. All you could eat buffet set up and it was just exclusive to us."

Irving quickly filled out, packing on fifty pounds of muscle. "I wasn't used to eating three meals a day," he explained. "Dinner for me would sometimes be a box of candy or something because we didn't have that much money. Usually on either Friday or Sunday there would be an actual dinner. Other than that was like scraps of whatever left over."

Thrown into 3/75 just when the Rangers were thrown into the thick of it themselves, Irving logged three consecutive combat deployments in Iraq during the period of its greatest severity, serving as a "door kicker, Machine Gunner, Stryker Driver, .50-Cal Gunner . . . any big gun is what my job was."

However, even as he was still learning exactly what it was that Rangers were and what Rangers did, he was reminded of his original schoolyard dreams.

◈

The real-life demonstration provided by 3/75's lethal sniper platoon in rapid succession near Tikrit during Irving's first deployment in 2005 was a better recruitment tool than any Charlie Sheen movie.

Two of the platoon's snipers—"SM" and "AC"—took out a sentry with a simultaneous 3-2-1 shot to kick off an assault that left seven foreign fighters dead. The snipers immediately transitioned to aerial overwatch, engaging a pack of insurgents who were attempting to swarm a downed Little Bird from the bench of another MH-6. And then the coup de grâce came when a terrorist on the roof of a three-story building attempted to maneuver on the Ranger element below.

SM and AC, back from aerial platform support duty and reintegrated with the rifle platoon, pulled off another coordinated 3-2-1 kill—this time a double headshot that created such force the combatant's head essentially exploded while his body cartwheeled to the ground below, landing right in front of Irving.

Irving looked at the man on the ground and then he looked up at the snipers.

"Holy shit. I want that job."

The young Ranger immediately started pestering the guys in the sniper platoon to try to find his way in. He said, "I started plucking their brains—what do I have to know and all this stuff? I never was a smart kid—graduated with a 1.7. I came out of high school and I sucked at math. I'm going to go fucking kill people, I don't need school. That was my mind-set. But once I saw that, it was game on. I wanted to be a full-fledged sniper at that point and I studied my ass off, worked out, read all the books, and talked to all the guys that I could."

◈

In 2005, after Jared Van Aalst became a platoon sergeant in a rifle company and Robby Johnson returned to the Army Marksmanship Unit, new leadership took over the 3/75 sniper platoon.

One of the major changes was the introduction of a selection process—something the Rangers already in the platoon saw as a step in the wrong direction.

"GM," a former 3/75 Ranger, explained, "Some guys came in who wanted a selection, where you had to ruck and do all this stupid stuff. 'We're going to have you do this song and dance.' Honestly, you didn't need all that. You just needed an interview to see a guy's character and the quality of the guy. You didn't get any better guys. Honestly, you got worse guys because you got away from what you were looking for.

"Hey, he's in shape. . . . Well, that's nice; we're all pretty much in shape. But is he going to be a thinker? Can he work by himself with just another guy and perform?"

Isaiah Burkhart concurred. "I actually didn't like that shit. I thought it was bullshit. The right guy may not be the best at whatever, but they are just a good fit. It just gave people a reason to judge other people. 'This guy did the road march faster than so-and-so.' I don't give a fuck how fast you road march."

However, having gone through the process himself, Irving saw its value. He explained, "It was a little smokefest. It was like a week long where you do this PT test in full kit, climbing ropes, different types of ladders, test to see if you're scared of heights—which I'm fucking terrified of—and you do that and take two psych evals. After that the veteran snipers interview you and decide if they want you on their sniper platoon. There's only like fourteen, fifteen guys that are snipers in the entire 3rd Ranger Battalion and they want to keep it a tightknit family.

"Looking back at it, I do think the selection was a good thing to have. At the time I thought it was pointless because we've all had three or four deployments under our belt and endured the suckfest. But guys can get lackadaisical back on the line."

Irving had put in his time and finally got a shot to become a 3/75 sniper. He had multiple combat deployments, earned his Ranger Tab, and now he'd passed sniper selection.

And with that, he became 3rd Battalion Sniper Platoon's first black sniper. As had always been the case in the Regiment, it was basically a nonissue. "When I first got to Battalion, there were three other black guys in Battalion. And after my first six months in, those guys were already gone. That made me and my 1st Sergeant the only ones there. I didn't get treated any different or anything like that. I went to Sniper Platoon and I was the first black sniper in 3rd Battalion's history. No one treated me any different. It was like, 'That's pretty cool, man,' but that's as far as it went. It was just, 'You have a job to do; you're a sniper like the rest of us.' "

Once in, Irving was loaded up with six months of consecutive sniper training, attending both military and civilian courses. They ranged from the standard U.S. Army Sniper School to various other courses that provided more specialized high-angle and urban training.

"We did the Army Sniper School and then after that we just sent the guys to every civilian sniper school we possibly could," he said. "I think out of those six months I was Stateside, I only had the chance to sit in my own home, like, one week total."

All of Irving's previous training and deployments led up to a particularly intense four-month run in Helmand Province, Afghanistan, in 2009. The platoon he and his spotter were attached to was engaged in brutal firefights on a nightly basis.

Irving was there to tip the odds in the Rangers' favor.

From March to July of that year, he tallied up thirty-three confirmed sniper kills, an enhanced reputation, and a new nickname with a considerably higher cool factor than "Stick Figure."

A couple of Rangers from 2nd Platoon sought Irving out at his compound.

"I heard you killed like seven-hundred-something guys."

"What?"

"Yeah, man. Everyone is calling you the Reaper."

The platoon actively jumped on the budding legend and Irving's accumulating feats were nightly discussions. "You're like the angel of death out there," he was told. "How many did you get tonight?" The Rangers kept tallies and continued to spread the word, although the "legend has it" number ballooned as word traveled, as it tends to do. In northern Afghanistan there was talk of a "reaper down south" with 150 kills.

◈

Irving is a huge sports fan and often speaks in football metaphors. His explanation of exactly where a sniper team fits in with the platoon it's supporting is a bit surprising. It's also quite apt in reflection.

"[Being a 3/75 Ranger sniper] is a full-time, dedicated job," he explained. "There's no real interaction with the line guys. We stay in our little cage and do sniper shit, which is pretty much math and free climbing.

"We're like the field goal kicker on a football team. The team needs you to step in to win the game and they'll call you out. You have this nice, good-looking uniform. . . . You know you're not really going to be in the shit and get beat up the whole game like the other guys. But you can either win the game for them or you can lose it."

He continued, expounding on the lonely existence of the specialist who is something of an outcast. A valued, critically important outcast, but an outcast all the same and only as good as their last shot.

"If we're in a big firefight and I can see the guys who are shooting at us but I can't make that shot, everyone looks at me. I've missed shots overseas—not many—but I've missed ones where you have that feeling where you want to walk away and go in a room and huddle into a little ball and cry."

This hero/goat discrepancy is typically determined by a matter of inches (or less). But in some cases, minutes are what make the difference.

◈

Irving and his spotter were presented with six prime targets—the Taliban commanders of Helmand Province. Frantically awaiting permission to take the shot, Irving finally gave himself the green light. (*"Fuck that—we're at war and they all have weapons."*)

All six were dropped in rapid succession. However, when the platoon went to examine the bodies, there was nothing to be found save for some intestinal tissue.

"So where's the bodies, Reaper?"

Taunted by the Rangers' equivalent to running backs and linebackers, the lethal field goal kicker responded, "Fuck you, I see the guts right here. I know I shot them."

The following day the Rangers watched an infrared camera feed from an UAV and spotted sweet—if gruesome—redemption for Irving. The drone picked up imagery of a large ceremonial funeral procession with six dead bodies—bodies that had, apparently, been collected from the battlefield by their tribesmen just ahead of the Rangers' arrival the day before.

"See, I told you. I knew we got those fuckers."

"Aww . . . shut up."

◈

When the 3rd Battalion Ranger snipers operated in the alien landscape of Afghanistan in 2004, they took on some expanded sniper ops in addition to the direct action role—stalking, setting up in hides, reconnoitering, and the like.

However, this was not out of any particular faith placed in the section by the line platoons. Rather it was largely driven by the snipers making themselves useful to demonstrate their worth.

The sniper platoon's value would become more than evident in subsequent deployments to Iraq. But at the same time, the scorching pace of operations and the urban nature of the conflict saw them transition into almost a pure direct action role where climbing skills and the accurate delivery of short-range, quick-twitch sniper fire were of paramount importance.

Now back in the open of Afghanistan—and with considerably more pull with the battalion—Irving helped push the snipers back to a more expansive mission set. However, this time it was highly prized by those above them.

"That was my claim to fame I guess, if you want to call it that," he said. "At that point it was normally only direct-action-type stuff. The longest shot you'd take is fifty or a hundred yards or whatnot. When we were in Afghanistan, the minimum engagement was like three hundred. I pitched this deal to my commanders—'Hey, let us go out on this op and actually do what snipers are trained to do, which is stalking, staying out for five days, just to go get a guy.'"

Irving was actually recruited himself for the mission he would later pitch to his commanders by the anonymous elite—the Regimental Reconnaissance Company.

Inside the Regiment, RRC is legendary. Outside, it's largely unknown. It exists in a role similar to Delta and DEVGRU's recce assets—specializing in close target reconnaissance—only minus the sniper capability.

In fact, their talents were so valued that in 2004 JSOC pulled RRC out from under the 75th Ranger Regiment and put it to work directly for the Command. In response, the 75th Ranger Regiment's sniper platoons reorganized so that the Rangers would retain an organic recon capability.

Former 3/75 Ranger sniper Pete Careaga explained, "Once we lost them we couldn't use them as much as we used to. So the reconnaissance mission had to be done in-house. At first, the snipers had to do the reconnaissance mission. I remember many days being out there all week just gathering information because [RRC] was busy doing more important stuff.

"So they took half of our platoon, the snipers, and made them a recon platoon. They also recruited some more guys from the line to plus up those numbers so they could become full platoon while also recruiting snipers a bit more heavily as well to make up for the shortfall. That didn't slow us down; it just kind of rearranged our numbers a little bit."

But now several years later and all but a distant memory to the 3/75 sniper platoon, the elusive RRC was back on the scene. A small team of RRC Rangers approached Irving and his spotter and presented them with a mission they could not refuse—a five-day mission behind enemy lines to track down an HVT.

On day four, Irving was positioned on a roof and overwatching 2/5 Marines as they attempted to take control of a hostile village. The suspicious arrival of a man on a moped with a bag of tools caught his attention. Minutes later, that bag of tools was revealed to be an RPG pointed directly at a Marine Humvee at point-blank range.

The Reaper sent a round from his cherished SR-25 from 743 meters away. *"Holy shit, dude; you blew him out of his sandals."*

The insurgent's sandals had not moved. His body, meanwhile, slumped on the ground several feet away. The Marines were suitably impressed.

On the fifth day, the hybrid RRC/sniper element was joined by a larger Ranger assault force to finally take down the targeted individual they had been tracking.

However, after breaking off from the assaulters, the smaller team found itself engaged in a sudden and overwhelming 360-degree ambush. Meanwhile, their potential reinforcements were engaged in a blistering firefight of their own as they approached the objective and were in little position to help.

It got worse—*much worse*—for the Reaper when he realized he had also come under the glass of an enemy sniper. He found he didn't much like being on the other end of the equation.

When he was with the Marines just before, he had heard tales of "the Chechen"—a sniper rumored to have logged some three hundred kills fighting against the Russians and now the Americans. While Irving knew how those kill count rumors went, he immediately recognized his hunter possessed serious skill.

"That one I still dream about to this day," Irving said. "At that point in my career, I had already killed a shit-ton of people, and it's cool. But when you're on the other end of a scope and he's really good too, it kind of puts you in your place. Maybe I'm not that good."

Pinned down in a small ditch with sniper rounds cracking inches away from his head, the Ranger sniper recalled the mental aspects of his training. He first sorted out the sniper's distance utilizing the snap/bang theory. "You hear the snap of the bullet and you count from one to five in under a second. When you hear the bang of the rifle, the number you land on gives away the distance. I knew how far away he was so I started to think about the different buildings, figuring out where I would be.

"If you're good, you're going to be a spot no one would ever think of, which is what I try to apply. If there's a big building and a pile of dog shit, I'm probably going to put myself in that pile of dog shit and cover myself as opposed to that big, tall building because that's where everybody is going to look. That's where he fucked up."

Irving had earlier noticed an odd building with a curtain hanging up in the window that was the correct range he was looking for. Suspecting he may have found the hide, he decided to make sure . . . by sticking his head up.

But only for an instant. The Chechen fired and missed, but Irving's spotter saw the telltale movement in the window.

"I knew it! I knew that's where that guy was at."

Irving identified the location but found the sniper was too experienced and too well trained to effectively countersniper. He explained, "It took quite a while to find him and spot him. He had everything down to a science but one simple mistake gave him away. But we still couldn't shoot him because he was shooting through small, little holes in the building. Special Forces guys use that a lot—they have a special school just for shooting like that, and he was applying it. He was damn good."

Still pinned down by the sniper, the ambushers started closing in on their position. Irving's spotter next noticed two men three hundred yards away headed in their direction. Irving was unable to make visual contact for fear of giving the Chechen sniper just the look he needed so he talked his teammate though the shot instead.

"Which way are they walking?"

"Left to right."

"Okay, what angle?"

"Thirty-five degrees."

"They are only three hundred yards in front of us and they are walking really slow. Give them a .3 lead."

The spotter squeezed the trigger of his .300 Win Mag.

"Oh fuck."

"What?"

" 'They're not moving. They just stopped."

"Well, fucking hit them then."

"Oh never mind. One of the guys has his hands in the air now."

"Roger that. What's he doing now?"

"He's strutting around."

"What? Did you hit him?"

"I don't think so."

Irving laughed when he recalled the conversation. "He has a .300 Win Mag and at a thousand yards that hits like a .357 at point-blank range." One of the RRC Rangers popped his head up and said, *"Fuck no. You hit him."*

"What do you mean?"

"His whole shit is red."

The sniper explained, "He was wearing a white man dress. I popped my head up a little bit and just saw this arterial spray of blood coming out this guy's arm."

"Hey man, how the fuck do you not see that?"

The wounded fighter's movements resembled an awkward dance, which Irving assumed was related to his brain suffering from the massive blood loss. Once he fell, the other insurgent attempted to apply a tourniquet with his turban.

"It was the worst tourniquet I've ever seen," Irving said. "It was a like a weird bow knot. That was the first time I've ever seen that happen."

◈

The eye-opening deployment continued to deliver fear-and-adrenaline-imprinted memories. On time, Irving's spotter knocked a combatant's head clean off with a shot to his upper chest. And the Reaper later collected his longest combat kill—883 yards.

Again ambushed and pinned down under the light of day, AH-64 Apache gunships arrived and engaged the fighters three hundred yards to the sniper team's left. Rounds then started to streak in from directly in front of their position.

Irving noticed a man dressed in all black. "I got down behind the gun and I'm looking at this guy and he's just spraying away—a long way away. Finally I'm like, 'Fuck it. I'm going to attempt this shot.'

"I'm shooting over this little stream and the stream is going from left to right and the wind is going from right to left. He was up on a hill a little bit. I dialed it for seven hundred and accounted for the slight wind. And I shot."

The bullet hit the ground just in front of its intended target. The Taliban tribesman looked directly where the round impacted and then traced his eyes up to where he intuitively calculated it must have come from.

"Instead of doing another equation, I just took where the bullet hit and basically did like when you copy and paste something," he explained. "I just held that much more to his body. By the time he looked up to where he thought the bullet came from I had already sent another round."

Just as the man's gaze came up, he was impacted in the sternum.

"When the bullet hit, there was no question. Sometimes guys run or spin around a little bit. This guy dropped like an eighteen-wheel truck was dropped from three thousand feet and landed right on his head. He just collapsed. It was weird. That was the cleanest, best shot I ever had. It was intense.

"That was the most memorable shot I ever had. I could see his face. I still know what he looks like to this day."

◈

Irving also helped expand and redefine the way that 3/75 Ranger snipers would operate during direct action missions, actively looking to engage targets during approach, ahead of the final assault.

He explained, "Every single night for four months we were in pretty good firefights. My whole mentality was that I knew I could cover the guys. Instead of having this long drawn-out firefight, it would only take one or two rounds to end the whole thing. So we started walking in front of our element and if we would spot guys, we'd call it up."

"Hey, dude, we got some guys five hundred yards in front of us that are armed."

"Roger that. Take them out."

Irving continued, "Before the team even reaches the building, I'm taking out targets. If possible, I don't want the entry team to have to worry about firefights indoors. I want them pretty much already covered.

"For most of the deployment, I was staying out in front and hitting guys," he said. "And when the actual raid happened, I would take my ladder off my back or free climb a building to cover my guys. Anybody ran out with a gun, I'd shoot those guys. Crazy deployment."

◈

The Reaper earned another title—Master Sniper—a rare honor that signifies an especially accomplished Ranger sniper with extensive school, combat, competition, and teaching experience.

Following the lead of his idol, Carlos Hathcock, Irving was inspired to relay what he had learned to the remainder of 3rd Battalion Sniper Platoon.

"As a Master Sniper, you're like the go-to guy. You've done it all, been to all the schools, and actually applied all that in combat. There are only a handful of Master Snipers.

"And as soon as I got out, I wanted to be training everybody now in the 3rd Battalion who is a BDM [Battalion Designated Marksman] or sniper. When I got back, one of my tasks was to write a handbook for everyone in the 3rd Battalion. I wrote that book and revised it and all the guys read it and applied it.

"That next deployment, a lot of guys came back with a significant number of kills—nothing wazoo—but several kills apiece."

During Irving's standout deployment, the thirty-five men in the platoon he was attached to killed "hundreds of guys . . . and not just regular guys, high-value targets."

That was nothing new for the 75th Ranger Regiment. "According to documents that the Ranger Regiment has put out, we've killed and captured more high-value targets than any other conventional or special operations unit out there," Irving said. "We've been constantly deployed and the numbers speak for themselves."

And now with Rangers of the 75th Ranger Regiment's GWOT golden age returning to civilian life, those numbers and the stories behind them are beginning to be told. Irving wrote about his wartime experience in *The Reaper: Autobiography of One of the Deadliest Special Ops Snipers.* Meanwhile, several other post-9/11 Rangers collaborated to provide firsthand accounts in *Violence of Action*, which leaves no doubt as to the Regiment's significance in modern warfare.

◈

The Reaper's half-mile kills were certainly no chips shots, especially considering the circumstances.

However, they were barely one-third the distance of the longest recorded sniper kill by an American serviceman.

Sgt. Brian Kremer of the 75th Ranger Regiment's 2nd Battalion Sniper Platoon struck down an insurgent like Zeus from a range of 2,515 yards in 2004 with his Barrett M82A1 .50-caliber rifle.

As previously noted, while generally similar, in terms of specifics, the battalion's sniper platoons exist independently of one another and have their own peculiarities. Each tends to favor different climbing tools and techniques and prefers different weapons systems.

And, as a former 3/75 Ranger sniper said, "They look way cooler than us. 2nd Batt has long hair and 1st Batt look like surfers. We just look like average guys."

Kremer's shot ranks among the five longest sniper kills ever recorded and pushes the boundaries of equipment, physics, and good fortune.

The sheer number of variables that can impact accuracy at that range is simply staggering. And it's not merely the wide range of factors that must be accounted for that makes things problematic, it's that they exert their influence simultaneously, each one varying and evolving based on location and/or time.

"A bullet and a weapon system inherently have limitations, driven by cost and a few other things," explained former Navy SEAL sniper Eric Davis. "You can spend $100 on a bullet that will shoot better than a minute of angle (MOA) and you can spend $5000 on a gun that will shoot better than a minute of angle. You put the two together and now the two have the capability of shooting within a one-minute angle of variance. That means that at five hundred yards, the gun and bullet have a five-inch spotlight that it's going to move within during flight. A human being is only like, what, nineteen inches wide? For the gun and the bullet itself, at two thousand yards, it's going to have a twenty-inch span. That means even if the shooter does everything perfect, the gun and the bullet itself may not be accurate enough to guarantee he hits the target."

A sniper attempts to understand his individual weapon as precisely as possible under a variety of conditions by logging and tracking the variables of each shot—a system called DOPE (data on previous engagement).

Both internal and external ballistics must be known. Muzzle velocity and ballistic coefficients (mass, diameter, and drag coefficient) are vitally important factors, and thus the design and consistency of the (match-grade) ammunition. These are further complicated by the fact that the round travels in an arch rather than a straight line, making aerodynamic compromises a necessity.

Of course, the shooter is part of the equation as well due to their body mechanics and recoil management.

And those are the easy, "controllable" factors. Mother Nature is more difficult to read and tame.

Something as simple as the temperature can make a significant difference. Irving said, "If it's really, really hot outside, I know I can shoot really, really far because the air is not as thick as it is when it's cold. Plus my powder is going to burn faster when it's hotter out, so I get way more pressure in my cartridge. If I set a bullet out in 120-degree temp for two days, and the factory box says it shoots twenty-five hundred feet per second, I'm going to tack on another forty to sixty feet per second because it burns so fast at that point."

It gets more and more complicated when you start to factor in distance, gravity, altitude, humidity, density altitude, barometric pressure, wind (both the velocity and the angle—at each and every point between the rifle and the target), and more esoteric concerns such as the Coriolis effect and the Magnus effect.

Irving talked through his thought process when approaching an extreme distance shot: "Anything under a thousand yards, I'm not too worried about all those variables like you are when you're shooting a mile. You have, of course, distance to the target as your first variable. If I dial my scope in to one hundred and I want to shoot someone at a thousand, that bullet is going to start dropping really fucking fast. It's going to hit the ground at three hundred yards. You have to counter the gravity. With a two-thousand-yard shot, I'm aiming forty feet plus in the air.

"Then you have your wind and there's different types of wind. The wind at your barrel, wind halfway, wind at the target, and then wind you can't see, which is where the bullet lives most of its life before it hits the target.

So let's say on a one-thousand-yard shot, I'm going to have an elevation of sixteen feet above the bore of my rifle set on my scope. I have no idea what that wind's doing. The only thing I can account for is what I see and feel on the ground. At that point, I'm like, 'If it's five miles per hour on the ground, it's probably somewhere around seven miles per hour at sixteen feet.'

"Then on a really long shot you have the Coriolis effect, which is the spin of the Earth. I'm accounting for the earth moving and deflecting the bullet, which is impacting the latitude and direction. When I pull the trigger on a one-thousand-yard shot with a .308, my flight time is going to be 1.2 seconds. Where is that target going to be with the rotation of the Earth 1.2 seconds from now? I'm adding on a little bit of a lead—tenth of a mil—plus the wind and all that shit.

"You also have the Magnus effect and spin drift but nobody gives too much of a shit about that. It's the torque of the bullet—like when a pitcher throws a curve ball. He puts a lot of spin on the ball. Same thing with a bullet—it spins to the right and when it starts to slow down and gets into its transonic state, that torque starts to tweak the bullet and make it want to pull to the right. You have to account for that at really extreme distances."

And while, as Accuracy 1st's Todd Hodnett likes to say, the bullet does not have a vote, the target certainly does. Even if the target is moving in a predictable, consistent fashion, the direction and speed must be taken into account. But over distances where the bullet must fly for seconds, there's plenty of time for those variables to change midflight.

Ballistic computers have automated many of the approximate equations and revolutionized accuracy in many respects.

The promise of even greater technological impact is on the horizon with weapons systems that themselves automate the process to a large degree.

With TrackingPoint, a user essentially "tags" a target, and the system then adjusts for multiple variables—humidity, temperature, barometric pressure, density altitude, and so on. Developed by John McHale following a frustrating safari hunt, the user simply pulls the trigger and the weapon fires once the adjusted crosshairs meet the tag.

Larry Vickers, a retired Delta Force instructor, Delta marksmanship instructor, and SOTIC grad, admitted, "It works great. I've heard of people hitting steel targets at eight hundred yards. But it doesn't adjust for wind, and that's an issue. But what somebody told me is, while it's very impressive, it works best with neophyte shooters. If you're a skilled shooter, you have trigger control, and the ability to align the reticle and hit the target."

Meanwhile, DARPA (Defense Advanced Research Projects Agency)—the world-altering DoD blue sky research and development agency that spurred the creation of the Internet, GPS, stealth aircraft, speech recognition software, etc.—has successfully demonstrated the effectiveness of EX-ACTO (Extreme Accuracy Tasked Ordinance)—a self-guided .50-caliber round.

EXACTO rounds adjust and change direction midflight, which has led some to predict that the current long-distance sniper records are about to fall and fall hard.

Vickers said, "There could be areas that a self-guiding round is beneficial for argument's sake. But it's going to be, the lower the skill set that the guy brings to the table, the more beneficial it's going to be, and the higher the skill set the less beneficial it's going to be."

Irving's knee-jerk reaction to the technological advancements at first comes across a bit like that of an assembly line worker about to lose his job to a manufacturing robot. However, his criticisms have merit, especially considering all that's required from modern spec ops snipers.

"I think it's fucking stupid," Irving said. "I think they should leave that alone. What DARPA's doing—I get it as far as technology-wise. But I'm a firm believer that technology fails at some point all the time. I've seen that happen. I've had laser range finders and cameras and all that just take a shit on a mission. And those basic mathematical equations you need to make a bullet go where it needs to go . . . it only takes a couple seconds to do if you're really good at it. But if you're not and the technology fails, what are you going to do?"

Irving contends that while many mistakenly believe the shooting aspect is far and away the largest determining factor for succeeding in the sniper role, that's actually far from the case.

"People think that sniping is shoot, shoot, shoot. Don't get me wrong—you have to be a good shooter. But 90 percent of our job is being able to get put in a situation—in a vehicle or in the woods or in the mountains—and blend in. And then you have to be able to take the shot without being seen or sometimes even heard.

"I've been through schools where you learn how to angle windows or doorways of buildings so when the shot goes off, it sounds like it comes from another room or even another building. You learn a lot about deception. Shooting the bullet—anyone can do that. If I gave a guy an equation and he plugged it into a calculator and applied it to the scope and pulled the trigger, eight times out of ten they're going to hit the target. But if they missed that first shot and didn't have the rest of it mastered, they'd be fucked."

13

Champions

The redirect away from Iraq also brought renewed attention to the parallel black-and-white SOF components in Afghanistan.

While the Joint Special Operations Command (and the collection of entities in its orbit) continued to serve as the primary CT force there and globally, Combined Joint Special Operations Task Force–Afghanistan (CJSOTF-A) had also operated continuously throughout the war.

Built on an Army Special Forces framework, and working in conjunction with other ISAF SOF such as Polish GROM and Canada's JTF-2, CJSOTF-A in part grew out of Task Force K-Bar.

While Adm. McRaven had taken control of JSOC, the larger United States Special Operations Command (USSOCOM) was now under the watch of Adm. Eric Thor Olson—the same SEAL officer who was awarded a Silver Star for his actions alongside the Black Team snipers in Mogadishu, Somalia, in 1993, just prior to his taking command of DEVGRU.

And just as McRaven had become the first SEAL in charge of JSOC in June 2008, Olson became the first SEAL to head SOCOM in July 2007, representing a pivotal shift in the nation's SOF powerbase.

Meanwhile, Army Special Forces directed CJSOTF-A, which had a new player under its watch.

Despite facing institutional obstacles on both sides, the performance of Det One in Iraq made a convincing, and ultimately winning, argument in favor of the addition of a full-time USMC component of SOCOM.

In late 2005, Secretary of Defense Donald Rumsfeld formally approved the formation of MARSOC. While it was heavily influenced by Det One, some were disappointed that it was not a direct outgrowth of the pilot program. Since its introduction, MARSOC's exact structure has fluctuated as it has sought to establish a niche among the nation's versatile and semi-redundant special operations forces.

Initially, MARSOC was split into two distinct operational elements. The 1st and 2nd Force Recon Companies were gutted to form the backbone for the new 1st and 2nd Marine Special Operations Battalions (MSOBs), which had a heavy direct action and special reconnaissance emphasis. Meanwhile, Marine infantrymen were tapped to man a foreign internal defense branch, originally called Foreign Military Training Unit (FMTU), and then rebranded Marine Special Operations Advisor Group (MSOAG).

Even though Det One had made its mark in Iraq and that theater was still erupting with volcanic intensity at the time of MARSOC's formation, from the start the MSOBs were tasked with preparing for Afghanistan operations in order to be declared mission ready as quickly as possible, leaving the SEAL Teams to continue supplying the direct action firepower in Iraq.

In early 2007, the Marine Special Operations Company-Fox from the 2nd Battalion was sent to Afghanistan marking the new command's first combat deployment.

It did not go well.

Feeling less than fully embraced or properly supported by CJSOTF-A above, the self-dubbed "Task Force Violence" eschewed the "lowly" reconnaissance missions it was assigned and instead shopped itself as a de facto black ops unit to the CIA, intent on running direct action missions against HVTs near the Afghanistan-Pakistan border.

In doing so, it concealed more than two dozen operations from the Special Forces commanders who controlled the task force. The MARSOC

Marines found themselves embroiled in further controversy after a major shootout broke out when their convoy was attacked in Nangarhar Province in March 2007.

The attack became an international incident. The Marines shot their way out of what they termed a coordinated ambush but others alleged they killed nearly twenty civilians in a retreating rampage.

CJSOTF-A kicked them out of country less than a month later.

Despite the inauspicious start, subsequent deployments were more successful and MARSOC continued its evolution as it found its feet.

In 2009, the FID component, MSOAG, was rebranded the 3rd MSOB and all three MSOBs were now under the Marine Special Operations Regiment (MSOR). A shared selection and training pipeline was developed for which to groom its Critical Skills Operators (CSOs), who form the bulk of each fourteen-man Marine Special Operations Team (MSOT)—effectively MARSOC's take on a twelve-man SF-ODA or sixteen-man SEAL platoon.

With MSOAG dissolved, all three battalions ostensibly focused on direct action, special reconnaissance, *and* foreign internal defense—again, positioning them somewhere between SF and SEALs. However, until the pipeline more fully repopulated and balanced each of the MSOBs, the 3rd continued to have an FID bent while the 1st and 2nd were designated DASR (direct action/special reconnaissance) battalions.

The rapid evolution on the young command has continued with additional significant changes. Most recently, after a long, consistent push (and informal internal adoption), the "Raider" tag was officially brought out of retirement. While the overall command retains the MARSOC tag (similar to the Army's USASOC), its subordinate units are now Raiders—for example, the Marine Raider Regiment, and the 1st Marine Raider Battalion.

The growing confidence of the Raiders inside SOCOM was made evident in '09 when the 1st Raider Battalion (then still 1st MSOB) assumed control of all CJSOT-A's SOF units and operations in northern and western Afghanistan.

Following continual deployments since its ominous debut, a number of Raiders have won glory or made great sacrifices—and all too frequently both.

◈

In March 2012, Gunnery Sergeant Jonathan Gifford was deployed to Badghis Province, located in the northwest of Afghanistan and sharing a border with Turkmenistan.

The thirty-four-year-old Gifford had nearly fifteen years of specialized experience and training with which to help guide and protect the men of MSOT 8232.

He was actually a pre-9/11 Force Recon Marine. He got out in July 2001 and moved back to Florida, only to see the world change and his talents in demand two months later.

By 2003, he was back with 2nd Force Reconnaissance and operating in the mountains of Afghanistan. His proficiency as a sniper was recognized in 2006, when he was assigned to serve as the chief instructor for the Marine Special Operations Forces Advanced Sniper Course (MASC) in the formative days of MARSOC.

MASC is a four-week course that prepares MARSOC Scout Snipers to effectively operate as special operations snipers. It not only refreshes them on the basics, but it also instructs on the use of advanced ballistic computers and weapons technologies, untraditional techniques, tactics, and positions, along with aerial sniping and urban and vehicle hides.

In '09, the CSO was made Team Chief for Team 8232 of the 2nd MSOB—the same battalion that got off to such a rocky start in '07—and deployed to Afghanistan in that capacity in 2010 and 2012, earning two Bronze Stars for valor for his actions.

Only July 29, Afghan Commandos from a Special Operations Kandak (battalion) who were being trained by Gifford's MSOT were struck by enemy fire. A half mile away at the time, the CSO raced to their location on an ATV, performed first aid on the downed soldiers, and then transported them to a location where they could be medevaced out.

He raced back across the field once more, this time to take the fight to their assailants. He eliminated an insurgent who was shooting through a window and then scaled the Taliban-held compound and put a grenade down through the chimney.

Gifford continued to press the advance until he was ultimately hit by fatal small arms fire.

Gunnery Sergeant Jonathan Gifford was posthumously awarded the Navy Cross—the second highest award for valor, ranked only behind the Medal of Honor.

◈

Numerous Marine Scout Snipers from the conventional Scout Sniper Platoons have also demonstrated remarkable bravery in Afghanistan.

2/8 SSP Team Leader Lance Corporal Joshua Moore received the Navy Cross for his bravery in March 2011, when he scooped up and threw a live grenade that had been tossed into their besieged compound back out the window to protect two wounded Marines. He then charged out of the building and countered with M4 and M203 fire of his own.

3/5 SSP Team Leader Sergeant Matthew Abbate was posthumously awarded the Navy Cross for the extreme heroism he displayed in October 2011 when a Marine patrol came under ambush. Matters were made considerably worse when they discovered they were standing in an unswept minefield and three members of the patrol were incapacitated by the explosives. Abbate raced through a minefield to draw enemy fire and repelled the ambush. He then cleared a landing zone so the wounded could be extracted and subsequently led another counterattack to fend off yet another ambush.

Abbate was killed in action less than two months later.

The Scout Snipers did not escape their share of controversy either, sparking a pair of international incidents. The ugliness of war, especially an unending one waged against a fanatical enemy, prompted even more ugliness. The same hate and anger that are often leveraged to fuel passion and bravery are not always easily confined in a neat little box. Nor are the realities of mortal conflict always easily understood by those living continents away.

Scout Snipers from 3/2s SSP were filmed urinating on the bodies of the corpses of Taliban fighters and the video later surfaced online, creating widespread uproar in January 2012.

Earlier, a different sort of image of hate caused outrage as photos leaked of Charlie Company, 1st Recon Battalion Scout Snipers posed in front of a flag displaying a Nazi Schutzstaffel SS logo in 2010. Additionally, it was discovered 1/7 SSP Scout Snipers were photographed using the logo as early as 2004. While believed to be indicative of ignorance rather than anything deeper, the usage was a very public black mark on the misunderstood and often maligned profession of sniper.

◈

The formation of MARSOC sealed the fate of the 1st and 2nd Force Reconnaissance Companies, which were deactivated in 2006 as its Force Recon Marines formed the core of the 1st and 2nd MSOBs. The remaining Force Recon Marines were funneled into Division Recon Battalions in the form of D Companies. These D Companies consisted of DRPs (Deep Reconnaissance Platoons), so that the USMC could retain direct control over at least a small organic Force Recon–style capability even as it handed off MARSOC to SOCOM.

By 2008, the D Companies had reconstituted to the point they were formally redesignated Force Recon, allowing USMC to have its cake and eat it in a way. However, the overlap also created confusion and competition, while further muddying MARSOC's place as it attempted to find its way, both in the larger SOF world and in service of the Marine Corps.

Those concerns were not in the minds of the Marines on the ground in 2008, certainly not during the course of a multihour chaotic clash that took place over the disputed village of Shewan in Farah Province.

A 2/7 Marine infantry platoon had been driven from the village located in southwestern Afghanistan. In response, an experienced team of Force Recon Marines was called in to reclaim it.

Despite fully expecting scathing resistance, the Marines had no idea they'd be facing down 150 organized Taliban insurgents as they cleared the village and rooted out the guerrillas.

As the force approached the village, they were subjected to a salvo of RPG and small arms fire from an entrenched force, emboldened by their recent rout of the Marine platoon.

With the team pinned down in a disabled Humvee and in the kill zone, Corporal Franklin Simmons braved the gunfire to established a superior position on a nearby berm.

The Force Recon sniper then proceeded to dispatch eighteen Taliban fighters over the next twenty minutes with his Mk 11 Mod 0 SR-25, despite rounds repeatedly impacting mere inches from his position.

He added two more kills to his tally that day as the Force Recon Marines—aided by the overwhelmingly effective close air support from a pair of USAF F-15E Strike Eagles—roundly defeated the enemy during a battle that raged for the next eight hours. In the end, sixty to one hundred Taliban were left dead versus no losses for the Marines and the village was reclaimed.

Simmons was awarded a Silver Star for his lethal accuracy and courage under fire. Another Force Recon Marine, Captain Byron Owen, also received a Silver Star, while twenty-eight awards for valor in all were earned in the battle.

◈

Throughout the long and sometimes overlooked engagement in Afghanistan, the contributions of the venerable Army Special Forces and Navy SEAL Teams have sometimes been overlooked. However, both have made obvious the extreme value of marrying special operations skills with sniper training.

These versatile force multiplier assets have routinely separated not only victory from defeat, but life from death. Countless American and allied troops' continued existence has relied directly on the ability of the men glassing and sending rounds downrange in their protection.

Besides anecdotes of feats that come across more like scenes from an action movie than real-world combat—such as the triple kill pulled off by a SEAL Team Three sniper who waited until just the right millisecond to pull the trigger, cleanly piercing a single round through three insurgents who were sitting alongside one another in a moving Toyota Hilux—there are also countless larger tales of such tremendous valor they would test credulity if portrayed on the silver screen.

The story of Marcus Luttrell, the "lone survivor" of his SDV-1 sniper team during Operation Red Wings, is not a solitary case. Rather it serves as an example of the level of heroism that's been demonstrated by SOF snipers in Afghanistan since 9/11.

◈

When the Afghanistan War was still in its relative infancy, Sergeants First Class Josh Betten and Andrew Lewis planned a six-day sniper mission to get a bead on a suspected enemy force so that they might provide early warning to their firebase ahead of an attack.

On the opening night of their op, they found themselves nearly overrun.

The two men hailed from ODA-2072 of the 20th Special Forces Group—one of two SFGs belonging to the Army National Guard—but they certainly didn't perform like part-timers in combat.

Lewis, who served as a Marine during the First Gulf War, immediately took out an attacker with a claymore mine and then dropped another with his sidearm. Betten, meanwhile, eliminated three others as the gun battle broke. The Guardsmen dumped rounds and grenades with abandon to keep the closing pack at bay, the two alternating between firing and reloading.

With machine-gun fire tracking them from both sides, the two sprinted to a cliff and slid five hundred meters down the side of the mountain to make their escape and report back to base.

Both were awarded Silver Stars. A decade later, they remain with the National Guard. Betten, in fact, remains with the 20th SFG's 3rd Battalion. Lewis went on to serve with the Army's Asymmetric Warfare Group and later became Deputy Director of the DoD's Counter Narco-Terrorism Task Force.

◈

In March 2004, Sergeant First Class Stephan Johns from the 3rd Special Forces Group was in heliborne sniper overwatch during an assault on an al-Qaeda and Taliban force in Northeast Afghanistan.

His helicopter was hit and forced down between the two combating elements. All on his own, he fended off numerous attempts to rush his position. Holding his ground more than a half hour, another bird was finally mustered to retrieve him. The Green Beret from ODA-334 killed nine fighters before finally making his escape.

Johns was also awarded a Silver Star.

◈

Another Silver Star was awarded to an SF sniper in July 2006. Sergeant First Class Eric Horton of ODA-776 disrupted an attempted ambush in Helmand Province with remarkable efficiency—and later grit.

The Green Beret immediately tore into the guerrillas with multiple killing strikes. He then repositioned himself to acquire a better vantage point and removed fifteen insurgents from the battlefield in thirty pulls of the trigger. That accuracy prompted a concentrated counterattack in his direction and was slammed by machine-gun fire in the shoulder. He was not out of the fight yet, however, initially refusing aid and engaging the enemy with a mounted M-240B machine gun and his one good arm, even as others attended to his wounds. Horton was credited with thirty-five sniper kills that night alone.

◈

Remarkably, Staff Sergeant Seth Howard of the 3rd SFG was just one of ten Green Berets from ODA-3336 to be awarded the Silver Star in a single battle in April 2008.

The team, joined by a squad of thirty Afghan Commandos, leapt several feet down from their hovering CH-47 Chinook helicopters and onto the snow below that draped the Shok Valley's jagged cliffs. Deep within the foreboding Nuristan Province valley, the daring assault plan called for them to penetrate the desolate mountain fortress never successfully invaded by U.S. or Soviet forces.

The target of Operation Commando Wrath was Gulbuddin Hekmatyar, the leader of Hezb-e-Islami Gulbuddin—a violent militant group that had made a most unwelcome resurgence in the preceding months.

The element of surprise was short-lived for the SOF assault team as the stronghold proved even more heavily fortified and defended than feared. While scaling the near-vertical cliffs in an attempt to reach the objective, they were attacked by an overwhelming force of nearly two hundred, who issued a flurry of RPG, small arms, and sniper fire.

Howard led a force of Afghan Commandos and fought through searing fire coming from multiple directions to reinforce critically wounded members of his ODA who were under threat of being overrun.

After climbing into position, Howard took cover behind the body of their slain interpreter, and, through the effective use of his sniper weapon and a recoilless rifle, personally accounted for the elimination of upward of twenty enemy combatants, including four trained snipers.

The team's attached USAF CCT, SrA Zachary Rhyner of 21STS, created the conditions to allow for the team's escape, directing close air support from F-15E Strike Eagles and AH-64 Apaches. During the seven-hour Battle of Shok Valley, Rynher controlled fifty dangerously close strikes, despite being wounded and trapped on a sixty-foot cliff.

Howard then defended the team's retreat down the mountain by providing precise overwatch fire before finally descending himself.

The team made a three-hour march to the extraction zone—which was only reached by helicopters that flew beneath power lines and took heavy fire, wounding one pilot.

Despite multiple injuries, every American soldier escaped with his life. All but three of the partnered Afghans survived.

Along with the ten SF soldiers, the ODA's Combat Cameraman was also awarded the Silver Star. And Rhyner, the CCT, received the Air Force Cross—just the third CCT to ever earn the medal. Two other Americans earned the Bronze Star.

◈

SEAL Team Seven Platoon Leading Chief Petty Officers Joseph Molina and Thom Shea were each awarded Bronze Stars with V devices for leading SEAL sniper teams in defense of a pinned-down SF ODA in July 2009.

Their QRF stormed over a ridgeline and, following a day-long battle, the ODA was able to escape unscathed. The SEALs accounted for twenty-two kills, including a high-angle, eleven-hundred-yard shot by Shea.

During that deployment Shea's BRAVO platoon was credited with 174 kills and six HVT captures. Shea also received a Silver Star during the deployment and returned to the States to serve as the Officer in Charge of the SEAL Sniper Course. Now a CEO and ultramarathon runner, he retired in 2014 following twenty-three years of service as a SEAL.

Molina too earned a Silver Star on that tour. The Southern Californian led his platoon through a two-day battle in which they eliminated fifty-six insurgents while taking no losses. His platoon was credited with 181 kills during their six-month deployment.

◈

SF soldier Chad Brack—an unapologetic nontheist existing in an overtly religious domain—earned his Silver Star with a series of life-saving and heroic actions over a three-day period in May 2011.

ODA-3332 was paired up with indigenous SOF of the 1st Company 2nd Commando Kandak, who cleared the Nuristan Province villages of Awlagal and Chapo. However, they were outmaneuvered by Taliban insurgents who had the team trapped in the valley below, utilizing the high ground supplied by three enveloping cliffs.

Sgt. 1st Class Brack gave up cover to throw down suppressive fire with his Mk 13 Mod 5 .300 Win Mag—including keeping the heads of two enemy snipers down—allowing the combined SF/Commando force to scramble to a more defensible position.

After fending back another attempted ambush, the SF sniper put the enemies nearby command and control position on notice by sending precise fire their way. He then swapped to his M4 to cover the retrieval of a wounded friendly solider and again set about denying the enemy snipers—this time buying time for the arrival of AH-64 Apaches which promptly obliterated their hide—as directed by Brack.

Later, the insurgents cleverly attempted to shoot and set off explosives left on a nearby roof during the initial clearing operation. Brack braved the fire to snatch them.

Finally, he braved the way up front to lead their escape from the valley—urging forward the Afghan SOF whose performance had instilled little confidence throughout.

In addition to the Silver Star, Brack has twice been awarded the Bronze Star, as well as a Purple Heart and numerous other commendations.

◉

While American SOF across the board enjoyed more than its share of victories in Afghanistan, the undisputed champion of the AO was the Naval Special Warfare Development Group.

SEAL Team Six had waited a long time for this . . . its entire existence in fact.

While Delta Force and DEVGRU notionally ranked side-by-side atop the nation's counterterrorism hierarchy as its preeminent direct action components, history spoke loudly to the contrary.

Whether down to merit or the men in command who made the call, Delta traditionally got the coveted mission taskings while SEAL Team Six got the consolation prize, if not the shaft altogether.

Even its position as the dominant hunter-killer unit in Afghanistan that it had been "gifted" was—well, not exactly a stocking full of coal, but perhaps at the same "gee, thanks" level of a package of socks from Grandma.

When JSOC gave its initial order after September 11, two Delta Force squadrons rotated through the country, one of them getting the first shot at bin Laden.

It was only when it became obvious that the serious CT work was going to take place in Iraq that Delta truly pulled up their stakes and replanted itself in the new theater. That left DEVGRU to slog it out in Afghanistan, a war zone that had frozen over operationally since its opening flurry, lacking both political will and ready targets.

While far busier than it had been at any point previously with endless three-month rotations for its squadrons and continual real-world ops—including some groundbreaking missions—there had to be that familiar sense of envy when it looked over to see how the other half lived.

In the mid-2000s, Delta Force broke new ground and shattered previously held beliefs about operational limits. Its operators brought dread, chaos, and lead in equal portions as it surgically dissected terrorist networks, blasting through doors and demonstrating its CQB prowess in live combat.

The sailors of SEAL Team Six, meanwhile, trudged through the snow and hiked miles on end across the spines of unforgiving mountain ridgelines in hopes that an al-Qaeda player of note had stuck his head out of hiding or wandered back across the border.

◈

DEVGRU did get its tastes of the blistering intensity of Iraq that was Delta's nightly existence—certainly enough to see what it had been missing.

A Warsaw Pact–trained sniper terrorized American troops in Iraq, killing several Army soldiers in the process. A number of snipers volunteered to take on the countersniper assignment, but one Black Team sniper from Red Squadron threw himself into the mission.

A former SEAL sniper instructor explained, "If you're on the glass all the time, it's going to happen, it's just a matter of when. Some guys slack off, but if you have the key attributes—you're patient, conscious, alert, and don't get fatigued—you'll get the results. This guy had them and he got them. He set up in a hide for six days drinking tea. He waited the sniper out and sure enough, a barrel finally appeared through the wall. That was all it took. He shot him right down the hole."

That was just one in scores of kills taken by ST6 in Iraq. Task Force Blue worked the western half of the nation and set its sights on putting bomb-making networks out of business the JSOC way—rapid successions of raids targeting midlevel and local leaders, which branched out through the network's spiderweb of connections as they snapped into focus.

Ultimately, DEVGRU killed and captured hundreds in these efforts while helping to drastically curtail IED attacks on coalition forces . . . but it's all relative.

SEAL Team Six's primary focus was Afghanistan and Afghanistan was not the place to be—not if you're at the top of the CT food chain anyway. But then, eventually, it was.

◈

DEVGRU had not only been the victim of the Army's institutional grasp over the nation's SOF hierarchy, some felt that it had also long suffered due to institutional issues much closer to home.

ST6 founder Richard Marcinko's rogue legacy had impacted the unit's standing in the wider special operations community—an effect that lasted for decades after the end of his command (Marcinko had only actually led the unit from '80 to '83).

Marcinko was brilliant in his theories but arguably less so in realizing them. A unit such as SEAL Team Six requires iconoclastic, independent risk takers . . . but also extremely professional, dedicated ones. While he may have found the sorts of cowboys he needed, he issued them black hats rather than gold stars and they readily followed his lead.

Robert Gormly was the first in a succession of officers who worked hard to retain the unit's edge but also sharpen its shark-toothed roughness into a finely honed blade. He faced a steep uphill climb.

Upon arrival, SEAL Team Six's XO warned him that despite Marcinko's boasts to the contrary, the unit had not been trained to an elite standard. Challenging exercises were often ended early because "as soon as things got tough, Dick would step in, abort the exercise, and take the troops drinking."

Another ST6 officer of the era recalled similar sentiments about the actual readiness of the unit, with whispers suggesting that it was "all show, no go" in those formative years.

It was said Marcinko had assembled a "personal fiefdom" around himself. Highly motivated and gifted SEALs could be turned away while "shit birds" were pulled into the flock and the officers (outside of Marcinko) were undermined, creating "a rigid meritocracy married to the worst sort of personality cult . . . that brought out the worst portions of cronyism, backstabbing, and flattery."

Gormly gave the arrogant yet underperforming maritime CT unit a reality check, requiring it to train and maintain standards in line with its extraordinarily demanding mission requirements.

However, Marcinko had assembled the unit from the ground up and his influence remained deeply ingrained in its DNA. The rogue warrior had constructed an inherently rogue organization. Subsequent leaders fought to exploit the inspired underlying concepts that drove his initial vision, while removing the less capable and less wholesome elements of what they had inherited.

But despite the dedicated and well-directed attempts of Gormly and those who succeeded him, in the eyes of some SEAL Team Six's reputation had largely been cemented. Even as DEVGRU enhanced its operational capabilities to a world-class standard, others in the military still viewed the unit as an enabled pack of outlaws—tremendously skilled outlaws, no doubt, but outlaws all the same. More worrisome, so too did some of its operators, who embraced the image and cultivated the belief that they were above the law.

◈

With two decades to change its culture, DEVGRU entered the post-9/11 world boasting professionalism and talent comparable to its Army counterpart, without having completely shed its inner rebel.

Leaders like Olson and McRaven elevated DEVGRU to a new level, directly through their leadership, and indirectly by pulling the unit up with them as they advanced through the ranks.

Ironically, McRaven was one of the junior officers Marcinko had run off back in the day, back when McRaven headed an ST6 squadron but refused to get on board with the commander's orders to conduct undisclosed "questionable activities."

Marcinko later criticized McRaven, claiming he "took the *special* out of *special* warfare." However, the argument could be made that the studious and measured Texan actually "brought the *special* out of *special* warfare" when he at last had the power to do so, rewarding DEVGRU with its golden age once it had come to more closely reflect his image than that of its founding father.

Even Delta alumni recognized the impressive transformation, citing "extraordinary efforts on the part of the SEAL community to enhance the professionalism and capabilities of the SEALs" and noting that "they're not the SEAL Team Six that Dick Marcinko put together."

◈

The Naval unit faced some serious growing pains as it first acclimatized to the harsh, mountainous backdrop presented by Afghanistan. While Delta Force had the luxury of extensive mountaineering training, Six had the heavy burden of maintaining its maritime capabilities, a time-consuming endeavor and one that suddenly paid few dividends.

As a result, initially, the Navy special mission unit was alleged to lack the training, gear, and mindset necessary to operate effectively and were roundly (and unsurprisingly) criticized by their Army counterparts, who might prefer ST6 stay in the water.

However, thrown in the deep end, over time DEVGRU learned how to "swim" in this very different setting. With a generation of operators who had grown up developing tactics in the barren land, by the time the Afghanistan War reclaimed the nation's focus, SEAL Team Six were masters of the mountainous terrain and more than ready to take the lead.

Afghanistan wasn't an ideal match for the tools JSOC had pioneered under McChrystal's watch and expanded under McRaven's in Iraq; it lacked the infrastructure, population density, and flat geography that had allowed Delta et al. to elevate their tempo to a prestissimo pace. However, the targeting and execution had become so efficient that the capability for exploiting these methods remained very much intact.

In an overwhelming display of kinetic intensity, the renewed campaign doubled its pace each successive year: coalition SOF killed more than thirteen hundred insurgents and captured seventeen hundred more during a four-month span in 2011, during which JSOC ran five hundred of the four thousand total missions and "had done most of the killing."

Afghanistan became SEAL Team Six's opportunity to showcase their ability to dominate compressed and chaotic kill zones.

"Nobody does CQB or direct action the way SEAL Team Six does— that's a fact," said former DEVGRU operator Howard Wasdin.

A former Six officer echoed those sentiments, claiming DEVGRU is not "just *good* at multiple-room CQB; there is no one else in the world that comes close."

"I'd be lying if I said that most of the people inside SEAL Team Six didn't think they were at that next elite level," Wasdin added. "If you go to SEAL Team Six compound, you have the billion-dollar trainer sitting right there off to the right and you can go in and shoot 360 degrees in any direction, throw a real grenade, take out an elevator, and have it all video recorded. You don't have that kind of training anywhere else."

Even in the early days following 9/11, the NSWDG CQB range featured eighteen HD monitors, quad video inputs, theatrical special effects, microwave motion sensors and pressure pads, and day and night camera tracking to capture it all on film (well, hard drive, actually). It's difficult to fathom what toys it may feature fifteen years and a budget explosion later.

In Afghanistan, SEAL Team Six's opportunities to put its prodigious combat marksmanship talents into practice often hinged on its ability to operate in the harsh environment unhindered. Armed not only with Hk416 and quad-tube NVGs, but also superior training, conditioning, and around a decade's worth of experience running ops in the nation's most unforgiving battlegrounds, DEVGRU routinely outmaneuvered the locals. They seized the initiative on enemy forces who previously considered their mountainside lairs all but unassailable by foreign forces.

To maximize this advantage, assaulting SEAL Team Six troops performed offset infils as standard operating procedure, disembarking from 160th SOAR helicopters out of hearing range and then hiking for hours across several miles of terrain in order to retain the element of surprise.

The responsibility for this game changer rested largely on the shoulders of Black Team, whose recce snipers mapped out potential LZs and paths to targets ahead of the missions. They then patrolled out ahead of the stealthy infiltration hikes and scouted the objective once in position. As the assault commenced, they would climb into position and pull overwatch duty (if not be included in the door kicking) and then assume the lead once again during exfiltration.

DEVGRU not only tore through Mullah Omar's Quetta Shura Taliban networks in the south, the Islamic Movement of Uzbekistan in the north, and the al-Qaeda-linked Lashkar-e-Taiba and Haqqani Network in the east, it also successfully pulled off a series of dramatic hostage rescue operations.

It was one they did not that underlined just how important their mountaineering talents had become in enabling their success.

◈

Intercepted communications suggested that, in October 2010, kidnapped Scottish aid worker Linda Norgrove, who had been captured and held by Taliban insurgents, was in imminent danger of either being executed in torturous fashion or transported to al-Qaeda-linked factions in Pakistan.

Held at eight thousand feet in northern Kunar Province, the urgent time frame prevented SEAL Team Six from utilizing what had become its preferred method; a silent ascent on foot from miles away was deemed impossible.

Coming in loud and fast in a predawn raid with an AC-130U gunship watching from above, the assault team fast-roped from Night Stalker MH-60 Black Hawks directly onto the compound grounds.

Recce snipers aboard the helicopters immediately dispatched multiple sentries, defending the assaulters' rapid descent to Earth.

With six insurgents taken out in the opening seconds by precise fire, Norgrove was nearly free. However, one of her captors had pulled her from the building, an act unrecognized by the rescue force. She broke free and curled into the fetal position as the gunfight raged just above her head.

An operator tossed a grenade at the sole remaining combatant from a nearby roof. The explosive killed the Taliban fighter but also severely wounded the hidden Norgrove.

She ultimately succumbed to her wounds.

It was initially reported by the assault team that Norgrove had been killed by a Taliban suicide vest. Only days later, following the careful review of drone and helmet cam footage, did the reality of the situation become apparent.

The culprit came forward and admitted the mistake. He was dismissed from Six while several others were disciplined for not speaking up immediately.

While the judgment of the SEAL at fault was a crucial factor, the rescue was made riskier and more complex than it might have been had the team not been forced to make a heliborne assault against awaiting captors.

Providing additional evidence of the hazards of the method was the more recent successful rescue of Dr. Dilip Joseph, whom SEAL Team Six freed from the Taliban in the mountains near the Pakistan border. However, Navy Petty Officer 1st Class Nicolas Checque was killed during the course of a gunfight that was spurred by the sound of incoming helicopters. While seven insurgents were killed and two others apprehended in the course of the successful rescue, the loss of Checque served as another scaring reminder of all that can go wrong during the course of such a high-risk mission.

But when tactically freed up by a recce-led offset infiltration, DEVGRU has shown it can execute even the most demanding of rescues with surgical exactness.

Four months following the attempted air assault on the Shok Valley by Special Forces ODA-3336, Gulbuddin Hekmatyar's militant group, Hezb-e-Islami, had taken an American Army Corps of Engineers worker hostage. He was being held in the mountains of Wardak Province with his captors convinced the treacherous terrain would shield them from any potential attack.

However, DEVGRU, with Army Rangers in support, set down and stepped out of the 160th SOAR MH-47E Chinooks some miles from the camp.

The troop leveraged its ability to conquer the terrain. Over a period of several hours and under cover of darkness, the element traversed the mountain path and approached the hut unseen at three a.m.

A small assault force took the captors completely unaware with suppressed weapons, killing them before they even realized a rescue attempt was in process.

It was a similar story in June 2012, when four aid workers—Briton Helen Johnston, Kenyan Moragwa Oirere, and two Afghani women—were successfully rescued in Badakhshan Province, near the Tajikistan border, in a joint HR operation conducted by ST6 and the British SAS.

Here, too, the commandos set down miles from the camp and hiked through the forested mountains in order to execute simultaneous nighttime raids. Completely outmatched in terms of training and technology, the Taliban captors were wiped out in mere moments. DEVGRU snuffed out seven kidnappers while the SAS killed four and saved all four aid workers.

◈

This mounting track record (including a dozen or so clandestine raids across the border into Pakistan) made SEAL Team Six the natural force of choice once HVT-1 had been pinned down to a compound in Abbottabad—intelligence that spurred the single-most coveted SOF mission ever embarked upon.

And it probably didn't hurt that former SEAL Team Six officers controlled the top two chairs in the nation's spec ops community.

Former Black Teamer Craig Sawyer, who suffered through the unit's leaner years, said, "Most of the JSOC commanders have been Army. In fact, most of them came through Delta. So it didn't matter which unit was appropriate for the job, it just mattered whose daddy ran JSOC at the time. Well, that's changed a little bit. A Navy Admiral was running JSOC for a while and SEAL Team Six got to show what they could do."

Operation Neptune Spear—the mission that killed bin Laden—was the most expansive, expensive, and ambitious manhunt in the history, requiring breakthrough technologies on multiple fronts plus a decade of concentrated effort from dozens of entities, thousands of experts, and millions of man hours.

It was the ultimate expression of the joint counterterrorism capability that had been founded in the wake of the Operation Eagle Claw humiliation and perfected following ten years of brutally relentless combat versus this new breed of fanatical adversary.

However, for the operators of Red Squadron, it was simply what they do.

Adm. McRaven said so explicitly: "It is what we do. We get on helicopters, we go to objectives, we secure the objectives, we get back on helicopters, and we come home."

"They do it constantly," added Sawyer. "They do it all the time, and a lot of times there is fierce resistance. And it's usually never heard about."

The unit had certainly pulled off more technical and challenging operations while shredding through much better prepared enemy defenses. The crash of the previously unknown modified "Stealth Hawk" required a bit of improvisation, but again, that is what they do.

However, the adjustment required an alternate method of bagging bin Laden. The original mission plan evoked one utilized by Delta Force to rescue Kurt Muse from Carcel Modelo prison in Panama City during Operation Acid Gambit in 1989.

There an operator was tasked with climbing down the side of the building to the window outside Muse's cell in order to neutralize the guard who was assigned to kill the American in the event of a rescue attempt.

However, the guard was not in position and was eventually taken out in the building interior by the assault force.

Operation Neptune Spear's slick mission plan—one that unraveled when the helo plummeted into the courtyard—planned for DEVGRU operators to enter the compound from both the ground and the roof simultaneously. The first opportunity to kill bin Laden was to belong to a Black Team sniper, who was slated to lean over from the roof and terminate bin Laden with an inverted shot.

◈

Technically, SEAL Team Six was "on loan" to the CIA during Operation Neptune Spear, a semantic solution made to justify JSOC's gray existence.

While the Joint Special Operations Command had limited its more industrial methods to the Iraq and Afghanistan AOs, it also engaged in more bespoke CT efforts in dozens of other nations.

These global terrorist hunts skirt the semi-philosophical border that separates Title 50, which governs covert intelligence actions traditionally associated with the CIA, from Title 10, which applies to the use of military force.

Title 50 is subjected to tighter, timelier congressional oversight but is significantly more expansive in its scope. Meanwhile, Title 10 is less restrictive in terms of supervision and approval, but it's traditionally only applied in narrowly defined war zones.

An argument has been made that GWOT has in fact transformed the entire planet into a battlefield to combat global terrorist networks. The AQN ExOrd and other similar directives have made that legally true in a number of nations to some degree. That fact grants JSOC liberty to send Delta Force and DEVGRU outside established war zones to execute a wide range of operations (including kill and capture missions) with relative impunity—and occasionally without even the CIA's consent or awareness.

However, should even the reimagined Title 10 not prove permissive enough, JSOC simply shifts its legal authority by placing its forces under the temporary control of the CIA—as was technically the case with Operation Neptune Spear despite JSOC retaining near-complete control over the tactical aspects of the mission.

◈

SEAL Team Six has been a central component of this black ops initiative, conducting confirmed kill-or-capture missions in not only Pakistan but also Somalia. Reports suggest that JSOC SMUs have operated with wide latitude inside a whole host of nations including Yemen, Lebanon, Libya, Madagascar, Bolivia, Ecuador, Georgia, Paraguay, Peru, the Philippines, Ukraine, Algeria, Indonesia, Thailand, Mali, Colombia, and even European nations.

There have even been suggestions that DEVGRU has been directed to place Mexican cartel drug lords in their sights, as concerns build regarding possible ties linking global criminal and terrorist organizations, a fear inflamed with the rise of ISIS.

Not surprisingly, reports have credited the Pakistan hunter-killer operations to ST6's Black Team. Similar operations have been mounted in Yemen and Somalia, where it's been reported that CIA/JSOC "omega teams" took out approximately half of the top fifteen al-Qaeda figures in the Arabian Peninsula (AQAP) in 2010.

JSOC snipers' unique hybrid skill sets, which unite the ability to operate in a low-visibility fashion with their extreme and multifaceted lethality, makes DEVGRU and Delta's recce operators attractive options for any proposed kinetic operations of an especially sensitive nature.

For example, the manner in which Delta's B Squadron recce troop was able to blend in and take out HVTs via surgical vehicle-to-vehicle target interdictions is one that it's easy to imagine translating to a wide variety of scenarios in a wide range of locations.

◈

The idea of weaving CIA and special operations forces in order to leverage the specialized skill sets needed to effectively conduct covert action while maintaining a reasonable argument for blurring the Title 10/50 separation is not exactly a new one.

Neither is it a post-9/11 invention to send small recon teams across borders and outside recognized war zones on conduct extreme risk close target reconnaissance or snatch-and-grabs.

MACV-SOG—Military Assistance Command, Vietnam–Studies and Observations Group—remains a legendary name in the special operations community. A spiritual predecessor to both JSOC and the CIA's Special Activities Division/Special Operations Group, SOG was *the* black ops unit of the Vietnam War, and one that redefined special operations during its day.

Former DEVGRU sniper Craig Sawyer sees a clear comparison between today's Delta Force and DEVGRU recce assets and SOG's recon teams.

"I'd say they are the closest equivalent, and I'd say their outlook and mind-set is the same. Very much so. Although, I will always look back upon the MACV-SOG operators with a prestige and reverence just due to the heavy operational climate that they were in. For some reason, it just seems like the culture and the climate in Vietnam and what those guys went in and did—what they were up against—it just seems darker and more dangerous than anything since.

"Not taking anything away from the lethal operations that have gone on for the last ten years, but it's just different. Those MACV-SOG operators in Vietnam will always be my heroes."

What Carlos Hathcock was for snipers, Jerry "Mad Dog" Shriver was for Special Forces. He didn't so much as live up to the stereotype of the daring-if-demented Green Beret as he did create it.

Idiosyncratic to say the least, he was also a fearless, driven operator. Shriver chased after the most challenging missions and pushed the operational limits. He may have "lived in his own orbit"—and slept on a bunk with weapons of every size and sort scattered about—but he also got results and was hugely respected by his peers.

Shriver earned two Silver Stars, seven Bronze Stars for valor, and a king-sized reputation. Legend has it that during one mission deep in enemy territory his recon team had enemy soldiers closing in on their position from all sides. When the FAC (Forward Air Controller) reported his concern from the sky, Shriver said, "No—I've got 'em right where I want 'em—surrounded from the inside."

In 1964, the 5th Special Forces Group established Detachment B-52—Project Delta. The following year, it got a new commander in a hard-charging officer named Charlie Beckwith, who recruited men for his outfit with a flyer that proclaimed: "Project Delta. Will guarantee you a medal, a body bag, or both."

Beckwith used Project Delta as a platform to test out his SAS concept with American forces—one he'd fully realize a decade later with the formation of 1st Special Forces Operational Detachment-Delta—Delta Force.

Project Delta undertook the most critical and perilous missions that existed in South Vietnam—long-range reconnaissance deep in enemy territory, hunter-killer missions, and direct action raids.

In 1966, two follow-up projects were established—Detachment B-50 (Project Omega) and Detachment B-52 (Project Sigma). 5th SFG initiated Project Omega and Project Sigma with the specific intent of conducting cross-border operations into Laos and Cambodia, but ultimately that mission became the exclusive domain of SOG.

SOG was a joint affair from its inception, drawing personnel from the CIA, Army Special Forces, Navy SEALs, USAF, and Marine Force Recon.

In an arrangement not entirely dissimilar to the one that would see SEAL Team Six operators assigned to the CIA to conduct cross-border operations three decades later, Project Omega transferred eight recon teams to SOG in the middle of 1967. Within months, they were running "Daniel Boone" operations—covert ops into Cambodia.

Given the highly sensitive nature of the mission, the recon teams were strictly limited in terms of size and equipment. Each recon team typically included two Americans and four or so indigenous soldiers and were instructed to take all possible precautions to remain completely invisible in "Indian country."

Serial numbers were filed off weapons—that is, if AK-47s weren't being used, indigenous Bata boots were worn, and so on—basically anything that could be done to mask the border penetrations. (Or at least that was the idea. After a few ops, the recon teams became lax on some of the finer points of the regulations because "if we get caught, what's it matter to us what boots we're wearing?")

Operations, which progressively went deeper and deeper into Cambodia, were to last four or five days. The recon teams would either infil or would "sneak and peak"—photograph anything of interest, count enemy forces, and generally assess the situation.

The mission set was not for the faint of heart, particularly for the men who went in at last light just as the jungle was coming to life around them. As a former SOG recon team leader explained, "When those helicopters left . . . You. Had. Nothing. *Nothing*."

If enemy contact was made and the team was compromised, by rule they'd call for immediate extraction. "Immediate" is relative term, of course, especially when machine-gun fire erupts from multiple directions deep in high-canopied, bamboo jungle. It could take as long as an hour for the birds to get to the team's location, and despite the concerted intent to remain undetected, more ops ended early due to compromise than ran the scheduled distance.

As SOG collectively gained experience and confidence, it began to expand its mission set. Photographs and numbers were no longer viewed as the most desirable source of intelligence—SOG's leaders wanted a prisoner snatched from across the border to interrogate.

The risk factor for what some would have already considered the most dangerous job in the world just went up. To give the recon teams a bit of additional incentive to make it happen, a prize was dangled before them—a free vacation in Taichung, Taiwan.

The recon team of Sergeant First Class Shriver, RT BRACE (note that the recon team names existed more for record-keeping purposes and were not commonly referred to by the men on the ground themselves), came close in late October '67—although it's debatable if that's "close" to snatching a prisoner or "close" to getting obliterated.

Mad Dog attempted to pose as a North Vietnamese soldier and lure an enemy to him but another NVA troop saw through the ruse. The recon team raced through the jungle with a large force in pursuit, and Shriver was forced to direct multiple runs of danger-close air support from SOG's USAF 20th SOS "Green Hornet" UH-1P gunships to pull off the narrow escape.

Shriver earned himself another Bronze Star for valor that day but no trip to Taiwan.

There was another recon team with ambitions of earning that vacation: RT AWL.

It was led by Staff Sergeant Tim Kephart and was a bit of an outlier among the other eight teams that existed in Project Omega at the time.

While all of the other teams used Montagnards to form their Special Commando Unit (SCU) —the indigenous component of the recon teams— RT AWL had Chinese Nungs. The Montagnards, who were from the Central Highlands of Vietnam, were generally preferred because they were genuinely motivated and at home in the jungle. Meanwhile, the Nungs were straight-up mercenary soldiers.

However, as the other recon teams transitioned to Montagnards, Kephart picked out the best of the lot who were displaced, assembling an all-star crew of Nungs.

Meanwhile, his assistant team leader was a bit different from most of the SOG SF guys as well. The Iowan was far younger than the others and had taken an atypical path to becoming a recon man.

Don Martin turned up at Long Binh Junction in Vietnam in August of '66 for processing as a member of the 101st Airborne facing his first combat deployment. After seeing a sign in the mess hall asking for Special Forces recruits, the young soldier sailed through the physical and written exam and was one of the thirty or so soldiers selected.

They weren't looking for recon recruits, though. They were looking for guys to work in the warehouse or cook the food, to free up the SF types so they could get out and do SF-type work.

Martin flew to the 5th SFG's in-country HQ, Nha Trang, and was assigned to B-50 Project Omega just as it was being put together—literally, as the camp was still under construction.

They put him behind a typewriter and it did not go well.

"This ain't gonna work, is it?"

"Naaah . . . "

"You don't wanna do this anyway, do you?"

"Naaah . . . "

Next, they moved him to the supply room. He had some carpentry skills and was able to help build counters that would be used to issue equipment.

He got to know some of the recon guys that way and soon wrangled his way into a position training the new Montagnard recruits as they got jump qualified. He was only a "five jump" guy himself at the time, so he gained some more experience, taking part in "Hollywood" (noncombat) jumps.

Around then the recon teams started running ops—basically training missions for what was to come. Martin next finagled his way onto the "Mike Force"—a largely Montagnard-manned force used to run patrols near camp and serve as a QRF. He then learned to fire the M29 81mm mortar, volunteering to take part in HIF (harassment interdiction fire) at night, which basically sent out random mortars just to make anything think twice about trying to sneak up on the camp.

Meanwhile, Kephart's teammate was leaving Vietnam and heading back to the States. Apparently he was impressed by the younger soldier's motivation and maturity and he invited him onto RT AWL, despite not having come up through the conventional path.

And, as Martin said, "Everyone else let it happen. But it wasn't really rocket science. You just had to have the guts to do it, you know?"

It was baptism by fire; Martin proved himself worthy of the position in a firefight that broke out in his very first mission with RT AWL. And the experience only stacked from there.

RT AWL was among the very first recon teams to go into Cambodia, and by the time SOG was hoping to snatch a prisoner in late '67, Staff Sergeant Kephart and Sergeant Martin were both highly decorated Green Berets—Kephart had earned a Silver Star and Martin two Silver Stars and a Purple Heart during their run as teammates.

Back at camp, they always had beds and mattresses while the other guys slept on cots. And, their lockers were stocked up with all sorts of off-the-book weapons, as was the norm with SOG, including some taken off enemy soldiers. Martin's locker had a half dozen AK-47s, one of (if not) the first CAR-15 XM177E2 Commandos issued, a suppressed Sten 9mm, a suppressed Swedish K submachine gun, and a couple Browning 9mms.

They bent the rules in the field, but they did so in order to operate how they determined best. For example, they ran the ridges even though they weren't supposed to. That's where the Viet Cong were, but that was also the quietest—and easiest—way to maneuver.

They used that resourcefulness to brainstorm a scheme to capture that prisoner. They located the perfect spot. During the night, they sat twenty feet away from a path and saw a large number of NVA troops pass right by their location.

"We had this big plan," Martin said with a laugh. "We were cowboys. *Big plan.* And we did it. We practiced it. We saw all these guys. . . . We sat there and watched like five hundred people walk by. They usually traveled at night. It would be quiet all day and then all of a sudden the jungle would come alive at night. They were smoking cigarettes and yakking and carrying big bags of rice and weapons and all kinds of stuff."

The idea was to string up a line of explosives. On either end there were grenades that had been taken apart and fixed with an electric cap so they could be set out with a detonator. And in the middle were concussion charges.

Martin explained, "We were going to sit there and wait until we saw someone who looked like an officer or someone who was really important. We were going to detonate this and get this guy with the concussion charge and not kill him, hopefully."

Everyone who happened to be flanked to either side of the officer, meanwhile, would meet a less fortunate fate. At least, that's how they figured they'd be able to complete the capture.

After the activity of the night had ended, the Green Berets went out to set their trap so they could carry out their plan the following night.

Martin was working one end of the trap while Kephart was down on his hands and knees at the other end, tying the line into place. There he was—very unexpectedly—engaged in conversation.

A North Vietnamese solider—a straggler—happened across RT AWL and walked up directly behind its team leader.

"We wore green fatigues, always," Martin said. "A lot of the other guys wore camouflage, but we always wore green because the North Vietnamese wore solid green."

That happened to be a wise decision. Instead of a discussion about the weather, the shocked and unlucky North Vietnamese found himself face-to-face with an American commando. He was immediately scooped up off the ground by Kephart, grabbed by the scruff of the neck and by the seat of his pants.

Martin heard the commotion and sprinted over from the other side of the line. Together, they pinned the enemy soldier down.

"So we called for immediate extraction and they were happy to come and get us," he said. "So the 'Guns' [UH-1P gunships] and the 'Slicks' [UH-1F troop transports] came. The Guns had to expel their ammo just for the hell of it and they shot all sorts of rockets. We said there had been several hundred that walked through the night before and they couldn't have been that far away. But they just shot the area for the hell of it and pulled us out. We didn't have any trouble getting out. And we took the poor guy back and they questioned him. He was just a low-ranking soldier."

Kephart and Martin got their trip. In fact, SOG was so happy they sent Shriver and some of the other recon guys along with them.

They ended up getting another trip out of the deal. Kephart and Martin were flown to Saigon where Colonel Ho Tieu, the Commander of Vietnamese Special Forces, awarded them the Gallantry Cross Medal.

They also had tea with Tieu, which was something of an uncomfortable affair, since he couldn't speak English.

Shriver continued pushing harder and harder, perhaps feeling a need to live up to his outsized reputation. Eventually, it caught up with him. In April of '69, he went out on a mission in Cambodia and never came back.

Kephart was a schemer off the battlefield as well and always looking for a way to turn a bit of profit. On their trip to Taiwan, he and Martin brought a stack of records thinking they'd be able to turn them for some quick cash back in Vietnam.

Although he was "one of the greatest soldiers you'd ever meet in your life," that proclivity may have caught up with him as well. The unverified rumor was that a remarkable military career that included several tours of duty ended prematurely when he was thrown in a Japanese prison. In any event, what happened to him remains something of a mystery.

Martin got out of the military in Oct '68, moved on, and never looked back, although he adds, "it was one of the best times of my life." He lives back in his hometown in Iowa with his wife Rita. While he remains a tireless worker, he also finds time for his grandchildren and enjoys an enviably normal life.

Unassuming and gregarious, relatively few people in his little town likely are even aware he's a veteran, let alone a highly decorated veteran of MACV-SOG. A true "quiet professional," that's perfectly okay by him.

◈

DEVGRU's growing proficiency operating in the Afghanistan/Pakistan AO actually led to concerns that its maritime edge may have been dulled with training and operational focus so heavily directed elsewhere.

The unit had shown the techniques honed in Afghanistan were directly applicable elsewhere. For example, in the successful rescue of American aid worker Jessica Buchanan and her Danish colleague, Poul Hagen Thisted, DEVGRU operators performed a HAHO jump into Somalia and intentionally landed several miles from the hostages' location. Once on the ground, they stealthily crept into location and then neutralized nine startled captors within seconds and saved both captives.

Still, the SEALs had largely been removed from sea—its counterterrorism raison d'être—for the better part of a decade. That trend was reversed somewhat due to the rising specter of international piracy, prompting some former areas of strength to be dusted off once again.

While the rescue of Captain Richard Phillips served notice to friend and foe alike of SEAL Team Six's continued ability to operate at sea, it was not the only maritime mission to have come along for DEVGRU in recent years.

Taking down pirate ships also led to a renewed interest in another old SEAL favorite: the knife as a CQB weapon.

Despite the "glamour" surrounding the use of fighting knives and their evergreen popularity in action movies, they have almost completely fallen out of favor among elite troops.

Retired Unit sniper John "Shrek" McPhee explained that the most realistic Hollywood portrayal is the scene in *Raiders of the Lost Ark* where an annoyed Indiana Jones casually shoots a sword-wielding showboat: "Knife fighting is bullshit. It has zero relevance in today's world. It takes three to five minutes for someone to bleed out and then you have an angry, dying man to deal with. Plus with all the blood, it makes it hard to hold the knife. It takes ten years of training to be good with a knife. You know how many 'gurus' have knife kills? Zero. The guys that do are in jail—it's a felony.

"Everybody in a knife fight goes to the hospital, even the winner. The SEALs think it's important because of ego. You never bring a knife to a knife fight."

While that may be the case for virtually every scenario a modern-day spec ops sniper is likely to encounter, that rarest of exceptions actually took place in February 2011.

Hollywood director Scott Adam, his wife, Jean, Phyllis Macay, and Bob Riggle had been taken hostage aboard Adam's fifty-eight-foot yacht, off the coast of Oman.

During the course of negotiations, the pirates unexpectedly executed their captives and fired a rocket-propelled grenade at the trailing USS *Sterett*.

A Gold Squadron boarding team was immediately launched in retaliation. The DEVGRU operators quietly set foot aboard the craft and cautiously began to clear the darkened cabin, fully aware the pirates would be expecting a counter for their murderous deeds.

Moments after the team began to flow into the room, a pirate uncoiled from the corner and leapt onto the point man's back, knocking him to the ground. SEAL sniper Heath Robinson, who was the second man through the door, instantly understood that the angle meant a round delivered from his carbine or his pistol would have endangered not only the Somali, but the DEVGRU operator under attack as well.

Brandon Webb—Robinson's former platoon mate at SEAL Team Three and later his instructor at the U.S. Navy SEAL Sniper Course—explained what happened next as part of his tribute to Robinson in *Among Heroes*:

Reacting faster than the speed of thought he slung his HK416, and in one smooth motion his custom Dan Winkler knife was out and slashing across the man's throat. Swift as a shark attack and just as deadly. Seconds later the pirate was on the floor without heartbeat or brainwave, and Heath's teammate was free and very much alive. I know, I know: you've seen moves like this happen in action flicks. But you have to remember: that's the world of fantasy and make-believe. In real life it's a split-second complex of exacting maneuvers that can go wrong in a thousand ways, and often do. Heath's flawless execution saved his teammate's life and left Heath with one of the few certified knife kills on record since Vietnam. (Heath's mom still has that knife.)

Within minutes, another pirate was killed by gunfire while the thirteen others found themselves on the other end of the captive/captor equation.

"A big thing we teach in sniper school is bullet path and exit path," Webb elaborated. "I have friends who have shot three guys with one bullet. If you line it up right, it can happen. At close range you have to be careful about the path of that bullet after it exits the person. He used that knife and just slit the guy's throat. Heath just happened to be the one guy who was in the right place at the right time . . . or the wrong place at the wrong time."

It was Hollywood fiction made reality, avenging the slain director who had worked on *The Dukes of Hazzard*, *The Bad News Bears*, and, ironically, *The Love Boat*.

Incidentally, Robinson's nickname just happened to be "Hollywood." However, that was more due to a combination of movie star good looks and ability to quote lines from his favorite flicks to lighten the mood than any John McClane or Jason Bourne-esque antics—though he certainly had executed his fair share of those as well.

He was a bit like legendary DEVGRU sniper Homer Nearpass in that sense. And, coincidentally, as a teenager in northern Michigan, Robinson was scarred by the images he saw on CNN . . . images of the bodies of American heroes being paraded through the streets of Mogadishu following a massive battle that Nearpass had taken part in.

It was that horrifying footage that inspired Robinson to carry on the family's Naval tradition and become a SEAL so that he could play an role in preventing—or at least avenging—future transgressions of the sort.

Dumped into the shambolic ECHO platoon at SEAL Team Three as a new guy in 2000, Robinson actively sought the mentorship of SEALs who could show him the right way to conduct his business. He found one such example in Webb, who had recently come to ECHO determined to right the ship.

Webb recalled, "It was the fuck-up platoon of Team Three. I remember going there and it was a disaster. All the experienced guys were off on hiatuses, going to schools. Meanwhile, the new guys were sitting back and they didn't even know how to wear their gear properly.

"Heath came up to me saying, 'Man, so glad to have you here. No one has mentored us properly. They are just yelling at us for being new guys.' He was that kind of guy. He always wanted to be squared away and do a good job. And for a new guy, he was exceptionally above average."

A short while later, GOLF and HOTEL would take down a terrorist ship—Alpha 117—Webb in aerial overwatch and Robison on the deck as part of the boarding team that took it down. He continued his meteoric rise from there; he was quickly ushered into combat in Afghanistan as part of Task Force K-Bar, became a plank holder at SEAL Team Seven, and again found himself under Webb's tutelage as one of the first students to graduate the revamped U.S. Navy SEAL Sniper Course.

All the while, however, the tenacious Robinson had his sights set on reaching the pinnacle of existence for a hard-charging and squared-away SEAL—the Naval Special Warfare Development Group.

He not only succeeded in beating the long odds (just 1 in 150 who attempt to become a SEAL ever actually make it to ST6), he also served for eight years with Gold Squadron and did so during an era marked by the most vicious, recurrent combat the unit had ever seen.

During that span Robinson earned four Bronze Stars (three with "V" devices for valor, the other for extraordinary heroism).

◈

In early August 2011—just three months after DEVGRU Red Squadron returned the favor by invading bin Laden's home and sending him crashing to the ground—Gold Squadron was in country and running coordinated operations with the 75th Ranger Regiment's 2nd Battalion.

On this particular night, the Rangers had assumed the lead in the strike force—tasked with hunting down a Taliban leader in Wardak Province's Tangi Valley by the name of Qari Tahir.

However, before the Ranger assault element had reached the objective, ISR tracked a small group of fighters fleeing the compound.

After the Rangers had swept and secured the OBJ (objective), killing or detaining all of the insurgents on site, and Tahir was still nowhere to be seen, the DEVGRU troop positioned as the mission's Immediate Reaction Force (IRF) launched in pursuit of those men who had previously bolted from the scene ahead of the assault.

With 160th SOAR overextended, they were ferried there by a National Guard CH-47D Chinook helicopter, call sign "Extortion 17."

As it approached the LZ, Extortion 17 was ambushed by a volley of accurate RPG fire. At least two struck the helicopter, including one that destroyed an aft rotor blade, and it plunged in a violent spin to the rocky earth below.

The Rangers hoofed over to the crash site. There were no survivors.

On board had been thirty-eight men—seventeen DEVGRU operators, three USAF 24STS Air Commandos, two West Coast SEALs, three NSWDG support personnel, five Army air crewmen, seven Afghan Commandos, and an interpreter, plus a U.S. military dog.

It was a crushing blow to the United States, still in a state of delirium following ST6's triumph in Abbottabad. The incident represented the single biggest loss of American servicemen throughout the entirety of the Afghanistan War.

The crash was even more shattering to DEVGRU, effectively erasing one-twelfth of the unit's operational force in one fell swoop.

"When you think about a helicopter crash, it's particularly devastating," Webb said. "The families are still grieving. It was heavy and it sucks because it's not like these guys went down like Glen Doherty on a rooftop in Benghazi fighting back. You're stuck in a helicopter and you get shot in the middle of the night and the next thing you know you're all dead. That's a pretty tough way to go."

Among the heroes killed on Extortion 17 was Special Warfare Operator Chief Petty Officer Heath Robinson.

◈

Another name on that list that so cruelly and unfairly starts to run together simply due to its inordinate length is that of Senior Chief Petty Officer Thomas Ratzlaff.

The antithesis of just another face in the crowd (although he could certainly be that when the situation required it), "Rat" was considered a legend among legends. Even to this day, the mere mention of the recce team leader's name is said to silence a room of DEVGRU operators, the reverence for him is so great.

Even as a youngster in Northwest Arkansas, all Tommy Ratzlaff wanted was to become a Navy SEAL. And he enlisted straight out of high school in 1995. However, like so many others who sign on the dotted line with the Navy dreaming of becoming one of its elite commandos, he instead ended up out in the fleet and served the next three years on a guided missile destroyer, the USS *Kidd* (DD 993).

The USS *Kidd* was originally to be the "Kouroush," ordered by the Shah of Iran. Plans changed for the boat—and for America's special operations forces—following the Iranian revolution. As a result, the U.S. Navy had a new destroyer and soon would have a new counterterrorist force as well.

Unlike so many others who end up on a ship, Rat's ultimate ambition to become a SEAL went undiminished. In fact, those who knew him at the time claim he only became more driven to do so, and in '98 he finally succeeded in attending, and graduating, from BUD/S.

Once in, there was no looking back. He did a relatively short stint at SEAL Team Two before he attended Green Team in '03 and earned his place on the "second deck." Over the next several years of continuous combat tours—twelve in all, nine in Afghanistan and one in Iraq—Ratzlaff worked his way up from Gold Squadron assaulter to recce sniper.

In April of 2010, Rat was set up in overwatch on a roof. He was watching over the assault element, who was arranged in a containment formation around a compound where a targeted insurgent was suspected to be hiding.

The team called the target out. A patrolling sentry responded to that request with a burst of AK-47 fire. Almost as soon as the Taliban guard pulled the trigger, Ratzlaff put him down. He had never lost a man in overwatch and had no intention of doing so on this night either.

The heavily fortified compound then erupted in small arms fire; the barrels of Kalashnikovs thrust out through the windows and sent a barrage of 7.62x39mm rounds at the ST6 assaulters hunkered outside.

Ratzlaff calmly went back to work, systematically silencing the enemy gunfire. Soon, the target and his guards were no longer a concern.

For that demonstration of battlefield acumen, Ratzlaff would receive the fourth of five Bronze Stars for valor he would ultimately be awarded.

That was just one of countless actions for which he became a near-mythical figure inside the black SOF community. However, it's the only one that's leaked outside of that small, secretive group in any detail.

In a family statement read by his nephew, Jeff Adams said, "As a Navy SEAL team member, my uncle was trained to keep a low profile and to do his job."

He took that vow to the grave and others have respected it ever since.

The stories yet to be told could almost certainly overflow several volumes, including whatever remarkable feat of bravery earned him the Star of Military Valour—the highest military honor the Canadian government has bestowed in the modern era.

That's an exceptionally rare honor—one less than two dozen soldiers, Canadian or otherwise, have earned.

The details of how Ratzlaff came to be awarded the Star of Military Valour are beyond sparse ("for actions in Afghanistan while supporting Canadian soldiers"), but in that sense, he stands as an ideal symbol for the dozens of extraordinarily skilled—yet virtually anonymous—men of the National Missions Force who dedicated, and ultimately gave, their lives in defense of their country.

14

The Tribes

With the battle versus AQI all but extinguished, Delta Force rejoined the rotation in Afghanistan more heavily toward the end of the decade. As the pace and fury ratcheted upward, the Unit saw more of its soldiers make the ultimate sacrifice.

Among them was one who was still a relatively new operator with just two years in the Army special mission unit. However, as is the norm in the Unit, he was not new to soldiering by any stretch.

Before joining Delta, he already had five combat deployments to his name. And among other assignments, he had previously been a 3/75 Ranger sniper, AMU competitive shooter, 3/75 Ranger Sniper Platoon Sergeant, 1st Platoon Alpha Company 3/75 Platoon Sergeant, and NCOIC of the 3/75 Reconnaissance, Sniper, and Technical Surveillance Detachment.

Delta Force operator Jared Van Aalst was killed in combat on August 4, 2010, in Kunduz Province, Afghanistan.

When Jack Murphy learned of VA's death, he was still bitter and struggled to let the old issues with his former (two-time) platoon sergeant go.

That changed in 2012 after he was contacted by one of Van Aalst's old friends, a former Ranger and active-duty Special Forces soldier:

"I don't know you, Jack, but I know all about you. Me and VA went way back and he told me all about you. He told me you were in all kinds of shit.

He said you were in trouble and asked for my advice. I asked if he thought you could Ranger through it, and VA said, 'Yeah, he can.' I told him he knows what to do."

"The reality was that VA was looking over my shoulder in a big way," a still-regretful Murphy said. "The reason why I was taken care of the way I was, was literally because of VA looking over my shoulder and making sure I did not get fucked. Anyone else would have been completely fucked. And what VA did was send me back to an infantry squad and looked after me there.

"I knew absolutely nothing about this at the time. I thought VA hated me. I thought VA hated me as much as I hated him. I only found this out after the fact and it's something that bothers me to this day that I was never able to put this stuff behind me. VA was the bigger man in the end and I could not let this anger and animosity I had go when I should have. We weren't at each other's throats, but it was something where, once I was out of the Regiment and out from under his chain of command, we should have been friends. It's something that eats at me inside to this day. But it is what it is."

◈

"One shot, one kill" has long been the sniper's creed. And it's one that's been joined in the military parlance by another, similar phrase that has risen in prominence during the Global War on Terror: "One team, one fight."

That sentiment is a truism of particular significance at the sharpest end of special operations where missions, campaigns, task forces, and commands are "joint" by definition.

As the overarching battle to counter global terrorist networks gained momentum, the nearly institutional feud separating the Joint Special Operations Command's Tier 1 units—Delta Force and DEVGRU—had subsided considerably.

September 11 and the resultant years of constant deployments and bloodshed flushed away much of the petty bickering. Besides lending renewed perspective, the attacks also changed the game for counterterrorist outfits. The old source of friction had become fiction, as both units were overloaded with more work than they could have previously imagined possible.

Rather than be locked in competition for the make-or-break op that might crop up once during the course of an operator's career, it was more a matter of deciding which unit would undertake the thousands of missions over here and which would undertake the thousands of missions over there.

Following 9/11, Delta and DEVGRU were both given plenty to "eat" and they feasted, racking up respective HVT kills and captures tallying into the hundreds of millions of dollars in terms of the bounties that had been placed on their targets' heads.

Additionally, a full decade before 2001, JSOC had mandated joint training exercises between its SMUs, and not just among the snipers. In the early days this was a rocky experience for both sides. But eventually a genuine sense of comfort and familiarity had been fostered between the two—both operationally and professionally.

"When we started to train together and play nice together, it was definitely us against them," admitted former DEVGRU sniper Howard Wasdin. "But the big thing is, after we trained with them for a while, we all got better. And after being in combat with them, Delta Force guys actually came to my hospital room and said, 'Hey man, I wish we bonded more with you guys before the firefight.' Once you're in the soup with somebody, you see theirs and they see yours and there's a mutual respect that's forged. I think with us being in Somalia with the Delta Force guys, that sharpened the tip of the spear and that was the springboard for how things are today.

"Is there still going to be sibling and professional rivalry? Of course there is. With any elite team there will be—that's like two Super Bowl teams playing. But the mutual respect and trust is there and that's what really matters."

This was borne out when DEVGRU lent out a handful of assaulters to serve as substitute Unit operators in 2005 after Delta had been rocked by a rapid series of causalities in Iraq.

◈

One pre-9/11 DEVGRU sniper actually became a post-9/11 member of the Unit.

In the '90s, a talented young country boy rose through the ranks to become one of SEAL Team Six's youngest ever operators. He continued his upward climb through the ranks at Red Squadron and soon became one of the youngest to ever become a sniper with Black Team.

However, frustrated with the interservice politics, he left SEAL Team Six following just four years and instead went to work for his father's company.

Then 9/11 happened.

He immediately sought out DEVGRU's Master Chief.

"Hey, I'm still in great shape and I shoot all the time. I'll go back through Green Team. I'll go through selection. I'll do whatever you want. Just let me back in, I want to contribute."

"Up yours. Go back to vanilla teams and work your way back up."

Next, he called the Army recruiter.

"What's it going to take to get me to Delta?"

"I don't know but we'll find out."

He was placed in the Army National Guard for twenty-four hours and then transferred to the Army to go to selection. He made the cut and deployed multiple times as a breacher.

Down the road, he crossed paths with some old ST6 Teammates while overseas.

"Damn man, what are you doing?"

"Hey, I got here any way I could."

"Roger that. Good on you."

◈

When Stanley McChrystal took command of JSOC, he attempted to integrate the units to an even greater degree. However, the respective operators bristled and flatly rejected his early attempts to shape and treat the two as if they were virtual doppelgängers—the same in all but name.

Leaders with the power to pull the trigger on national-level missions have largely treated the two as interchangeable. They are both viewed as far exceeding the tactical threshold necessary to execute even the most technical and challenging CT taskings. The parsing beyond that might not go much deeper than, "Who's available?" or "Who's there already?"

But what may seem like small nuances to outsiders—irrelevant details—can be considered mission critical gulfs—in talents, in capabilities, and in mind-set—to those more on the inside.

And it's obvious that even if the relationship is stronger than it once was, the animosity still smolders (largely) under the surface.

Unsurprisingly, operators on either side of the equation contend their unit's superiority is self-evident and that the most-high profile missions are practically their birthright.

SEAL Team Six was criticized for basking in the spotlight after finally having their "daddy" decide who got to pitch in the big game and being awarded the one op everyone wanted.

Following suggestions that future missions of the sort should instead go to Delta Force or the Ranger Regiment due to the Army units' track record of offering a more discreet solution, an anonymous DEVGRU operator struck back in an open letter to *SOFREP* editor Jack Murphy.

In the somewhat ironic counter, the active-duty SEAL wrote, "First I will give credit where credit is due. Delta is one of two (the other being DEVGRU) of the most hard core and prolific group of warriors ever assembled in the history of warfare. . . . That said, let's break things down to a digestible level. Ask your CAG friends about the highest profile op they've done lately . . . and you'll hear the crickets chirping loudly. It's not because they are not talking about it, but because they are not being chosen to do them.

"And don't even try and use the excuse that it was only because

McRaven was running the show. There have been some other ops (post-Bin Laden) that were way more technical than the Bin Laden op and it was an Army General that chose our Navy element to do it.

"The real answer is . . . it was, and still is, OUR time. Period."

Not surprisingly, retired Unit sniper John McPhee had a vastly different take.

The operator opined that the vast differences separating their respective selection and training methodologies, along with the average experience of the units' respective operators, results in a cavernous separation in terms of capability.

"I'm only willing to talk because I'm tired of the bullshit training," McPhee said. "I'm tired of people dying because of ego. Ego has killed more guys than this nation's enemies. I'm not for or against SEALs—I'm against bad training. SEAL training is based on hazing to be the best you can be. In the Unit, you prove yourself and then they treat you like a man.

He continued, "To get to a SEAL Team, there's no selection, no psych evaluation, board selection of any kind. [Without those] you will almost never get the *right* guy. A couple buddies say you're good and you're good.

"In the Army, you want to be a Ranger, get a Ranger Tab, and go to a battalion, you get selected and evaluated. Rangers that have gone to BUD/S call it pool fitness and say it's not that hard. After a few years, maybe you want to become a Green Beret, you think they're cool. So you go to SF selection, get a psych evaluation. It's the same thing as you move on. By this time, you've probably had six years of the most intensive training in the world. It's a stepped professional system. Four to six selections, evaluations—oral, psych, physical—on the way up. The Army is just more professional.

"Human nature says if you have two guys who are the same age and have the same natural abilities, the guy with the best training is going to be the one who performs the best."

McPhee, who now instructs cutting-edge gunfighting techniques utilizing frame-by-frame video review that would leave NFL teams envious, also claimed that SEAL snipers are years behind their Unit counterparts in terms of tactics and technology (a sentiment supported by another former

Delta operator): "SEAL Team snipers only switched to first focal plane sights about two years ago. They're like a decade behind. They still had that Vietnam mind-set—dial in the DOPE and all that bullshit."

Ultimately, results are what matter and McPhee was unconvinced in that area as well.

"The problem with SEAL Teams is they kill everyone," he said. "That only creates more problems and makes more enemies. The Unit only kills those who need to be killed."

Even the much vaunted Operation Neptune Spear did not escape his harsh judgment. "These guys were running their mouths. It was ego and lies. They high-fived and then raced to see who could make the first million from a book deal or movie. They put us at risk, not just on the battlefield but at home. They put our families at risk. They need to learn to shut the fuck up. They compromised technology to our nations' enemies because they didn't plan for total destruction. They could have just asked the pilots, 'How do I destroy this?'"

He was particularly critical of the atypical grouping for the operation, which teamed Red Squadron's most senior men as an "all-star" troop of sorts. While that may have put a great deal of experience on the ground, it also meant they were not a well-oiled, cohesive squad who had run dozens of ops together.

"If they would have run into any real resistance they would have gotten chewed up," he said. "You can't just pick teams and expect everything will be okay. And they broke their only rule—don't shoot the guy in the face."

◈

Despite being just a few dozen men strong and deeply classified, DEVGRU's Red Squadron is perhaps the single-most recognizable symbol of both the triumphs and the sacrifice of the Global War on Terror.

Even before GWOT, its snipers distinguished themselves with heroism in Mogadishu, Somalia.

And then one of its own—Neil Roberts—was the first SEAL to die following 9/11, doing so with great bravery under horrifying circumstances.

Reports indicate that it was Red Squadron that then lit up CNN at the start of the Iraq War, rescuing Jessica Lynch.

And then Red Squadron's Black Team snipers demonstrated their remarkable capabilities with a simultaneous triple headshot that again had the world watching on in awe.

And finally, the squadron was made the centerpiece of what can only be termed the most high-profile and high-priority special operations mission of the century: the cross-border elimination of Osama bin Laden.

It's perhaps something of a fluke of fate that so much has fallen Red Squadron's way, enabling them to rack up multiple missions that have inspired bestselling books and Hollywood blockbusters.

But these assignments and accolades also seem to lend credence to the reports of DEVGRU's transformation from a rough-edged hatchet into a finely honed blade. From highly suspect to highly professional. From Marcinko to McRaven.

However, some special operations sources allege that the squadron adopted an eye-for-an-eye mentality following the brutal killing of Roberts and has been pushing boundaries ever since—a band of skillful yet ruthless heroes/outlaws.

Even its greatest triumphs have the asterisks—such as the $30,000 in cold cash ransom money that seemingly vanished from the lifeboat in the confusion following the rescue of Captain Richard Phillips.

And there are reports that ST6 operators ventilated bin Laden's corpse, unloading more than a hundred rounds into him.

The raw and relentless nature of an unending war has unsurprisingly pushed many to (and beyond) their breaking point. Home lives have been destroyed and far too many friends and comrades have given all.

Whether Red Squadron is an out-of-control outlier, an example of wider trends, or merely an innocent victim of inaccurate allegations and genuinely the virtuous champions portrayed by the mainstream media is an intriguing if unanswerable question at this point.

Delta's recce troop hasn't escaped the SOF grapevine completely unscathed either.

Army Special Forces have sometimes found themselves marginalized during the Global War on Terror—brushed aside by JSOC's long reach and tip-of-the-spear-sharp elbows.

Despite its sterling start in the early days in Afghanistan in 2001, SF's unconventional warfare capabilities have not always been as prized as the direct action talents of the Joint Special Operation Command's special mission units in what has often been a largely kinetic conflict—at least in the headlines.

There were reports that opportunities to kill or capture Mullah Mohammed Omar and Ayman al-Zawahiri were missed because of JSOC's refusal to allow nearby SF ODAs to take on the hits, instead insisting they wait for strike teams from Delta Force or DEVGRU to arrive from hours away.

On another occasion, "one of the most senior Taliban leaders" was located and SF attempted to go in pursuit—but they were never given permission to utilize the helicopters necessary to take up the chase.

CJSOTF-A has lacked sufficient organic lift aircraft, and the 160th SOAR's 3rd Battalion—which was specifically stood up to support white SOF—came to be just another asset monopolized by JSOC. The Command's breakneck OPTEMPO continually tied up all available birds and its national-level priority status trumped all others competing for those assets.

Even as the wars have shifted, Special Forces has been frustrated by JSOC's ability to throw its weight around—even in SF's own arena.

Delta recce operators have reportedly pushed their way in to claim some of the more fancied FID (foreign internal defense) missions, snatching them away from SF.

However, with the Unit increasingly stocked with operators who came straight up from the Ranger Regiment, not every one of them has the necessary background or training to execute the mission, at least not at a Special Forces level.

A former SF soldier explained, "You'll have Delta recce guys doing FID and it turns into a bit of a mess in some ways. Some of them came from SF but a lot of them came from the Rangers. So some guys have previous experience and understand FID and some guys have not a clue."

He continued, "Those guys were doing FID with their element in Afghanistan and, like, six of those recce dudes got fired because they got caught removing firing pins from the Afghanis' weapons. I guess they didn't want to get shot in the back or something. So they got canned.

"And then in Libya, a SF guy said, 'Can you believe these fuckin' guys? They can't even use a compass. They don't know how to read a map. What the fuck?' Yeah, I know that. No shit. It's a completely different mind-set and these guys just don't have that experience.

"These recce guys definitely do some pretty hard-core stuff behind enemy lines. But I think they also get swiped into all sorts of other different stuff."

15

End of the Beginning

By 2011, the Joint Special Operations Command's terrorist network disassembly line was decelerating in Afghanistan as it had before in Iraq, but for different reasons.

With the successful assassination of Osama bin Laden and the latter-day impotence of the central al-Qaeda organization, conditions were ripened for America to declare victory—accurate or not—and remove itself completely from an intractable situation. Instead, it remained heavily engaged in Afghanistan, gradually drawing down its forces. The endgame remains murky and the means to achieve it even murkier.

In 2012, after more than a decade of the heaviest SOF usage in military history, the nation's black and white SOF were put under a unified command structure—Special Operations Joint Task Force–Afghanistan (SOJTF-A)—to better coordinate their operations in country.

The SOJTF-A commander also was placed in charge of NATO Special Operations Component Command–Afghanistan (NSOCC-A), further streamlining the hydra-like effort.

However, that effort had become progressively stymied. The rules of engagement (ROE) were made restrictive to the point of handcuffing assault teams. Worse still, they were known to, and actively manipulated by, the insurgents.

Mission approvals were no longer instantaneous nor did they necessarily drive the next or the one after that. And those stealthy takedowns in which DEVGRU SEALs slinked into compounds while their targets slept were ruled out altogether. "Tactical call-outs" had evolved naturally in Iraq due to the extreme danger associated with suicide bombers and booby-trapped homes. However, they were forced upon even Tier 1 assets in Afghanistan.

Perhaps most frustratingly, Afghanistan's president Hamid Karzai demanded an end to night raids—further handicapping the powerful tools JSOC had pioneered.

The nation's (and SOF's) relationship with Karzai had been an interesting one to say the least. Fluid almost by nature, it grew increasingly antagonistic in the later years of his presidency.

Shortly after 9/11, Karzai was hand-selected by the United States to lead the new regime following the defeat of the Taliban. He was ushered back into Afghanistan and watched over by Army Special Forces ODA-574 and CIA Special Activities Division Paramilitary Officers as the first wave of the invasion rippled throughout the country.

Installed as the nation's leader before 2001 was even out, Karzai's life was spared when a DEVGRU VIP Security Detail element foiled a close-up assassination attempt on the then-interim president with overwhelming force.

However, as the war steamrolled forward and JSOC implemented the rapid-pace CT system it had developed in Iraq, civilian casualties—particularly those linked to special operations raids—had become a fracturing point. While the United States placed immense value on JSOC's ability to surgically target its enemies, the practices by which it did were considered invasive by the local populace and Karzai played on those sentiments.

There is no doubt that JSOC's raids resulted in civilian casualties. The sheer number of raids—missions that are inherently violent and chaotic—practically demands that be the case. The real question is if those numbers were being minimized to an "acceptable" degree.

There is also no doubt that the genuine statistics were less than those claimed by the Taliban and related groups, who imagined, inflated, or created civilian death tolls as central strategies in their propaganda campaigns.

And Karzai too treated the claims—even dubious ones—as political grist to further his standing and leverage.

By the time Karzai was set to leave office following thirteen years in power, he offered no thanks to the United States—which had paid for Afghanistan's continued development with $100 billion in aid and two thousand lives. Rather he claimed the U.S. had no desire for peace in Afghanistan and warned his successors to be cautious in their dealings with the West, perhaps one final attempt to publicly cut any strings in the eyes of those who viewed him as a puppet.

By 2014, the industrial age was over. Two wars that revolutionized not only special operations, but warfare, were all but ended. And with it were retiring warfighters who had spent three-quarters of their twenty years spent engaged in mortal combat, looking to transition to the next stage of their lives.

◈

Chris Kyle returned to Iraq in 2008 for a fourth and final deployment. SEAL Team Three's aura of invincibility had been shattered during his last deployment, and the Texan returned to battle perhaps a bit less enthusiastic than before—although he maintained an unrepentant love affair with war.

His body was breaking down after years of stress and mounting injuries, and there was a growing sense that the bullet with his name on it was tracking him down.

While Kyle returned to Iraq with a new platoon—DELTA, as CHARLIE, had been split up and its experience filtered throughout Team Three—he once again found himself attached to conventional units. The new generation of SEAL snipers had worked miracles in the eyes of the forces they had augmented. And they were now, quite naturally, in high demand.

"You had such a hostile environment in Iraq with that house-to-house urban environment," explained former U.S. Navy SEAL Sniper Course

Manager Webb. "Employing sniper teams to sneak ahead of the conventional movement really provided a tremendous amount of value. We started to augment those guys and they saw how effective it was and started making the request for the snipers more and more—and they were specifically asking for SEAL snipers."

That growing reputation provided the SEAL sniper program with widespread awareness, prompting contact from the Army and USMC sniper programs. "They were calling us, wanting to know how we were training these guys. Just given the nature of that invasion, it was just Chris being in the right place at the right time. SEALs aren't designed to do the stuff these conventional units were doing, but we sure as hell can sneak in ahead of a movement, set up, and provide overwatch protection for these guys."

An "all-star" task force drawn from SEAL Teams Three and Eight united SEAL snipers from both coasts and set them loose in Sadr City. The hellish urban hole had grown even fouler over the years, now every bit as perilous as Fallujah or Ramadi in their worst days.

However, rather than cut through the Shia militias the way they had the Sunni insurgents west of Baghdad in his previous deployments, Kyle and his element found themselves on the receiving end of things this time around. Under massive assault by RPGs, IED, and machine-gun fire, they scurried from building to building.

The guardian angel that Kyle credited with knocking him over in order to dodge a bullet like the one in Ramadi had seemingly forsaken him. First a bullet struck him in the head, ricocheting off his NVGs but temporarily blinding him as his helmet shifted over his eyes.

Moments later, a heavier round burrowed through the ceramic armor plate on the back of his carrier. While the armor slowed the round so that it caused nothing more than a superficial wound, it was just another sign to Kyle that he was living on borrowed time.

But then the unexpected happened—he survived the vicious battle in Sadr City and his kill count continued into the stratosphere. After the Sadr City mission was completed, he went to work alongside the Army's 10th

Mountain Division, hunting down makeshift bomb shops near Baghdad and tallying up another twenty kills in the process.

That elevated his final confirmed total to 160—with another hundred or so on top of that unconfirmed—the most ever notched on the butt of an American sniper's rifle.

The bullet with his name on it wasn't in Iraq after all. He made it back home safe and sound. And, after receiving an ultimatum from his wife, he finally parted ways with the Navy and the Teams. Kyle ended his service ranking among the most decorated heroes of the war, having been awarded two Silver Stars and five Bronze Stars for valor.

However, the near-pathological drive to protect others continued to burn inside him. He felt guilty that he would no longer be going to combat—convinced that American servicemen were destined to die because he was not there to watch over them. That haunted him.

His former SEAL sniper mentor, Eric Davis, could sympathize. He said, "That's what drives me. I want to help other people—I want to save lives. I want to impact the world greatly, so when you leave that, it's torture. You do feel like—again, it's not arrogance—but you're like, 'Okay, I'm a SEAL, I'm a sniper, is there anything higher end? Is there anything better? Is there anything more I could do?' The answer is no. So when you leave all that you feel like you're letting people down and people could die as a result. It's horrible."

One way he managed this guilt was by continuing to protect in the best way he could—training military and law enforcement personnel through Craft International. Kyle imparted his hard-earned wisdom so that others would be better able to defend not only themselves, but others as well.

The Legend found a way to have an outsized impact even when he was no longer in a position to deliver lethal and lifesaving fire downrange.

The Texan later stumbled into a second life as a celebrity. An uneasy celebrity to be sure, but a celebrity none the less. His memoirs, *American Sniper,* was a massive hit—a mainstream sensation. And his legend, combined with his charismatic mix of swagger and humility, made him the closest thing a sniper can be to a household name.

He braved even the talk show circuit (growling at anyone who dared attempt to plaster makeup on his face). This was not to raise his profile, but rather to drive sales for the book. And in Kyle's case, this was an act of remarkable selflessness, and he donated his share of the book's earnings in its entirety to "America's Mighty Warriors"—the foundation created by Debbie Lee, the mother of Kyle's friend, Marc Lee, who was the first SEAL killed in Iraq back in 2006.

Kyle was tireless in helping his fellow veterans too. There was never any lip service. What he said, he not only meant, he lived.

"He truly cared about veterans and not just spec ops veterans," Webb said. "He cared about the guys, period. I think a lot of that comes from the fact that he supported a lot of conventional units in Iraq—whether it was the Army or the Marines. He was in the trenches with these conventional guys and he really cared about them. He talked to me in private about it and I knew it wasn't bullshit. It was definitely a cause that was important to him and close to his heart."

Tragically, it was due to an inability to turn off this drive to help that the bullet finally did catch up to him. Kyle and a friend, Chad Littlefield, were murdered on a gun range by a mentally disturbed ex-Marine named Eddie Ray Routh, whom Kyle was attempting to help.

"The fact that Chris and his buddy gave their time to pick this guy up and take him to the range just shows you what kind of guy Chris was," Webb said. "He didn't have to do that for that guy. I wouldn't have done it. Chris was out there on the front line with that stuff."

Davis found the shocking killing difficult to rationalize or accept. "Somebody who is doing straight humanitarian help and helping you in particular? It's got to be the most deepest rooted evil there is. The most selfish, pyscho . . . It's really just gross. It's dirty. You're taking someone off the planet.

"Chris didn't sign up for that. You become a SEAL and you sign up for that. You go to war and you have the clichéd 'I wrote a check up to and including my life.' But when you're taking someone out on the range to help them, the only thing you signed up for is a potentially shitty afternoon when you could have been home with your family. That's the sacrifice he signed up for there. The very thing he fought for, you're taking it away from him. That wasn't Chris's choice to die."

Former SEAL "Drago" added, "I want people to see that Chris was a man dedicated to saving lives on and off the battlefield. And even after leaving the Navy he continued that work. He was dedicated to making a difference in other soldiers' lives. He used his expertise in the field to train them. When they went back in the theater, they were better trained soldiers. He helped others to deal with PTSD. He was saving lives on the battlefield and off the battlefield.

"I would like to tell Chris's kids that their daddy is now guarding angels in heaven. He is protecting them and making sure they are safe, just like he was protecting us."

Even in death—perhaps especially in death—Chris Kyle remains the Legend.

"There are all kinds of stories about SEALs and snipers and the military, and stories are cool," Davis explained. "Stories excite us and are interesting. But legends inspire us and change us forever. Legends stick. You can have all those kills—who cares? That's just pulling a trigger and executing your job. But when you're a guy like Chris, who lived his life like he did and held the ethics that he did and stood for something like he did, then the spectacular event becomes more than just a story. Then it becomes a legend."

◈

The post-9/11 spec ops snipers not only continued the tradition of excellence established by the likes of Carlos Hathcock during Vietnam, they added legends of their own, and even helped to rewrite the book on what it means to be a force multiplier—a one-man implement of mass influence on the battlefield.

What becomes clear is that, contrary to one's natural inclinations, snipers like Chris Kyle are not driven to dole out death so much as they are consumed with the preservation of those placed under their protection. That's a heady calling that does not simply shut off.

Some are able to transition to more indirect methods, such as Howard

Wasdin. The former DEVGRU sniper explains that his decision to pursue a career as a chiropractor was driven by the need to find a way to continue helping people.

And there's former 3/75 Ranger sniper Isaiah Burkhart, who recently became a paramedic.

Meanwhile, Unit snipers John "Shrek" McPhee and Don "Kingpin" Hollenbaugh, along with 3/75 Ranger sniper Nick "the Reaper" Irving, are more direct in their approach, passing the lessons learned in blood down to a new generation of shooters through forward-thinking instruction.

And DEVGRU operator Homer Nearpass, who played such a pivotal role both in Mogadishu in '93 and in the formative days of JSOC's AFO activities in Afghanistan in '01, continues to contribute to the NSWDG sniper community in a meaningful way. Brought back by the command as a civilian government employee following his retirement, Nearpass is there to push DEVGRU's snipers to the bleeding edge by, for example, testing and selecting new ballistic trajectory apps for use by ST6.

Others still find themselves continually drawn back into the chaos in order to protect others, even after their military careers have ended.

On September 11, 2012, former SEAL Team Three sniper Glen Doherty frantically scrambled from Tripoli as part of a small joint CIA/JSOC element to reinforce the locally placed CIA GRS (Global Response Staff) team in Benghazi, Libya. The U.S. consulate had come under terrorist attack from aggressors later identified as hailing from al-Qaeda in the Lands of the Islamic Maghreb (AQIM), Ansar al-Sharia (ASL), al-Qaeda in the Arabian Peninsula (AQAP), and the Mohammad Jamal Network (MJN), underlying just how nuanced and multifaced the amorphous threat of terrorism had become.

Doherty was naturally gifted across a wide range of activities and an instant charmer. Equally at home with surfers and skiers as he was with SEALs, to those who met him, the gregarious Massachusetts native did not appear to be the type who could bring down great violence—unless those who met him were the ones on the other end of that violence.

Always in search of that next adventure, Doherty found one equal to his vast ambition when he became a Navy SEAL in the mid-'90s.

Benghazi wasn't the first time Doherty had rushed in in response to a shocking terrorist attack. He and sniper partner Brandon Webb were emplaced on the bridge of the USS *Cole* with a .50-caliber rifle and given very liberal ROE within hours of its attack in October 2000.

"Bub" was ready for his next escapade in 2001 and on his way out of the military when 9/11 happened. That pulled him back in for several years of combat before finally making good on his threat to get out and move in '05.

"Out" was relative in Doherty's case. He took on a long series of contracting gigs, putting himself in the most dangerous places on the planet for months at a time and balancing that with some beach or mountainside R & R. He worked and played as hard as human endurance would allow.

His contract as a member of the CIA's Global Response Staff posted in Libya was supposed to be the last time he'd put his life on the line for money and adventure. GRS had provided plenty of both. Formed in the wake of 9/11, GRS sought established SOF vets to serve as, essentially, high-speed bodyguards for its case officers operating in the darkest corners of the planet. GRS was similarly split between blue-badged staffers and green-badged contractors like the Agency's Special Activities Division/Special Operations Group. It offered men with the right training and talents six-figure deals for relatively short stints overseas. In other words, GRS and Doherty were a perfect fit.

Or at least they had been. Now in his forties, Doherty was ready to move on to a position where small objects were not regularly flung at his head at 2,350 feet per second. But he still had one last job to complete.

With Benghazi in chaos, Doherty and the rest of the GRS/JSOC team commandeered a plane with $30,000 cash and threw themselves into the madness. By the time they arrived, U.S. Ambassador J. Christopher Stevens and U.S. Foreign Service Information Management Officer Sean Smith were already dead, but the GRS team was still desperately needed. They arrived at the CIA annex, which had now come under the ire of the terrorist mob.

Doherty made his last stand on the annex's roof. He was hit with indirect fire moments after fellow former SEAL Tyrone Wood had suffered the same fate. It was the final actions of two men who had worked tirelessly and courageously in the shadows in defense of their nation.

Their sacrifice, along with the efforts of the remainder of the rescue force, prevented any further death, enabling the narrow escape of dozens of cornered Americans. One of the Delta Force operators from the Tripoli-based rescue team was awarded the Distinguished Service Cross, while the other, a Marine, earned the Navy Cross for their extraordinary heroism in Benghazi.

◈

As the attacks in Benghazi so clearly illustrated, the successive winding down of the wars in Iraq and Afghanistan did not mark an end so much as a transition.

The United States' global war had become exactly that. And while parallel drone programs run by the CIA and JSOC, working in concert with its radically enhanced special operations capability, had repeatedly demonstrated the nation's vast reach and capability to erase its enemies in a highly selective manner, there was no end in sight to what had become a self-perpetuating, endless state of conflict.

President Clinton was right back in 2000. America's "black ninjas" and its air force of faceless robotic killers did in fact "scare the shit" out of al-Qaeda and its equivalents.

The United States's CT apparatus—and JSOC and its SMUs in particular—had become, in the words of a former Delta Force operator, the "terrorist's terrorist."

But there's also an argument that claims the manner in which they've been used has transformed them into a terrorist factory at the same time.

JSOC has killed thousands upon thousands of "bad guys," but how many new ones have been created by the very execution of the process?

Somewhat ironically, in the wake of enhanced interrogations and indefinite detention controversies, killing was made more politically palatable than capturing, and the kill-capture ratio shifted heavily as a result. But

Predator missiles that materialize from the sky and commando teams who come in the night incite fear and confusion even among the innocents they are actually serving, creating a steady stream of replacements from even the most targeted strikes.

And yet inaction is equally damaging as a nebulous array of quasi-related terrorist organizations with global ambitions continue to fester and spread.

While al-Qaeda proper had been largely decimated by the Unites States' relentless campaign, a mass of networks have emerged to both follow its lead and fill its void. Lashkar-e Tayyiba (LET), Asbat an-Ansar, al-Qaeida in the Islamic Maghreb (AQIM), Al-Shabaab, al-Qaeida in the Arabian Peninsula (AQAP), the Haqqani Network, Boko Haram, and Al-Nusra Front are just a small sampling of the constantly evolving terrorist situation that threatens to strike United States' interests both at home and abroad as AQ's brand of violence and radical ideology continues its expansion.

Discouragingly, the unwinnable war that had been won in Iraq has since been "unwon." Without the United States to exert its influence, the new Iraq government almost instantly proved corrupt. Politicians instinctively fell back on long-established ethnic and religious divisions, setting renewed conditions for renewed sectarian conflict.

And without JSOC to "mow the lawn" and systematically cull al-Qaeda in Iraq, AQI morphed into something even darker—ISIS (Islamic State of Iraq and al-Sham)—a grotesquely brutal self-proclaimed caliphate with grandeurs of global domination.

According to Secretary of Defense Chuck Hagel, "They are beyond just a terrorist group. They marry ideology [with] a sophistication of . . . military prowess. This is beyond anything we've seen."

Joint Chiefs Chairman Gen. Martin Dempsey added, "This is an organization that has an apocalyptic, end-of-days strategic vision and which will eventually have to be defeated."

ISIS has brought renewed violence to the region and effectively undone all that was accomplished in JSOC's revolutionary campaign against its predecessor.

Meanwhile, JSOC has continued its evolution as well. The old "daddy" is running the show again following years of SEAL leadership. Adm. McRaven, who succeeded Adm. Olson as SOCOM Commander, retired in 2014 and became the new Chancellor of the University of Texas System. He was replaced atop SOCOM by Gen. Joseph Votel, the former 75th Ranger Regiment Commander who previously succeeded him as JSOC Commander. And Votel's position at JSOC was assumed by Gen. Raymond Thomas, a former Delta squadron commander.

Delta operators corralled the vehicle of Abu Anas al Libi—an AQ planner with alleged ties to the 1998 embassy bombings—and snatched him off the streets of Tripoli in October 2013. They then nabbed Ahmed abu Khatallah—a ringleader of the Benghazi attacks—in another low-vis operation June 2014.

And in July of 2014, the Unit mounted a complex hostage rescue attempt of journalist James Foley, descending on a remote ISIS-held oil facility near Raqqah, Syria. The operators neutralized a large terrorist contingent but found it to be a dry hole and extracted.

Despite the mission's execution being described as "flawless" and "magic," it failed to rescue Foley, who is believed to have been moved just days before the operation. He was viciously beheaded in the sort of unspeakable act typical of ISIS, further amping up the already stoked tension.

With ISIS tempting the repowering of JSOC's industrial killing machine, and precision, clandestine operations dotting the globe in response to the continued scourge of terrorism, the nation's elite snipers are destined to remain as valuable as they've ever been.

They are tide-turning human weapons custom fit for this new age of warfare—men who can operate unseen or undercover. They are uniquely capable of operating both in preparation for larger forces or with unilateral lethality.

There will be no shortage of work for America's special operations snipers in the foreseeable future. In fact, despite making the most outrageously disproportionate contributions of any troops throughout the Global War on Terror to date, this exceptional breed of warrior may very well prove even more critical in the next phase than it was the last.

Update

Since the original release of the hardcover version of this book, special operations snipers have been thrust into—and occasionally basked in—the spotlight like no time before.

The feature-film adaptation of Chris Kyle's autobiography, *American Sniper,* was released and immediately established itself as a monster success—both commercially and critically. With a $350 million–plus domestic gross (pulling in nearly $550 million globally), the movie was among the very biggest box office draws of 2015, outmuscling even the latest releases in the hugely popular Hunger Games and Hobbit franchises. Adored by mainstream audiences, *American Sniper* proved to be a favorite of critics as well. It reeled in a litany of awards and accolades along the way, among them six Academy Award nominations, including recognition in the prestigious Best Picture and Best Actor categories.

Nick "The Reaper" Irving also captured the nation's imagination. His autobiography, *The Reaper: Autobiography of One of the Deadliest Special Ops Snipers,* was a breakout hit in 2015. The *New York Times* bestseller was subsequently snatched up by NBC, and now a small-screen adaptation is being readied to air on network television in the fall of 2016.

Meanwhile, CBS is in the early stages of developing a series based on

The Red Circle, the autobiography of former U.S. Navy SEAL Sniper Course Manager Brandon Webb.

Despite this unprecedented level of public attention, the shadow warriors still out in the field have continued to silently ply their trade. Over the past year, the world has shown itself to be an increasingly volatile place, particularly for those who operate ahead of the tip of the spear.

Tension among the world's major powers has not been this acute in decades; the United States, China, and Russia are angling for the control of hearts, minds, and territory (land, sea, and space—cyber and actual), while the South China Sea and Ukraine take shape as next-gen battlefields.

Meanwhile, the threat presented by the Islamic State—AQI mutated into something even more vile—has not diminished in the slightest. The opposite has occurred in fact, as ISIS has become further entrenched in its land grabs and ideology.

A convoluted multinational war against ISIS—ranging across Iraq, Syria, Libya, Nigeria, and Afghanistan—picked up momentum late in 2014 and into 2015. The United States and a coalition of nations engaged in a series of air strikes in an attempt to somehow shape this chaotic set of wars—wars that offer few, if any, immediate or obvious positive potential outcomes.

All the while, ISIS has reveled in its atrocities—alternately capturing and massacring any it deems not tightly aligned enough with its belief structures. Men are routinely beheaded or burned alive, while women are taken as sex slaves.

One of those hostages was a young American named Kayla Mueller. Mueller was taken as the "wife" of Abu Bakr al-Baghdadi, the emir of the Islamic State, and repeatedly tortured and raped as a result. Al-Baghdadi personally delivered Mueller to one of his chief lieutenants, Abu Sayyaf, who kept Mueller under his watch while al-Baghdadi was away.

The enslaved aid worker was held for a year and a half before she finally perished on February 6, 2015, at the age of twenty-six. ISIS claimed the cause of death was a Jordanian airstrike although that remains in question by Western intelligence agencies.

Mueller was kept captive alongside a small number of teenaged Yezidi sex slaves. One, a fourteen-year-old, escaped and made her way to Iraqi Kurdistan, where she was directed to the headquarters of Task Force 27.

Task Force 27 was an American special operations unit built around Delta Force. TF 27 had been pre-positioned with the goal of targeting and striking ISIS HVTs, and now this young girl finally empowered it to live up to those ambitions. Following multiple interviews, the girl's story (and Mueller's involvement) was pieced together, and Sayyaf's critical standing within ISIS became more and more clear.

Abu Sayyaf—"the bearer of the sword"—was described as something akin to ISIS's chief financial officer. He was known as "the emir of oil and gas" and, in that capacity, managed the terrorist network's vitally important black market dealings.

TF 27 zeroed in on Sayyaf's location—finally identified as a multi-story building in Syrian town of al-Amr, near the old fields east of Deir ez-Zor. The task force monitored his activities starting in March with satellite overwatch and electronic surveillance methods. In May, Delta Force (and reportedly British SAS) recce elements obtained eyes-on confirmation of Sayyaf's presence inside the compound.

On the night of May 15, 2015, the Unit finally unleashed a virtuoso direct action raid on the target building. A strike forced was ferried in by Bell Boeing V-22 Osprey and Black Hawk (allegedly of the so-called "MH-X" stealth variety) aircraft, targeting Sayyaf for capture.

Some of Sayyaf's men were said to have offered fierce resistance, while others attempted to hide rather than face the American commandos. Some adopted a tactic somewhere in between those two, utilizing women as human shields. Whatever the preferred methods of confrontation or evasion, all proved futile in the face of the opposition's experience, training, and technology.

Approximately fifteen ISIS fighters were killed in the ensuing battle. Some were gunned down by rounds that deftly skirted past the heads of the makeshift human cover, while others were eliminated in frenetic hand-to-hand combat that took place inside the tight confines of the base.

Sayyaf himself ended up on that list of EKIAs—raising a weapon in anger rather than allowing himself to be taken alive.

No Delta operators were injured in the raid.

While Sayyaf was killed, his wife, Umm Sayyaf, was successfully captured. Rumored to be directly related to ISIS ruler al-Baghdadi, Umm Sayyaf proved to be a surprisingly well-connected, informed senior ISIS figure, not to mention a deep well of information upon interrogation.

The raid also freed an eighteen-year-old Yazidi slave and netted several terabytes of data. ISIS computers, cell phones, and various other materials provided the United States with a wealth of intelligence—information that helped to shed light on ISIS's organizational and financial details, the network's tactics, techniques, and procedures, and valuable tracking information.

The actionable intelligence harvested from the scene resulted in a drone strike of another ISIS leader before the month was out.

Acknowledgments

First of all, I want to thank my girlfriend, Kristin, who showed immeasurable patience and offered endless support despite all the weeks of my coming to bed at 4 A.M. to complete work on this book. I'd also like to thank my writing assistant, Koda, for reminding me that it's necessary to take a break every now and then.

Also, thank you to Brandon Webb and Jack Murphy and the entire gang at SOFREP for showing the faith in this "been here, done jack" to create something worthy of their name.

The same goes for my editor, Marc Resnick, and St. Martin's Press. I had pored through any number of books he's edited and it's pretty cool to be on the other end of things. The operational tempo and intelligence fusion required on the publisher's end to pull this off would have left Stanley McChrystal dizzy.

Thanks to the dozens of guys who were willing to share their experiences downrange, both anonymously and on the record. The personalities were wide-ranging, but to a man, they were extremely generous with both their time and what they were willing to share.

I'd also like to say thanks for the dozens of incredible reporters whose work served as sources of both inspiration and knowledge. Writers such as

Sean Naylor, Mark Urban, Marc Ambinder, Mark Bowden, and David Brown really do amazing work in a difficult field. There are too many others to mention—if not pared down, this title's bibliography could be longer than the rest of the book.

Finally, I want to thank all of my friends and family, but in particular, my parents, Don and Rita, who have always been more supportive than I could have dreamed.

This book would have never happened if not for my dad and on multiple levels. He was the young MACV-SOG Green Beret featured in chapter 13, and his service sparked my lifelong interest in special operations—particularly black ops. It was the same story over and over again when I approached spec ops snipers about possibly participating in the book. "Who are you?" "I'm a motorsports journalist." "Why are you writing this? Why you do care?" After I'd give them a brief background, the standard response was, "Wow! MACV-SOG, those guys are my heroes. . . ."

I never wanted to make it seem as if I was trading on my dad's achievements, but I think that history made them understand the sort of respect I have for the type of work they do and made it a bit easier to trust someone they didn't know.

Bibliography

Ackerman, Spencer. "Actually, Special-Ops 'Night Raids' Are Rather Gentle." *Danger Room* (June 28, 2011). http://www.wired.com/dangerroom/2011/06/actually-special-ops-night-raids-are-rather-gentle/.

Ambinder, Marc. "Then Came 'Geronimo.'" *National Journal* (May 7, 2011). http://www.nationaljournal.com/magazine/practicing-with-the-pirates-these-navy-seals-were-ready-for-bin-laden-mission-20110505.

———. "The Secret Team That Killed Osama bin Laden." *The Atlantic* (May 2, 2011). http://www.theatlantic.com/international/archive/2011/05/the-secret-team-that-killed-osama-bin-laden/238163/.

Ambinder, Marc, and D. B. Grady. *Deep State: Inside the Government Secrecy Industry.* Hoboken, NJ: John Wiley, 2013.

———. *The Command: Deep Inside the President's Secret Army.* Hoboken, NJ: John Wiley, 2012.

Anderson, Jon R. "Appsolutely." *Navy Times* (May 18, 2010). http://www.navytimes.com/article/20100518/OFFDUTY02/5180303/Appsolutely.

"Assessing U.S. Special Operations Command's Missions And Roles." *Terrorism, Unconventional Threats and Capabilities Subcommittee of the Committee on Armed Services House Of Representatives, One Hundred Ninth Congress, Second Session* (Hearing Held June 29, 2006). http://www.fas.org/irp/congress/2006_hr/soc.pdf.

Beckwith, Col. Charlie A. *Delta Force: The Army's Elite Counterterrorist Unit.* New York: Avon, 1983.

Bergen, Peter L. *Manhunt: The Ten-Year Search for Bin Laden—from 9/11 to Abbottabad.* New York: Crown Publishers, 2012.

Biscuiti, Scott M. "Marine Scout Snipers Scope Out New Tactics." *11ᵗʰ MEU* (January 30, 2008). http://www.11thmeu.marines.mil/News/NewsArticleDisplay/tabid /2683/Article/21971/marine-scout-snipers-scope-out-new-tactics.aspx.

Blaber, Pete. *The Mission, the Men, and Me: Lessons from a Former Delta Force Commander.* New York: Berkley Caliber, 2008.

Blehm, Eric. *Fearless: The Undaunted Courage and Ultimate Sacrifice of Navy SEAL Team Six Operator Adam Brown.* Colorado Springs: Waterbrook Press, 2012.

Borger, Julian. "Linda Norgrove: US Navy Seal Faces Disciplinary Action Over Grenade Death." *The Guardian,* October 13, 2010. http://www.guardian.co.uk /world/2010/oct/13/linda-norgrove-us-commando-disciplinary.

Bowden, Mark. *Black Hawk Down.* New York: Atlantic Monthly Press, 1999.

Branigin, William. "Iran's Quds Force Was Blamed for Attacks on U.S. Troops in Iraq." *The Washington Post,* October 11, 2011. http://www.washingtonpost.com /world/national-security/irans-quds-force-was-blamed-for-attacks-on-us -troops-in-iraq/2011/10/11/gIQAPqv0dL_story.html.

Brennan, Julie. "The Lives Behind the Banners." *The Express,* January 5, 2009. http:// www.lockhaven.com/page/content.detail/id/507866/The-lives-behind-the -banners.html.

Bronstein, Phil. "The Shooter." *Esquire,* September 10, 2014. http://www.esquire.com /features/man-who-shot-osama-bin-laden-0313.

Burton, Janice. "Fierce Battle Above Shok Valley Earns Silver Stars." *Army.mil,* December 15, 2008. http://www.army.mil/article/15160/fierce-battle-above-shok -valley-earns-silver-stars/.

Chesney, Robert. "Military-Intelligence Convergence and the Law of the Title 10/ Title 50 Debate." *Journal of National Security Law & Policy* (February 9, 2012). http://www.jnslp.com/wp-content/uploads/2012/01/Military-Intelligence -Convergence-and-the-Law-of-the-Title-10Title-50-Debate.pdf.

Cote, David J. "Army Master Sgt. Robert M Horrigan." *The Summit Project.* http:// mainememorial.org/media/those-we-honor/army-master-sgt-robert-m -horrigan/.

Coulson, Danny O. *No Heroes: Inside the FBI's Secret Counter-Terror Force.* New York: Pocket Books, 1999.

Crumpton, Henry A. *The Art of Intelligence: Lessons from a Life in the CIA's Clandestine Service.* New York: Penguin Press, 2012.

Dillion, Nancy, Phillip Caulfield, and Corky Siemaszko. "Four Americans, Including Ex-Hollywood Director, Killed by Somali Pirates Before SEALs Boarded Yacht." *New York Daily News,* February 22, 2011. http://articles.nydailynews.com/2011- 02-22/news/29441911_1_somali-pirates-sailing-event-yacht.

Dozier, Kimberly. "Navy SEAL Raid in Somalia Shows Campaign Ahead." *Associated Press,* January 26, 2012. http://www.foxnews.com/us/2012/01/26/navy-seal-raid -in-somalia-shows-campaign-ahead/.

———. "Petraeus Highlights Special Ops Successes in Afghanistan." *Associated Press,* September 4, 2010. http://www.fayobserver.com/articles/2010/09/04/1027918?s ac=Mil.

Dreazen, Yochi J. "Shadow War Unlikely to Slow Down After SEAL Deaths." *National Journal,* August 9, 2011. http://www.nationaljournal.com/shadow-war-unlikely -to-slow-down-after-seal-deaths-20110809.

———. "Rolling Out Global Hit Teams." *National Journal,* September 3, 2011.

Durant, Michael, and Steven Hartov. *In the Company of Heroes.* New York: Putnam, 2003.

Eversmann, Matt, and Dan Schilling. *The Battle of Mogadishu: Firsthand Accounts from the Men of Task Force Ranger.* New York: Presidio Press, 2004.

Fury, Dalton. *Kill Bin Laden: A Delta Force Commander's Account of the Hunt for the World's Most Wanted Man.* New York: St. Martin's Griffin, 2009.

———. "The Pope." *Small Wars Journal,* May 14, 2009. http://smallwarsjournal .com/mag/docs-temp/243-fury.pdf.

Gellman, Barton. "TIME Person of the Year, Runner-Up: William McRaven: The Admiral." *TIME* (December 14, 2011).

Golgowki, Nina. "Marine Filmed Urinating on Bodies of Dead Taliban Has No Regrets and Would Do It Again." *New York Daily News,* July 16, 2013. http:// www.nydailynews.com/news/national/marine-regrets-urinating-taliban -article-1.1399764.

Gordon, Michael R., and Bernard E. Trainor. *Cobra II: The Inside Story of the Invasion and Occupation of Iraq.* New York: Pantheon Books, 2006.

Gormly, Captain Robert A. *Combat Swimmer: Memoirs of a Navy SEAL.* New York: Dutton Group, 1998.

Graff, Garrett M. *The Threat Matrix: The FBI at War in the Age of Global Terror.* New York: Little, Brown and Company, 2011.

Grant, Will. "The Longest Shots." *Sniper Ready* (May 12, 2012). http://sniperready .com/modules/propack/blockblog-post.php?post_id=5.

Gup, Ted. *The Book of Honor: The Secret Lives and Deaths of CIA Operatives.* New York: Anchor, 2007.

Haney, Eric. *Inside Delta Force: The Story of America's Elite Counterterrorist Unit.* New York: Random House, 2003.

Henderson, Charles. *Marine Sniper: 93 Confirmed Kills.* New York: Berkley, 2001.

BIBLIOGRAPHY

Irving, Nick. "DARPA GPS Guided Sniper Bullets?" *The Loadout Room* (September 8, 2013). http://loadoutroom.com/6131/darpa-gps-guided-sniper-bullets/.

Irving, Nick, and Gary Brozek. *The Reaper: Autobiography of One of the Deadliest Special Ops Snipers.* New York: St. Martin's Press, 2015.

"'Jacque' 100% Colombian Mission to Free 15 Hostages." *CNN.* Posted to YouTube on July 4, 2008. http://www.youtube.com/watch?v=PoIutiSHYPs&feature=pla yer_embedded.

Johnson, M. L. "Vets Kill in Train Crash Were War Heroes." *Associated Press,* November 17, 2012. http://www.military.com/daily-news/2012/11/17/vets-killed -in-train-crash-were-war-heroes.html.

Kyle, Chris, Scott McEwen, and Jim DeFelice. *American Sniper: The Autobiography of the Most Lethal Sniper in U.S. Military History.* New York: William Morrow, 2012.

Lamothe, Dan. "Marine Scout Sniper Who Tossed Live Grenade from Compound to Get Navy Cross." *Marine Times* (October 23, 2013). http://www.marine corpstimes.com/article/20131023/NEWS/310230023/Marine-scout-sniper -who-tossed-live-grenade-from-compound-get-Navy-Cross.

———. "Marine Scout Snipers Used Nazi SS Logo." *Army Times* (February 9, 2012). http://www.armytimes.com/article/20120209/NEWS/202090327/Marine -scout-snipers-used-Nazi-SS-logo.

Lardner, Richard. "Socom Nominee Is 'Quiet Warrior.'" *The Tampa Tribune,* May 13, 2007. http://news.tbo.com/news/metro/MGB56AYSM1F.html.

Lindsey, Fred. *Secret Green Beret Commandos in Cambodia: A Memorial History of MACVSOG's Command and Control Detachment South (CCS) and Its Air Partners, Republic of Vietnam, 1967-1972.* Bloomington: AuthorHouse, 2012.

MacPherson, Malcolm. *Roberts Ridge: A Story of Courage and Sacrifice on Takur Ghar Mountain, Afghanistan.* New York: Delacorte Press, 2005.

Mann, Don. *Inside SEAL Team Six: My Life and Missions with America's Elite Warriors.* New York: Little, Brown, 2011.

Marcinko, Richard. *Rogue Warrior.* New York: Pocket Books, 1993.

Maurer, Kevin. "Army Unit Receives 10 Silver Stars." *Associated Press,* December 13, 2008. http://www.utsandiego.com/uniontrib/20081213/news_1n13stars.html.

Mazzetti, Mark. *The Way of the Knife: The CIA, a Secret Army, and a War at the Ends of the Earth.* New York: Penguin Books, 2013.

———. "U.S. Is Said to Expand Secret Actions in Mideast." *The New York Times,* May 24, 2010. http://www.nytimes.com/2010/05/25/world/25military.html?_r=1.

McChrystal, Stanley. *My Share of the Task: A Memoir.* New York: Portfolio, 2013.

———. "It Takes a Network." *Foreign Policy* (March/April 2011). http://www .foreignpolicy.com/articles/2011/02/22/it_takes_a_network?page=full.

Michaels, Jim. "Cliffhanger Afghan Mission Is Heroes' Tale." *USA Today,* December 12, 2008. http://usatoday30.usatoday.com/news/military/2008-12-11-silverstar _N.htm.

Military Times Hall of Valor. http://projects.militarytimes.com/citations-medals -awards/.

Miller, Greg. "Strike on Aulaqi Demonstrates Collaboration between CIA and Military." *The Washington Post,* September 30, 2011. http://www.washingtonpost. com/world/national-security/strike-on-aulaqi-demonstrates-collaboration -between-cia-and-military/2011/09/30/gIQAD8xHBL_story.html.

Munoz, Carlo. "Defense Department Seeks New Authorities for Counterterrorism Fight." *DEFCON Hill* (March 3, 2012). http://thehill.com/blogs/defcon-hill /operations/219343-defense-dept-seeks-new-authorities-for-counterterrorism -fight.

Murphy, Jack. "Why the White House Hasn't Released Photos of Osama bin Laden's Corpse." *SOFREP* (March 10, 2014). http://sofrep.com/33599/why-us-govt-hasnt -released-photos-ubl-corpse/.

———. "Jack Murphy Lands on SEAL Team Six's Target Deck." *SOFREP* (September 6, 2012). http://sofrep.com/11055/jack-murphy-lands-on-seal-team-sixs-target -deck/.

———. "SEAL Team Six Throws OPSEC to the Wind, Next Time Use Delta Force or Rangers . . . " *SOFREP* (August 24, 2012). http://sofrep.com/10674/seal-team -six-and-the-white-house-throw-opsec-to-the-wind/.

Muse, Kurt. *Six Minutes to Freedom.* New York: Citadel Press, 2006.

National Commission on Terrorist Attacks. *The 9/11 Commission Report.* New York: W. W. Norton, 2004.

Naylor, Sean D. "Chinook Crash Highlights Rise in Spec Ops Raids." *Army Times* (August 21, 2011). http://www.armytimes.com/news/2011/08/army-chinook -crash-highlights-rise-in-spec-ops-raids-082111w/.

———. "NSW source: Crash 'Worst Day in Our History.'" *Navy Times* (August 6, 2011). http://www.navytimes.com/news/2011/08/navy-special-warfare -community-in-shock-and-disbelief-080611/.

———. "SEALs in bin Laden Raid Drawn from Red Squadron." *Navy Times* (May 5, 2011). http://www.navytimes.com/news/2011/05/army-seals-in-bin-laden-raid -drawn-from-red-squadron-050511/.

———. "JSOC Task Force Battles Haqqani Militants." *Army Times* (September 13, 2010). http://www.armytimes.com/news/2010/09/army-haqqani-092010w/.

———. "Exclusive: Inside a U.S. Hostage Rescue Mission." *Navy Times* (November 7, 2008). http://www.navytimes.com/news/2008/11/military_air_rescue_110708w/.

————. "Wide Support for SEAL Tapped to Lead JSOC." *Navy Times* (March 4, 2008). http://www.navytimes.com/news/2008/03/navy_jsoc_mcraven_030408w/.

————. "Inside the Zarqawi Takedown: Persistent Surveillance Helps End 3-Year Manhunt." *DefenseNews.com* (June 12, 2006). http://integrator.hanscom.af.mil/2006/June/06152006/06152006-11.htm.

————. "Closing in on Zarqawi." *Army Times* (May 8, 2006). http://www.armytimes.com/legacy/new/0-ARMYPAPER-1739369.php.

————. "Bin Laden Raid a Triumph for Spec Ops." *Navy Times* (April 28, 2006). http://www.navytimes.com/news/2011/05/military-bin-laden-raid-a-triumph-for-special-operations-050911/.

————. *Not a Good Day to Die: The Untold Story of Operation Anaconda.* New York: Berkley Caliber, 2005.

"The Necessity of Faith." *Samaritan's Purse* (September 16, 2012). http://www.samaritan.org/article/the-necessity-of-faith/.

Nordland, Rod. "In Farewell Speech, Karzai Lashes Out at US 'Agenda.'" *The New York Times,* September 24, 2014. http://www.bostonglobe.com/news/world/2014/09/23/farewell-speech-karzai-lashes-out-agenda/qqq4tBpPh2LxPQY8eUNRsI/story.html.

Owen, Mark. *No Easy Day: The Firsthand Account of the Mission That Killed Osama bin Laden.* New York: Dutton, 2012.

Peritz, Aki, and Eric Rosenbach. *Find, Fix, Finish: Inside the Counterterrorism Campaigns That Killed Bin Laden and Devastated Al-Qaeda.* New York: Public Affairs, 2012.

Pfarrer, Chuck. *Warrior Soul: The Memoir of a Navy SEAL.* New York: Ballantine Books, 2004.

Pharrer, Chuck. SEAL *Target Geronimo: The Inside Story of the Mission to Kill Osama bin Laden.* New York, 2011.

Piedmont, John. *DET ONE: U.S. Marine Corps U.S. Special Operations Command Detachment, 2003–2006: U.S. Marines in the Global War on Terrorism.* Washington, DC: History Division, USMC, 2012.

Priest, Dana, and William M. Arkin. *Top Secret America: The Rise of the New American Security State.* New York: Little, Brown, 2011.

Rayment, Sean. "How the British Hostages Were Rescued in Afghanistan." *The Telegraph,* June 3, 2011. http://www.telegraph.co.uk/news/worldnews/asia/afghanistan/9307833/How-the-British-hostages-were-rescued-in-Afghanistan.html.

————. "Linda Norgrove: How the Rescue Operation Was Bungled." *The Telegraph,* October 17, 2010. http://www.telegraph.co.uk/news/worldnews/asia/afghanistan/8068530/Linda-Norgrove-how-the-rescue-operation-was-bungled.html.

Runkle, Benjamin. "The 'Mogadishu Effect' and Rick Acceptance." *Command Posts* (August 27, 2011). http://www.commandposts.com/2011/08/the-mogadishu -effect-and-risk-acceptance.

Scahill, Jeremy. *Dirty Wars: The World Is a Battlefield*. Nation Books, 2013.

———. "JSOC: The Blacks Ops Force That Took Down Bin Laden." *The Nation* (May 2, 2011). http://www.thenation.com/blog/160332/jsoc-black-ops-force-took -down-bin-laden.

———. "The CIA's Secret Sites in Somalia." *The Nation* (July 12, 2011). http://www .thenation.com/article/161936/cias-secret-sites-somalia?page=full.

———. "Obama's Expanding Covert Wars." *The Nation* (June 4, 2010). http://www .thenation.com/blog/obamas-expanding-covert-wars.

Scarborough, Rowan. "SEALs Were Sent to Stop Fleeing Taliban." *The Washington Times,* August 10, 2011. http://www.washingtontimes.com/news/2011/aug/10 /fatal-seal-mission-was-not-a-rescue/.

———. *Sabotage: America's Enemies Within the CIA*. Washington, DC: Regnery Publishing, 2007.

Schmitt, Eric, and Mark Mazzetti. "Secret Order Lets U.S. Raid Al Qaeda." *The New York Times,* November 9, 2008. http://www.nytimes.com/2008/11/10 /washington/10military.html?pagewanted=1&_r=1.

Schroen, Gary C. *First In: An Insider's Account of How the CIA Spearheaded the War in Afghanistan*. New York: Presidio Press, 2007.

Shelton, Hugh. *Without Hesitation: The Odyssey of an American Warrior*. New York: St. Martin's Press, 2010.

Shultz, Richard H. Jr. "Showstoppers: Nine Reasons Why We Never Sent Our Special Operations Forces After Al-Qaeda Before 9/11." *The Weekly Standard,* January 26, 2004.

Sileo, Tom. "Bigger Than Life." *Creators.com*. http://www.creators.com/opinion/the -unknown-soldiers/bigger-than-life.html.

Skovlund, Marty Jr. *Violence of Action: The Untold Stories of the 75th Ranger Regiment in the War on Terror*. Colorado Springs: Blackside Concepts, 2014.

Smith, Michael. *The Killer Elite: The Inside Story of America's Most Secret Special Operations Team*. New York: St. Martin's Press, 2006.

"Special Interview with Admiral William McRaven." *The Situation Room, CNN*. July 28, 2012. http://archives.cnn.com/TRANSCRIPTS/1207/28/sitroom.01 .html.

Stetz, Michael. "Navy SEAL from IB Awarded Silver, Bronze Stars." *San Diego Union-Tribune* (February 17, 2011). http://www.utsandiego.com/news/2011 /feb/17/navy-seal-iimperial-beach-wins-silver-and-bronze-s/.

Talton, Trista, and Sean Naylor. "The Story of 'Task Force Violence.'" *Marine Times* (February 15, 2008). http://www.marinecorpstimes.com/article/20080215 /NEWS/802150317/The-story-8216-Task-Force-Violence.

Urban, Mark. *Task Force Black: The Explosive True Story of the Secret Special Forces War in Iraq.* New York: St. Martin's Press, 2010.

Von Zielbaurer, Paul. "Snipers Baited and Killed Iraqis, Soldiers Testify." *The New York Times,* September 25, 2007. http://www.nytimes.com/2007/09/25/world /middleeast/25abuse.html?_r=0.

Wasdin, Howard E., and Stephen Templin. *SEAL Team Six: Memoirs of an Elite Navy SEAL Sniper.* New York: St. Martin's Press, 2011.

Webb, Brandon, and John David Mann. *Among Heroes.* New York: Penguin, 2015.

Webb, Brandon, and John David Mann. *The Red Circle: My Life in the Navy SEAL Sniper Corps and How I Trained America's Deadliest Marksmen.* New York: St. Martin's Press, 2012.

West, Bing. *No True Glory: A Frontline Account of the Battle for Fallujah.* New York: Bantam, 2011.

Woodward, Bob. *The War Within: A Secret White House History, 2006–2008.* New York: Simon & Schuster, 2009.

About the Author

Evan Williams

Journalist Chris Martin has covered the motorsports world since the late '90s. More recently he added special operations coverage and science fiction to his slate. He writes for SOFREP, and is the author of the episodic military sci-fi series *Engines of Extinction* and the e-books *Shaping the World from the Shadows* and *Beyond Neptune Spear*.

www.sofrep.com